GREEN
THOUGHTS

GREEN THOUGHTS

A WRITER IN THE GARDEN

Eleanor Perényi

Vintage Books
A Division of Random House
New York

*Grateful acknowledgment is made to the following for permission to
reprint previously published material:*

Atheneum Publishers, Inc.: James Merrill, from "From the Cupola"
from *Nights and Days*. Copyright © 1966 by James Merrill. Reprinted
with the permission of Atheneum Publishers; Farrar, Straus and Giroux,
Inc.: from *Henry James at Home* by H. Montgomery Hyde.
Copyright © 1969 by Harford Productions Ltd. Reprinted by
permission of Farrar, Straus and Giroux, Inc.; International Creative
Management: from *The Unquiet Grave* by Cyril Connolly. Copyright
© 1944 by Cyril Connolly. Reprinted by permission of International
Creative Management; Alfred A. Knopf, Inc.: from *Journals of
André Gide* by André Gide, translated by Justin O'Brien. Copyright ©
1947 by Alfred A. Knopf, Inc. Reprinted by permission of Alfred A.
Knopf, Inc.; Oxford University Press: from *The Pillow Book of
Sei Shonagon*, translated by Ivan Morris. Reprinted by Permission of
Oxford University Press; Rodale Press, Inc.: reprinted from
The Encyclopedia of Organic Gardening © 1978 by Rodale Press, Inc.
Permission granted by Rodale Press, Inc., Emmaus, Pennsylvania 18049;
A. P. Watt Ltd. and William Heinemann Ltd.: from *Mapp and Lucia*
by E. F. Benson. Reprinted by permission of A. P. Watt Ltd.
and William Heinemann Ltd.

Library of Congress Cataloging in Publication Data
Perényi, Eleanor Spencer Stone, 1918-
Green thoughts.
Includes index.
1. Gardening—Addresses, essays, lectures.
2. Organic gardening—Addresses, essays, lectures.
3. Gardening—United States—Addresses, essays, lectures.
I. Title.
SB455.3.P47 1983 635 83-47805
ISBN 0-394-71714-7 (pbk.)

Contents

Foreword vii

A Note on References ix

ANNUALS 3

ARTICHOKES 8

ASHES 9

ASPARAGUS 10

ASTERS 12

AUTUMN 14

AZALEAS
AND RHODODENDRONS 18

BEANS 21

BELGIAN FENCE 24

BIENNIALS 25

BIRDS 28

BLUES 31

COMPOST 39

DAHLIAS 46

DAYLILIES 54

EARTHWORMS 55

ENDIVE 57

EVERGREENS 59

FAILURES 63

FENNEL 66

FROST 67

FRUIT 68

GARLIC 70

GOOSEBERRIES
AND CURRANTS 72

HEDGES 74

HELP 79

HERBS 83

HYBRIDS 101

INVITATIONS 104

IVY 105

JAMES VS. BENSON 107

LAWNS 108

LILIES 116

LONGEVITY 121

MAGIC 123

MAKING NOTES 126

MAZES 130

MULCHES 130

NATURALIZING 135

NIGHT 141

ONIONS 143

ORIGINS 146

PARTLY CLOUDY 148

PATHS 153

PEONIES 156

PERENNIALS 161

PESTS AND DISEASES 166

POISON 175

POPPIES 177

POTATOES 179

PRUNING 181

REWARD 187

ROCK GARDENS 188

ROSES 193

SEEDS 202

SEED TAPES 207

SEEING EYE 208

STANDARDS 209

STRAWBERRIES 213

SWEET PEAS 214

TOADS 216

TOMATO 217

TOOLS 221

TREE HOUSES 225

TREES 227

TULIPS 228

TWO GARDENERS 235

VEGETABLES 242

VINES 250

WEEDS 253

WILD FLOWERS 256

WOMAN'S PLACE 259

Catalogues 271

Index 281

Foreword

I have had only two gardens in my life. The first was a large rather mournful park in the style called a *jardin anglais* on the Continent, attached to my husband's castle in Hungary. A *jardin anglais*, contrary to what you might think, has no flowers: it is an adaptation of the English landscape style, all grass, winding walks and forest trees. Those wanting a little color might find it in the formal rosary planted around a wrought-iron gazebo—or feast their eyes on three tremendous mounded beds cut into the south lawn and filled first with tulips, then with annuals in serried ranks and municipal colors, lastly with cushion chrysanthemums. All these were raised in the greenhouse, which also sheltered a collection of tropical plants in tubs that in summer were brought out and disposed artistically about the grounds or stood on trestles by the entrance to the castle. No flowers had ever been grown for the house, nor was there any question of a flowering plant being taken there in winter. It would have died of cold.

My efforts to change all this met with limited success. Like Elizabeth in her German garden, of whom I often thought, I was up against a tradition that was totally opposed to—indeed had never heard of—the wife of the Herr Baron grubbing among the flower beds. English duchesses can cover themselves with dirt and lose their diamond rings among the peonies. In central and eastern Europe such conduct was excused only if one was a foreigner, and then only barely. Unlike Elizabeth, I had an indulgent husband but unlike her, too, we were poor, much too poor to embark on ambitious remodeling schemes, which anyway would have had to fight a savage climate, for we lived under the brow of the Carpathians with winter winds that seemed to come straight from Siberia. Nevertheless, I managed to make the beginnings of a perennial garden and to plant a host of bulbs. But even as I did so, the first guns of World War II were booming on the other side of the mountains at our backs, in Poland. I could hear them while I worked, and the premonition I had then was fulfilled. I knew I wouldn't see my plantings come to maturity, and I didn't. The property is now a state farm, the castle, minus most of its looted furnishings, a museum; that part of old Hungary is now incorporated into the Soviet Union.

My second garden, as readers will see, is on the Connecticut coast. I took it up with reluctance, not because it was less grand than my Hungarian one, but because I am one of those unfortunates who when they lose something they love can't immediately replace it with a new model. I grieved over my lost garden and all that went with it, and I didn't want, ever again, to be attached to a piece of ground. But it didn't work out like that. Gradually I did become attached. Gardening became my avocation and greatest pleasure. But I am no horticultural expert and wouldn't want to pass myself off as one. All I can claim is some thirty years of amateur experience, which is to say that I know something about a lot of things and not enough to call myself a specialist in any. I grow herbs but am not an herbalist, roses but am not a rosarian. I haven't a greenhouse.

Why, then, presume to write a book about gardening? The simplest answer is that a writer who gardens *is* sooner or later going to write a book about the subject—I take that as inevitable. One acquires one's opinions and prejudices, picks up a trick or two, learns to question supposedly expert judgments, reads, saves clippings, and is eventually overtaken by the desire to pass it all on. But there is something more: As I look about me, I have reason to believe I belong to a vanishing species. Gardens like mine, which go by the unpleasing name of 'labor intensive,' are on their way out and before they go, I would like to contribute my penny's worth to their history.

A Note on References

The four encyclopedias I most regularly consult are: The Royal Horticultural Society's *Dictionary of Gardening* in five volumes (including the Supplement), 1956 edition, published by the Oxford University Press; *Hortus Third*, in one 1290-page volume, compiled by the staff of the Liberty Hyde Bailey Hortatorium at Cornell University and published in 1976 by Macmillan; *Wyman's Gardening Encyclopedia*, by Donald Wyman, published in 1971 by Macmillan; the Time-Life *Encyclopedia of Gardening*, of which I own twelve volumes (they may have added some since my original purchase), all but one—*Pruning and Grafting*—written by the late, beloved James Crockett of *Crockett's Victory Garden* fame. They were published between 1971 and 1978. In my text these are referred to respectively as the *R.H.S.*, *Hortus III*, *Wyman*, and *Time-Life*.

GREEN THOUGHTS

ANNUALS

Plants that flower, set seed and die within a single season, they can perform prodigies in their brief lives. A morning glory will throw a blue mantle over a small building in no time, tithoniums and castor plants make hedges tall as a man by midsummer. All annuals require full sun for most of the day and their flowers to be regularly cut off—one reason I prefer the tall, which give me flowers for the house, to the short, which don't but have to be deadheaded anyway. For once annuals are allowed to set seed, they are finished.

Annuals used to be, and in England still are, classified as hardy, half-hardy, and tender, distinctions that are important to gardeners who grow their own because they determine how the plants are to be cultivated and what to expect of them. Hardy annuals are sown outdoors in late fall or early spring where they are to grow. They bloom early and can't be counted on to last through a hot summer. The other two must by northern gardeners be started under glass and only transferred to their places in the garden after the nights are warm. Rightly cared for, these will bloom furiously until the frost kills them. Now American cata-

logues no longer use the terms 'hardy' or 'tender'—either from
the fear that they aren't understood and so will be off-putting, or
because they realize that the majority of Americans don't grow
their own. They buy them from the garden center in flats, without
knowing or caring what class the little plants belong to. Some
catalogues leave out the word annual altogether (Harris Seed
does), making you guess that unless otherwise stated the plant in
question must be one. Only a little less annoying is the locution
'Grow as annual.' Is it an annual or isn't it? Many plants—wax
begonias and geraniums among them—we call annuals in the
North are actually perennials in their native South, and are so
grown by southern gardeners. Up here, they can often be dug up
and potted before a freeze, to be grown indoors all winter and
returned to the garden the following year. A friend of mine has
produced an impatiens the size of a small shrub by this means,
and surely others would like to do the same. Why, then, is impatiens listed solely as an annual even in a southern catalogue like
Park?

The Victorians meant hardy annuals when they spoke of old-
fashioned flowers, a term that used to puzzle me: In *Little
Women*, Beth grows 'old-fashioned flowers,' and I always supposed this was part of Alcott's goody-goody emphasis on out-of-
date virtue. That isn't the case. The sweet peas and larkspurs and
pinks beloved of Beth actually were old-fashioned by the middle
of the nineteenth century—having been superseded by the newer,
smarter, tender annuals imported from the tropics and sub-tropics
of Mexico, India and South America. The old annuals in contrast
were natives of the north temperate zone, age-old denizens of
cottage gardens where familiarity and the folk imagination bestowed on them their common names: love-in-a-mist, pincushion
flower, bachelor's buttons, sweet sultan. I love their long stems,
cool colors and sweet fragrance but they won't do for formal
bedding. They have the loose habits of wildings and soon lapse
into untidiness. You don't see them marked 'New!' or 'Improved!' in catalogues because they aren't. The breeders don't
bother with them and never did. Their efforts are concentrated on
the tender annuals, far and away the most popular today.

These are zinnias, marigolds, petunias, red salvia, ageratum,
coleus, etc., in character mostly bushy, scentless and brilliantly
colored. They owe their success to improved greenhouse con-
struction about the middle of the nineteenth century, and new

techniques of mass production that made it possible to market them on a huge scale. Victorian taste did the rest and they quickly became the basis for the only really hideous gardening style on record. In England it was called carpet-bedding because the low-growing plants could be packed into patterns like those of an Oriental rug—but also be made to spell out mottoes, depict clocks and maps, even the human face. Blatant colors and that labored ingenuity the nineteenth century so often mistook for art made carpet-bedding irresistible to philistines of every degree: royalty, the new rich, stationmasters and municipal gardeners were the chief exponents and given the opportunity, might still be. Examples survive at Balmoral, the Boston Public Garden and in many a municipal planting on the Continent. Communist regimes, those perpetuators of *démodé* capitalist styles, are also partial to carpet-bedding, which I am distressed to read now figures prominently in Peking's once-elegant parks.

One group, though, did resist—the English cottage gardeners who obstinately went on planting their hollyhocks and primulas, roses and pinks as of old, rescuing in the process many species that the rage for carpet-bedding would have thrown on the dust heap. They were vindicated toward the end of the century when their informal plots came under new scrutiny. William Robinson and Gertrude Jekyll, who are chiefly credited with the revolution that killed off carpet-bedding, were under the influence of the arts-and-crafts movement led by Ruskin and William Morris, and one of their precepts was the return to 'nature' and native materials. This led Jekyll in particular to a careful examination of the cottage gardener's plants and methods. The impulse was essentially romantic but Jekyll was no dreamer. Her knowledge of plants and techniques was vast, her books and articles widely read, her garden designs copied all over the world. Here is one of her tributes to the cottager's art: 'I have learnt much from the little gardens that help to make our English waysides the prettiest in the temperate world,' she wrote. 'One can hardly go into the smallest cottage garden without learning or observing something new. It may be two plants growing beautifully together by some happy chance or a pretty tangle of creepers that one always thought must have a south wall doing better on an east one.'

Jekyll's great contribution to gardening was the herbaceous border—her own was two hundred feet long—which at first glance might not seem to have derived much from the cottager's tuzzy-muzzy. The connection was in the use of mostly hardy plants, informally arranged, and the effect was to render forever out of date the garish rigidity of carpet-bedding with its regiments of bushy little plants needing to be renewed every year. All the more curious then that a version of carpet-bedding called the ribbon border, graduated rows of tender annuals, should be the prevailing way to plant flowers in American yards to this day. Dwarf marigolds and zinnias, wax begonias (not annuals but treated as such in this context), scarlet salvia, petunias, ageratum, clash together beside a million driveways, are backed against countless fences. What can their attraction be? They aren't cheap and they aren't labor-saving. Perennials could take their place at half the cost and work of replacing them each spring. Their ready-made air is a sad advertisement of the fact that ours is a throwaway culture, and that I suspect is their charm. A garden of store-bought annuals is as temporary as a plastic pool and can be abandoned without a qualm when the owner moves on.

If that is the situation, it is abetted by those in charge of the mass market, where annuals far outnumber perennials and standardization is total. Only a few years ago it was possible to find a considerable variety of annuals at garden centers, many of which had their own fields out back: white zinnias, tall snapdragons, schizanthus, nasturtiums, salpiglossis. Today, most seedlings are trucked in from a central source, wear identical labels and are confined to the fewest possible varieties in mixed colors—nine plants to a flat (it used to be twelve), five of which will turn out to be fiercely, horribly red or orange. Except of course for the petunias. No flower in the universe can have received as much attention from the breeders in the last twenty years, and it beats me to understand why. They are pretty, very pretty—and as hopelessly impractical as a chiffon ball dress. Rain soils and bedraggles them; they are mostly too short and floppy to make a good cut flower, need constant shearing if they are to bloom through a summer. They must be popular or they wouldn't have swamped the market as they have, often at the expense of annuals that are just as attractive, and a better buy. Or would they? It is permissible to wonder how much of their popularity is due to propaganda and their overwhelming presence at the point of sale. If you don't care for petunias you are pretty much out of luck if you depend on a garden center to supply you with annuals.

The remedy that occurs to most of us sooner or later is to raise our own. The catalogues are full of tempting offerings (and another mystery to me is who buys them when I don't see them in gardens or sold commercially). My advice is: Don't, not unless you have a greenhouse. Some require as many as nine weeks from sowing to setting out in the garden, others as few as six. Either way there will soon be a forest of little pots, each with its tenant straining toward the light, and not a habitable room in the house. Don't count on light units to help. The plants outgrow them. By the first of May you will be ready to show the whole lot the door, and it can't be done. They must first be taken outside for about a week (longer if the weather is cold) to harden off, and brought indoors every night lest they freeze to death. Do this for a couple of years and it's back to the garden center.

Outdoor planting is less of a bore but risky. Hardy annuals have a better chance of making it than tender ones, but an icy spring rain can wash out a sowing in no time—or it may be wind and drought that take their toll. The seeds of tender annuals can't, as noted, go into the ground until weather and soil warm up, and in a climate like this one that can mean they won't come into bloom until the summer is half over. So what with one thing and another I have pretty much given up on annuals, which in any case I only want for cutting. The few I grow go among the vegetables: striped and particolored zinnias, including the charming brown-and-yellow model called Chippendale; tall, mop-headed marigolds in lemon shades; ruby nicotianas; spidery cleomes; asters; and the beautifully named swan river daisy.

Others drop from heaven. I tried for years to grow larkspur and couldn't until the birds planted a large crop. (They also plant sunflowers, some of which I leave.) But my pride is a wine-dark opium poppy that has always been here. We like to imagine that the seed was brought from China by a local sea captain who caught the habit there, perhaps as long ago as the eighteenth century. A more modern habit has been represented by *Cannabis sativa*, whose appearance not miraculously coincided with the arrival of adolescents in the house next door. Unlike the opium poppy, it was rooted up. I have to draw the line somewhere.

ARTICHOKES
(*Cynara scolymus*)

The true or globe artichoke is a giant thistle, as one discovers when the buds (the part we eat) aren't picked. The bristly choke shoots up like startled hair and behold—not the fat green calyx that waits to be drizzled with hollandaise but a splendid purple flower. I first became aware of what artichoke plants looked like at Paestum, where fields of them lap at the bases of the temples— a most beautiful crop, with leaves somewhat like acanthus—and I have wanted to grow them ever since. No one was prepared to say that it couldn't be done, and a friend insisted he had raised a number of plants, pulling them through our Connecticut winters under heaps of straw. But I never saw the proof and the suckers I ordered from a dealer who advertised them as hardy came to nothing. I am now convinced they can *not* be grown this far north.

Jerusalem artichokes (*Helianthus tuberosus*), however, can, and there are those who think they taste alike. I don't and see no reason why they should since they aren't remotely related. Jerusalem artichokes are sunflowers, whence their name, which is a corruption of *girasole*, the Italian for sunflower. On the other hand, *girasole* isn't what Italians call the Jerusalem artichoke: that word is *topinambur*, which has a Turkish ring. So the whole thing is baffling, especially as the plant doesn't come from Europe. It is an American native and was widely grown by the Indians, who introduced it to the early settlers, few if any of whom can have been Italian.

However that may be, and having decided a few years ago to try it, I have been trying to rid the vegetable patch of its presence ever since. I have prepared it in every way suggested by Marcella Hazan (*The Classic Italian Cookbook*, Volume I), sliced it raw for salad, pureéd it for soup. Diabetics, I understand, value it as a substitute for potatoes because it is low in glucose. Perhaps that is what ails it. To me it's a vegetable without any pronounced character and no substitute for anything. In the garden it is a nuisance. Uproot the tubers as you will, they elude you and spread underground, to reappear the following year with all the aggressiveness of the unwanted, sending up their big stalks and little sunflower heads. Even the flowers are inferior. Away with it, I say.

ASHES

Water leached through wood ashes in a hopper makes lye. (Add fat to the lye and boil and you have soap.) So why is it a good idea to spread wood ashes around plants where they can be rained on—or, as cottage gardeners do, toss deluges of soapy water on flower beds? Nobody seems prepared to say. All I know is that wood ashes contain up to ten percent potash, which makes them the highest natural source of this vital ingredient in fertilizer, and that potash helps plants to resist disease, build strong root systems, ripen fruit. (Muriate of potash, America's main source of the potash in chemical fertilizer, is something else. Though 'natural,' it comes from huge deposits of potassium chloride salts in our western deserts and is the residue of ancient seas, therefore salty, and it leaves a certain amount of chlorine in the soil.) Wood ashes are alkaline and not recommended for use near acid-loving plants like blueberries. All others benefit from scatterings around them, and I only wish I had a large supply. Since I haven't, I use them chiefly to deter slugs, who won't expose their soft bellies to a gritty barrier of ashes next to the young shoots of delphinium, or near lettuces and cabbages, both potential hiding places for these loathsome pests.

The emphasis is on wood ash, not coal, which, depending on the source of the coal, may or may not contain poisonous amounts of sulphur and iron and be harmful to soil. In old communities where coal furnaces were the rule until well after World War II, many gardeners have inadvertently planted on top of old dumps, and been disagreeably surprised. And when you come to think of it, this is peculiar too: coal, after all, is nothing more than a kind of solidified compost made of decayed plant material. It only goes to show that not all natural processes are benign. Black walnut trees, for example, secrete a chemical that has a toxic effect on certain plants grown near their root systems. Pliny noticed this, though exactly how and when it occurs is still in dispute. Oats, the Jerusalem artichoke, sunflower hulls, some kinds of cherry, and cucumber, all have the capacity to slow or stop the growth of plants in their neighborhoods and could be—if the chemical involved were understood—used to develop natural herbicides. Meanwhile, anyone who spoils the birds with sunflower seeds will have observed that the grass beneath the feeder turns yellow and that even nearby shrubbery begins to look peaked. The hulls should be raked up, while serving as a reminder that not everything 'natural' can be indiscriminately tossed into a garden.

——————— ❧ ———————

ASPARAGUS
(*Asparagus officinalis*)

———————

Asparagus is one of the oldest vegetables in cultivation: Cato the Censor (yes, he who wanted Carthage destroyed) gives directions for growing it in his manual *De agricultura*. The Emperor Augustus used to say 'quick as boiled asparagus,' a hint that only the tenderest young shoots reached his table. Or he may have preferred the wild asparagus, which looks like bundles of little green faggots, and is served in Roman *trattorie* today. (In South Carolina the same delicacy is called chainey briar and is a good excuse, apart from the azaleas, to visit Charleston in spring.) Wild asparagus grows in lots of places, but only Europeans and Americans have domesticated it, and the European varieties I'm sorry to say are greatly superior to the Washington strain, now standard in the United States. Not all are green. Italy has its purple Genoa, and in northern Europe people often prefer their asparagus blanched, which turns it pale gold with a blunt tip and imparts a delicately acidic flavor. While nothing on this side of the water compares to the Genoa, the blanched, or the sumptuous

French Argenteuil, asparagus is still very much worth growing if you have the space.

Putting in an asparagus bed is like planting a tree. The hard work comes at the beginning, and you need faith in the future to accomplish it because nothing much happens for several years—three if you start with one-year-old roots, four if with seed. Meanwhile, you mulch, feed, weed and water, cut down the foliage in the fall and leave the young shoots uneaten. Harvest them too soon and the plants won't build the strength they need for their long lives. Notice, also, which ones produce berries. They are females, whose sprouts are skimpier than the males', and they will self-sow, crowding the bed with still weaker seedlings. Pull them out. These chores are leading up to the spring day when you go out and reap enough asparagus to pile on a platter. You do this by snapping off the stalks (never with a knife, which might damage the underground shoots you can't see), and I know of no more pleasurable operation.

A well-made asparagus bed can last for fifty years—double that in a few legendary English gardens and on the Continent. So the size and location are important. The bed doesn't have to be in or even near the vegetable garden, but it must be distant from trees and in the sun. That much is easy. On size, no two books agree. Fifty plants are considered about right for a family of four with moderate appetites. Two people with a passion for fresh asparagus could use the same amount. With fifty plants as the gauge, the proper dimensions for an asparagus bed can be eighteen by twenty feet, twelve by sixteen feet, ten by ten feet, depending on how far apart the roots are set and the distance between the rows; the more you study the question in various sources, the more it begins to sound like those mathematical problems that involve two trains traveling at different speeds. Jim Crockett's formula, given in *Crockett's Victory Garden,* called for trenches eighteen inches wide with a distance of four feet, center to center, between them, and he liked his crowns (roots) eight to ten inches deep at two-foot intervals (other schools of thought prefer shallower planting five to six inches below the surface and different dimensions). Actually, I don't believe any of these details are as important as the materials that go into the bed itself, which should be made to last forever.

Ancient asparagus beds sat upon uncounted loads of rubble, ashes, sand, and most important of all, rotted manure—all dug in to a depth of several feet. The crowns were placed on top of these riches, about ten inches below the surface, the trench to be filled in as the roots developed, preferably with compost. Such a daunting prescription can't be followed today. Now the practice is generally to dig a trench twelve to eighteen inches deep. Crockett would put 10-10-10 fertilizer at the bottom, compost the top four inches and fill the intervening space with loosened earth. The English, mindful of good drainage in a damp climate, like to scratch in rubble, sand, and other lightening agents and incorporate manure with the soil to be replaced. All American sources mix manure and/or compost with commercial fertilizer at some point. My own procedure is a compromise. Digging deep trenches being of all gardening chores the least attractive to the help who must do it, I settle for about a foot deep, rake in sand and ashes, then mix as much well-rotted manure and compost as I can lay hands on with the soil I put back. The crowns I set at about five inches and cover them at once. At that depth they have no trouble emerging, and I make up for the shallowness with liberal applications of seaweed and salt hay (any mulch would do) each year.

Whenever I write about gardening I am struck by the amount of physical labor I seem to be describing. On paper it sounds overwhelming—but that is the nature of written directions. The reality is not so onerous. Two companionable people who have assembled their materials can prepare an asparagus bed in a long springtime afternoon, and enjoy it for years without much additional effort.

--- ❧ ---

ASTERS

Plants that bloom in cloudy masses are a boon to the perennial border because with no effort on your part they produce 'drifts of color.' The phrase is Gertrude Jekyll's. Jekyll, like Monet, was a painter with poor eyesight, and their gardens—his at Giverny in the Seine valley, hers in Surrey—had resemblances that may have sprung from this condition. Both loved plants that foamed and frothed over walls and pergolas, spread in tides beneath trees;

both saw flowers in islands of colored light—an image the normal eye captures only by squinting. The difference was that Monet made his garden in order to paint it: Jekyll intended the garden itself to be a picture, which isn't as easy as it sounds. One has only to look at a photograph of an actual garden (Monet's for one) to see the balkiness of nature: details stand out, blocks rather than drifts appear. One longs for a brush to blur it all over, and that, in effect, is what plants like asters (and gypsophila and the silvery artemesias) do for a border.

Perennial asters, better known as Michaelmas daisies, grow wild and tall in this country. *A. novae-angliae* and *A. novi-belgii* are their Latin names, and most garden hybrids descend from them. *A. Amellus* is a European of shorter stature. Whatever their ancestry, the best were hybridized in England—Harrington's Pink, for example came from a *novae-angliae* seedling shipped to England in 1938 in exchange for a rare fern. And somehow, with their palette of clear, cool colors they *look* English. There are blues, lavenders and purples, crimsons and pinks, whites, but no yellows, whatever an occasional catalogue may say. This color range makes them awkward with chrysanthemums, with which they bloom concurrently, and many people prefer the sunset tones of chrysanthemums. I don't. The only kind that interest me are the Japanese giants with heads like whirling nebulae, those with spoon-shaped petals, or the ostentatious doubles called football, and I have no luck with any of them. So I concentrate on Michaelmas daisies instead, and am rewarded with fleets of monarch butterflies, who prefer them to any other flower.

To save money and because perennials ordered by mail are a risky business, I grow nearly all of mine from seed. Michaelmas, however, are tough enough to stand delays in shipment, and I get them from Wayside, whose selection of English cultivars is the finest I know. They are easy to grow, most of one's efforts going into taming the underground stolons that form dense mats and creep out to strangle everything around them. The plants must be sheared back, the short varieties once, the taller at least twice before the end of July, in order to make them branch into little bushes. They should then be tied to stakes, or the drift of color will be prostrate. Michaelmas would rather be in a sunny place but are otherwise not difficult to handle.

I wish I could say the same for the annual or China aster (*Callistephus chinensis*), which I find infuriating. Fussier than orchids, they don't seem to know they are ordinary. They can't be put near pot-marigolds, nor more than twice in the same place. They are subject to a virus called yellows, and to another sinisterly known as black neck—which I haven't seen. What I dislike about them is the length of time they take to bloom, and their refusal to renew themselves after the first cutting. With most varieties you might as well pull up the whole plant and make a bouquet of it (some catalogues actually advise this), because you won't get a worthwhile second crop of flowers. For a steady supply you should in fact sow them like beans, a row every two weeks. I have neither the time nor the space for that, and year after year tell myself not to bother with them at all. Then the catalogues arrive. The charm of asters is their fluffy heads and ravishing colors—dusty pinks and powder-blues, strawberry reds and amethyst purples—and the way they arrange themselves in a bowl. I can't resist them and invariably let optimism get the better of judgment, which come to think of it may be the first principle of gardening.

AUTUMN

As the natural world prepares to shut up shop, the gardener may be inclined to do the same. But as most of us know, fall is the busiest season of the year. Where I live, it is also one of the pleasantest to be outdoors. The scent of burning leaves is, alas, no longer with us—burning trash is forbidden in the village. (I don't really mind because I can now either beg or steal the bags of leaves unwisely set out for collection by the inorganic neighbors and add them to our store.) There are epiphanies to make up for that loss. Swans are on the increase in our marshes and on a misty autumn morning when I am hard at work, a wedge of them may fly overhead, so low that I hear the rustle of their pinions, a heart-stopping sound. Hummingbirds, too, visit at this time of year, pausing in their incredible flight to Central and South America; and the warblers, likewise en route from wherever they spend the summer. There is a feeling of suspense: When will the final curtain fall? Heavier dews presage the morning when the moisture will have turned to ice, glazing the shriveled dahlias and lima beans, and the annuals will be blasted beyond recall. These deaths are stingless. I wouldn't want it otherwise. I gardened one year in a tropical country and found that eternal bloom led to ennui. Up here I bury my bulbs in the same spirit that the squirrel, my enemy, goes about his work. He will find the chestnuts he has hidden in the rose garden when he needs them (so will I when they sprout next spring), and my bulbs will come up in due course.

Meanwhile, there are the chores. Now is the time to remove the compost from the bins and spread it around. Invariably there look to be several tons of it, and just as invariably we run a little short. By the same token the emptied bins appear large enough to hold any amount of leaves and refuse and are soon overflowing. By spring, the level will be reduced by half. A compost heap has that resemblance to a bottomless pit: it can always absorb more. You see why when you think of a forest floor, but it amazes me that a flower bed composted for thirty years shouldn't be a centimeter higher than the surrounding lawn. Leaving out lava, how are cities buried? Such idle thoughts come easily to the gardener. There was Newton. . . . But the apple story derives from Voltaire, an untrustworthy source.

Apples: They must be raked up, too, because we were unwise enough to plant a wild apple tree on the lawn. It has a dancer's posture and the pippins make superior jelly. Pomace is said to be a desirable additive to compost. An alternate opinion says the opposite. The apples, however you view them, are a nuisance. Luckily, the tree blooms every other year, what one of my books calls 'the disconcerting biennial habit.' I would prefer it not to bloom at all, because in all those years it showers fruit for yards around, bringing bitter complaints from the help and the recurrent question: Should it be felled? Memories of *The Cherry Orchard* make that impossible to face. The ring of the axe would be harrowing enough; nowadays it's the whine of the chainsaw, heard all too frequently in the village as the elms have gone down. The apple tree will stay, and the fruit be deposited in the compost.

I once believed grass should be left long over the winter, and that the foliage of autumn-blooming perennials would dispose of itself somehow. Wrong. Long grass deprives the roots of oxygen, and all dead stalks are to be cut to the ground when they have finished flowering. But look carefully. Many perennials have formed the crowns of next year's growth and these are on no account to be tampered with. Only the tops come off. Many weeds on the other hand are perennials too, and must be yanked out *now*. They will still be the first thing up in spring but fewer by half than if the beds go into winter unweeded. That done, I apply the compost, taking care not to smother the plants still showing—and the herbaceous border is locked up for the winter.

Herbaceous borders are managed differently in England. They divide, reset and put in new perennials in the autumn. I mention this because too many American garden books repeat these and other hand-me-down directions that won't serve in North America. I am hardly the first to complain. The Reverend Jared Eliot of Killingworth, Connecticut, in a manual written in 1748–49 pointed out that the difference in climate between new and old England make English advice impractical in this country. Yet the prestige of English horticulture is such that we are still being told to do things their way.

Dividing established perennials in the fall is safer than putting in new ones ordered from a nursery, and I have got away with transplanting biennials from the seedbed to their places in the border (see BIENNIALS), but the risk is great. In the northern United States, wait for spring to divide old perennials and be prepared to waste your money if you put in new ones. The same applies to the planting and pruning of roses. I shudder to recollect a supposedly experienced hired gardener cutting our bushes to within a few inches of the ground one autumn. He assured me that was how it was done and I believed him. The wipeout was nearly complete among the modern hybrids. (So-called old roses are tougher but shouldn't be cut down either.) Rose canes up north lose about half their length to the cold whatever you do, and if they go into winter already shortened, by spring they are blackened to the point of imminent death. Some people put baskets filled with leaves over their bushes, but having listened to a friend who does this complaining every year about his losses, I can't recommend that method either. To fit under a basket, a bush must be pruned quite severely, and it is clear to me that the leaves aren't enough to protect the stumps. Trial and error have taught me to leave the tops of rose bushes alone until spring (when the dead parts are cut off) but to mulch the bases heavily with compost and salt hay. The process is called hilling-up and instructions usually call for 'a mound of soil,' or 'rich top soil'—a good example of how unhelpful books can be. Where is the soil to come from? Not from around the roses, which would expose the roots. And not from elsewhere in the garden, where it would leave a large hole. In fact, compost is about the only thing you *can* use, and it is most efficient, slowly breaking down over the winter to the point where it is easily brushed aside when the weather warms up.

Further bad advice from books: Don't prune shrubs in the fall; it stimulates new growth that will be killed back. Again, trial and error and a little observation of how plants respond to approaching cold has demonstrated to me that this isn't so. Pruning (and fertilizing) in midsummer is indeed a poor idea. Trees and shrubs have formed next year's buds by the end of July and thereafter begin to prepare themselves for winter. Pruning or fertilizing them before the end of September does mess up the action, start new growth. But by the end of October or early November they are going into dormancy and won't react even to quite heavy pruning. I am not, of course, speaking of those shrubs such as lilacs that bloom in late spring. To prune them in the fall is to eliminate the next year's flowers. The time to work on them is immediately after the flowers have faded. A shrub that blooms after June 30th is safe to trim in late fall.

The kitchen garden is the last to be cleaned up and composted and is never quite out of service. After the bean vines have been disentangled from their wires and carted away, the cabbage stumps pulled up, seaweed piled in the empty rows, my final act is to mark with tall stakes those spots where carrots, leeks and parsnips are buried under their straw comforters. These signposts will guide me to them after the heaviest snowfall, and armed with an iron fork, I can pry them loose even when the ground is frozen. A bunch of carrots enclosed in what feels like solid rock spangled with ice crystals might not seem worth the trouble. But once it has thawed in the kitchen, there is a special kind of triumph. Not only are these frozen vegetables sweet as sugar, they answer an ancient instinct for survival. They would scarcely keep us alive in a pinch, but there is the sense that a step has been taken in the right direction.

AZALEAS AND
RHODODENDRONS

Most of us think these are different plants. Catalogues list them separately, and gardening journalists clearly distinguish between them, with reason. Rhododendrons are evergreen with large, leathery leaves; azaleas are mostly deciduous and have finer foliage. Rhododendrons like shade, azaleas don't. Even the pests and diseases that attack them aren't the same. Such distinctions don't impress botanists—they count stamens. Azaleas were once thought to have five, rhododendrons ten or more. When this criterion was found not to be invariable, azaleas were summarily moved into the genus rhododendron.

The fact may seem of little consequence to the layman until he wants to look up an azalea—say, *A. calendulacea*—in a modern encyclopedia. He will have to locate it under RHODODENDRON, with its name changed to *R. calendulaceum*, neuter under the rules of botanical nomenclature. In a dictionary like *Wyman*, it will then be revealed that *R. calendulaceum* is the flame azalea, native to our southern mountains. But should he be seeking a hybrid, he will usually find that azaleas are suddenly azaleas again. The Knapp Hill and Exbury hybrids are so listed in *Wyman*, while their ancestors are called rhododendrons, as if they were a bastard line. And this is clarity itself compared to the way the subject is handled in the magisterial *R.H.S. Dictionary*, where more than three hundred rhododendrons are described in detail, and the azaleas among them so cunningly concealed you might never discover them. The azalea hybrids are ignored.

There must be a better way to help out the curious gardener, and I would stay with the older sources if they weren't equally confusing. I happened on one recently that was a bible to American gardeners in its day: Richardson Wright's *Practical Book of Outdoor Flowers*, published in 1924. Wright studied under E. H. Wilson, the plant explorer who helped revolutionize modern gardens with his discoveries of rhododendron species in western China. Wright should therefore have been up on the subject if anyone was. Yet his book is so riddled with mistakes one can only hope they were misprints. Among others, he calls *A. indica* (now *R. indicum*) an American native when it comes from Japan, and identifies *R. ponticum* as a Ghent hybrid (which makes it an azalea), though of course it is the intoxicating shrub that made Xenophon's Ten Thousand drunk on the shores of the Euxine.

Classification aside, no gardener is going to confuse the somehow eminently Victorian rhododendron with shiny leaves that roll up like cigars when the cold strikes them and big, globular flowers, with the airier, more fragile-looking azaleas that seem to belong on a Japanese screen. Even the color ranges are different, indeed opposed, as Gertrude Jekyll long ago pointed out, and would she had been heeded. Rhododendrons are at the blue end of the red spectrum—mauve, purple, blush pink—azaleas at the yellow: peach and copper, hot reds and oranges. (Both, of course, also have white varieties.) Mixed plantings of the two, distressingly common in suburbia, are positively awful in their ugliness and have greatly contributed to my stand-offish attitude to plants I really prefer in the wild. America has beautiful native varieties of both: *R. catawbiense* that lights up the forest primeval in the Great Smokies, the scented azaleas called *arborescens* and *viscosum*, and many more. But the most spectacular come from China and Japan. They are magnificent shrubs in their way, and I wish I didn't have the feeling I would like them better in their own mountains. Partly, it's the way they have been used in, for example, English landscape parks, that I object to. Russell Page has observed (in *The Education of a Gardener*) how disfiguring is the introduction of hybrid rhododendrons to the approach to the lake at Stourhead in Wiltshire; and they are no less unbecoming at Brode Hill and other places. Gardens, we are told, must move with the times, and in principle I agree; I am no advocate of Shakespearean borders. But these blazing introductions don't belong in classical gardens. Worse even than Stourhead is what has happened at the Villa Lante near Viterbo, where someone has seen fit to plant azaleas on the upper terrace at the approach to the *bosco*. In the context of that Renaissance masterpiece, they are an insult.

Where then would I plant them—if at all? Rhododendrons are to me essentially *fin-de-siècle*. They remind me of Newport and Long Island estates of that period, which isn't, as they say, mine. Nevertheless I tolerate a couple of them in what Jane Austen (who never saw a rhododendron) would call a small shady shrubbery, where not many other flowering shrubs will grow. One is white, the other a clear pink rare in rhododendrons, too many of which have a sickly mauve cast. (Scintillation is its name.)

Azaleas aren't well represented either in my garden. I had until this year a large specimen of an Exbury hybrid called Gibraltar whose blossoms, glowing like orange light bulbs, had been too favorably represented in the catalogue. The Exburys were bred from American species on the English estate of Lionel de Roths-child, and I'm sorry to say this noble provenance had its influence when I ordered it. Gibraltar throve, calling into question the theory that plants know what we think of them and cringe at an unkind word, for I hated it and sighed with relief when I at last found the courage to cut it down. What remain are five dense, low-growing little shrubs that Park Seed calls Satsuki azaleas (a name not in my dictionaries), which bloom late and in candy colors: rose madder with darker marking; rose striped with white, etc. I might, one day, replace the Exbury with *A. schlippenbachi*, a species native to Korea and Japan that is pink as the heart of a seashell. But azaleas in colors I like are few and far between, and anyway I don't feel I have the right setting for them.

I have said they look Japanese, though I would be hard put to it to say what I mean by that, except that many are native to Japan and have been painted by Japanese artists. On the other hand, sunflowers painted in Provence by Van Gogh don't 'look' either French or Dutch. It may be that the art of some countries —and Japan is one of them—has been so specialized along certain lines that it automatically imposes itself on natural objects. (I was struck at a recent revival of the ballet *Orpheus* by the disturbingly Japanese aspect of Noguchi's sets: a few rocks, a moon, no more—yet they could have come only from a Japanese hand.) Or is it the other way around? Do the objects themselves teach artists how to paint them? Japanese flora, like those of most islands, have a style of their own. I have an iris, royal purple with yellow markings, that is exactly the made-up face of a Kabuki actor. Was it bred to have this resemblance, or did the flower inspire the make-up? Who knows? In any case, when a race of artists has succeeded in imposing its vision on a plant, it is usually a wise idea to copy that way of handling it. The Japanese treat azaleas as they grow in nature, in wildwood settings with pines and other evergreens, where they both elude and beguile the eye, like a light flickering in the distance. Our azaleas are at their loveliest in somewhat the same context: the swamp-forests of the South, where they are reflected in water black as marble, and their brilliance is dimmed by veils of Spanish moss. They overpower a small garden, especially one where other flowering trees and shrubs are grown. Blooming fruit trees suffer from the clamor of azaleas nearby (unless, of course, they are white); flowering shrubs like lilac and weigela make hybrid azaleas look cheap. Worst of all in my opinion is the modern habit of tucking baby azaleas into beds with tulips and other perennials. More than the colors clash: two genres that ought to be separate collide with painful effect. Azaleas call for more discretion than any other flowering shrub because of their assertive colors; but because these are also the source of their popularity, they seldom get it.

———————— ❧ ————————

BEANS

Haricot and Romano beans, lima beans, French horticultural beans, kidney beans, *garbanzos*, pinto beans, *fave* or broad beans, black beans, *flageolets* all arouse in me the deep primordial appetite the average person has for meat. The only member of the pulse family I don't like is the soybean. *Tofu*, a sort of bean curd, and *miso*, a fermented paste, are to me nauseating contributions to health-food diets, as to Japanese cuisine itself, to which early exposure gave me a fixed dislike. I spent hours in a Japanese kitchen as a child, watching with delight the carving of vegetables into baubles fit for a Christmas tree; but few European children can be persuaded to eat raw fish, seaweed or gluey rice—or *tofu*—and I might easily have starved in Japan. The prejudice has stuck, though I am otherwise an addict of the cuisines of poverty and especially those that exalt the bean. A *chateaubriand* is wasted on me. Give me *frijoles refritos*, *cassoulet*, Boston baked beans, *pasta i fagioli*, *hummus* or a *caldo Gallego*, whose cousin in Portuguese New England is called Holy Ghost soup. Best of all, give me a dish of garden limas or string beans no bigger than match sticks, briefly boiled and rolled in sweet butter.

Limited space and northern climate are all that keep me from growing every imaginable bean, including the tropical varieties one sees heaped into pyramids in Mexican markets, each the basis of a delicious dish. At one time or another I have tried most of the types commonly grown in the United States, including the shell beans southerners call cow peas, but one has to stop somewhere and my repertory is now limited to what I consider the essentials. I don't, for instance, grow the broad beans Europeans wrongly insist are superior to the American lima. No bean in the world can compare with a freshly picked lima. But limas, like corn, begin to deteriorate the instant they are harvested, and those usually found in markets are almost another vegetable, coarse and yellowed when cooked. The perfect lima looks like a little purse made of *eau-de-Nil* satin, keeps its color in boiling water and is only faintly, exquisitely mealy. I grow the aptly named King of the Garden, a pole variety that supplies us for two months if the weather is kind. No bush and no baby limas—neither is as good as the big pole lima.

Limas, however, take a long time to mature, and to have a shell bean earlier in the season I make a small planting of French horticultural beans. (I can't discover why they are called this as I have never seen them in France and anyway, why 'horticultural'?) They can be eaten green but are better when left on the vine until the pods acquire their characteristic magenta markings. The beans inside will then also be stippled pink like tiny marble Easter eggs, a color that unfortunately disappears in the cooking, when they turn brown. Richer than limas in flavor, they are boiled and buttered in the same way and are helped by a final garnish of freshly clipped sage.

Further choices must be made between what should now be called snap beans, the 'string' having been bred out of them. Italian gardeners hereabouts can be told by the forests of rough poles reared in support of the flat green Romano type they prefer. Yankees like the yellow wax snap bean. I have grown both, and after a summer in England sent for the seeds of the scarlet runner, an ornamental for us, there for eating. (In fact, the varieties are slightly different, and American runner beans aren't a substitute for the English if you intend to eat them.) At other times I have experimented with purple-podded snap beans and a southern type (carried by Park Seed) called Old Dutch Half Runner. Where space counts, none is a substitute for the plain green snap bean as developed in America. I get mine from Harris and always order white-seeded varieties—Blue Lake for the bush and Kentucky Wonder for the pole growers. This is because, when the inevitable surplus occurs, I leave the pods on the vine to produce shell beans. Why more gardeners don't do this I can't think, except that they seem not to know it can be done. When the beans are overgrown, they pull them out, unaware that the white bean inside is splendid to eat, much better than the pea beans sold in boxes, and unequaled for *cassoulet* and *fagioli alla Toscana*.

Choosing the beans I want is now routine. Growing them isn't. Even southern New England is too far north for limas, and I never know how they will turn out. Planted too early, they rot—leaving a little shroud behind them. Put in too late, they won't make a crop before Labor Day, a woefully short season. Bush limas are supposed to mature earlier. I don't find they do, or not enough to matter, and in the meanwhile they occupy more space than I can spare. Both kinds are chancy and cold isn't their only enemy. Most beans sprout quickly and a few vacant spots don't matter. Limas, which must be pushed into the soil with the 'eye' down, come up in slow motion—two fat paddles on a stout green stalk that cutworms will demolish in a trice. If the cutworms don't get them, two leaves presently unfold which the birds consider the ultimate salad. Often the row must be filled in again and yet again, until each plant has four leaves and is properly launched. (After that, neither the cutworms nor the birds will take any further interest in them.)

To get around this agonizing cliff-hanger, I tried for a time to start lima seed indoors in peat pots, setting them out only when the vines were well on their way. This foiled their enemies but accomplished very little. They didn't outstrip their mates planted in the ground as a control but simply sat there, clinging feebly to their trellis, until the others caught up. So I no longer fuss with pots.

Snap beans are easy by comparison, or would be if I could master the laws of succession. No matter how short the rows or how long the intervals between plantings, mid-July finds us overpowered. It is the classic experience, compounded by my refusal to pick any but the slimmest, youngest pods. I don't 'French' them—any more than the French themselves do. They stay on the vine, getting bigger and bigger and this is how I discovered that I could have a crop of shell beans. I leave them only until the pod has swollen and turned yellow. Allowed to shrivel to the crackling stage, they often mildew and are hard to shell, but the yellow casing slips off like a glove. Spread on a paper towel, the beans dry nicely in a few days and keep for six months or more in a tightly lidded glass jar. (*Flageolets*, which I first tried this year, are managed in the same way.)

This drying is my only attempt to prolong the life of beans. I don't freeze them. My one attempt, which may have been badly done, was no better, perhaps not as good, as the store-bought. The limas I don't even dry, for the simple reason that there are never enough. We eat them all, and my final act before a predicted killing frost is to pick every last pod with a visible bean in it.

❦

BELGIAN FENCE

Of all the ways to plant espaliers, this is the one I most want to try. It is also one of the simplest—nothing more than a series of Y-shaped dwarf fruit trees set at two-foot intervals to make a diagonal lattice. Not less than five are needed, but the fence can then be extended indefinitely. One could hunt around for saplings of suitable size and prune them oneself to the right shape. (Directions are given in the *Pruning and Grafting* volume of the *Time-Life Encyclopedia*.) But it would be easier to order them from Leuthardt Nurseries (see CATALOGUES), the only firm I know in the eastern United States to specialize in espaliers.

The most elaborate, the four- and six-armed *palmette verriers* are spectacular candelabra. Already pruned and shaped, five to six feet high, carefully bound in burlap and lashed to a framework, they are wonderful things to receive in the mail—horticultural works of art that only need a hole dug for them. The individual trees to make a Belgian fence are much simpler in form but would presumably be a little more complicated to set up. The space I have in mind, the dividing line between the working part of the garden (vegetables, berries, etc.) and the croquet lawn, is fifty feet long and would therefore require twenty-five trees, a lot of digging. A lot of money, too, you might imagine, but the cost would actually be the same or less than replacing the dilapidated trellis that occupies the space. (The 1979 price for individual trees, either apple or pear, was $9 to $11, which compared to what lumber costs is an extraordinary bargain.) And think what you get: a leafy crosshatching that in May is covered with blossom, in autumn with fruit. It would be formal without being oppressively so, and modest enough to adorn a *jardin de curé*.

Still, if I wanted it I should probably have ordered myself a Belgian fence years ago, when I first saw the photograph in the Leuthardt catalogue. There comes a point in the gardener's life when he feels he has made his bed and had better lie in it. I am getting on. So I ask myself if I really care to cope with twenty-five little trees eager to start a new life under my aegis, needing to be pruned, supported, and no doubt mended after a bad winter storm. And I guess I don't. But in the meantime, a curious thing happens whenever I look at that space. I seem to see the Belgian fence superimposed on the existing trellis, like a double exposure. Another step and the trellis would disappear, leaving only the fence in my mind's eye. And that would be perfect, better than the real thing.

BIENNIALS

In the golden age when a flower garden was looked at as a kind of stage, biennials were important to the *mise-en-scène* of the herbaceous border. Canterbury bells like ruffled pagodas, sweet Williams and wallflowers, each with its distinctive perfume, bannered armies of foxgloves—these were the principals. They bloom in June after the bulbs are over and the midsummer perennials are still in the wings, an interlude that needs filling. But their day may be over. Biennials bloom for about a month (Canterbury bells a little longer if the first flush of bloom is plucked, allowing a second to take its place), then die. And to achieve this brief performance they must be started from seed the year before, then thinned out and reset to winter either in the seed bed or the border where they are to flower—in New England, the former is best—and they should be transplanted in early spring. They are rarely to be had ready-made. Few garden centers carry them, and those that do put them on sale too late, toward the end of May, as half-grown plants. A biennial should by then be full size and about to flower or it will be a poor thing in the garden. So there is really no alternative to raising them yourself if you want them.

I sometimes think I don't. There have been years when I was ill, absent, or lazy and didn't sow the seed. I always regretted it. Nothing quite takes the place of biennials, even if those places are empty by July. I say *if* because of the anarchy surrounding the subject of what is and what isn't a biennial. The plant you expected to pull up and throw away will often live on, causing you to plume yourself on having wrought a miracle when all you have done is enter the world of plants that are actually short-lived perennials but are labeled biennial because that is how they are likely to behave. Sweet William and dame's rocket (*Hesperis matronalis*) are of this order and in my garden have survived for years, far outlasting the short-lived Pacific hybrid delphiniums which are true perennials but in many parts of the country act like biennials.

Vegetable biennials are easy to identify. They are those that, if left to winter in the ground, flower and go to seed the following summer. Parsley, beets, Swiss chard, carrots and onions are all biennials. It is among the flowers that confusion reigns, and the incontestably biennial are few. Foxgloves, Siberian wallflowers, Canterbury bells, some of the evening primroses (*Oenothera*), honesty (*Lunaria biennis*), whose purple flowers are metamorphosed into papery silver discs, the mulleins, Brompton stocks, alpine and woodland forget-me-nots complete the list.

But what of hollyhocks, English wallflowers (*Cheiranthus Cheiri*), Himalayan and Iceland poppies, the common pansy? They may be anything depending on which authority you consult, which catalogue you order from. Iceland poppies are biennials to the *R.H.S.*, perennials to *Wyman*, 'best treated as biennial or annual' in the *Time-Life Encyclopedia*. *Wyman* calls the English wallflower an annual, the *R.H.S.* says it's a perennial, *Time-Life*, again, that it does best grown as a biennial. And so on, down the line.

The catalogues compound the confusion, labeling plants at will. Most of them don't like the word biennial; maybe they think the average person doesn't know what it means—and maybe they are right. Take the common hollyhock (*Althaea rosea*), which in American garden encyclopedias is generally agreed to be a biennial. (The *R.H.S.* says perennial, but ignore that for the moment.) Turn to three standard catalogues for 1980 and study their hollyhock offerings: Burpee has five perennials and three annuals; Park Seed, seven perennials; Harris, two annuals and one perennial. Then choose a specific variety—let us say Summer Carnival, a handsome five-foot specimen with double pompoms. What is it? To Burpee, it's an annual; to Park, a perennial that will bloom in its first year; Harris agrees it will bloom in the first year but calls it an annual, which is impossible. If it's an annual, the first year will be the last.

Obviously something is the matter. No gardener should have to cope with such obfuscation, particularly when it would be easy to clear it up. The missing link is climate. When the *R.H.S.* calls a plant a perennial that in America is a biennial, the *R.H.S.* is correct for England, an offshore island. We are a continent, with no less than ten zones of hardiness, not to mention high mountains, deserts and coastal lowlands, and it stands to reason that no plant will react identically to such enormously varied conditions. To oversimplify somewhat: A short-lived perennial may last for some years in the warmer parts of the country, become a biennial under more severe conditions, and in the far north behave like an annual. Conversely, certain lovers of cold (some dianthus, for example) are perennial in the North but best treated as biennials where summers are hot. Nearness to the sea will also make a difference. Why then do American reference books and catalogues take so little cognizance of climate or geography? *Time-Life* is the honorable exception, and I now use it almost exclusively on that account. Jim Crockett, who wrote most of the volumes, was first of all a practical gardener, and it shows. The catalogues should at least follow his admirable example instead of pretending that climate is of no consequence. Where doubt exists, they fall back on that catch phrase 'grow as,' and without an explanation of where and why, the admonition is pointless. The statement 'grow as annual in Zones 5–8,' or 'likely to be biennial in the Northeast' is all that is needed.

Gardening can't be an exact science, and we wouldn't enjoy it if it were. It would be like gambling without odds. But the odds are long enough as it is. The growing of flowers is in decline. The theory behind the vagaries of the catalogues may be that the less we know the more inclined we will be to rush in where the informed would fear to tread. They should realize that disappointed customers have no incentive to order again. Tell us the facts, I say, and let us make our own judgments.

————— ◇ —————

BIRDS

There are several schools of thought on birds. Commercial growers resent them for the damage they do to fruit buds, berry crops, seedlings, even flowers. Others argue that they destroy pests and help maintain nature's balance in the garden; still others want them around for sentimental reasons. I share all these points of view to some extent. The blue jay is a feathered fiend when he goes after the robins' eggs and screeches at cats. (I prefer the cats.) I am furious when birds get into the pea patch or eat up the grass seed. At the same time I cherish the mourning doves, the cardinals whistling farewell to the day, and the rare visitations of evening grosbeaks and bluebirds that make one feel, quite unjustifiably, like one of the chosen.

I have also begun to fear for birds, and in recent years taken steps to encourage them. I removed the scarecrow from the vegetable garden, which I was glad to do anyway. Dressed in my cast-off clothes, this figure had become an increasingly derelict version of myself, and though it didn't really keep off the birds, it had begun to frighten me to death. I installed feeders and a wren house, unvisited to this day; made a rococo birdbath out of clam shells; planted berry-bearing shrubs. But I am far from convinced that any of these measures is effective. The quality of the bird population is clearly in decline, for while the grackles, cowbirds, starlings and sparrows multiply, I count fewer and fewer of the more desirable specimens.

Though I am in no sense a bird-watcher, I do make occasional notes on their appearance in the garden, and from these I see that we have nothing like the variety we had ten years ago. Only the toughest are winning the war against pollution, pesticides and the slow destruction of their habitats; and in the face of these larger threats, efforts like mine are pathetically inadequate. If the blue-bird, 'who carries the sky on his back' in Thoreau's fine phrase, is getting to be rare as the roc in this part of New England, it isn't for want of feeders, but because he isn't among those fittest to survive the hostile world we have created. I have watched a Boy Scout troop attaching bluebird houses to trees along the road that connects us to Interstate 95. They might as well have been build-ing tepees to entice Indians. The birds and the Indians are dying out for not dissimilar reasons.

This doesn't, of course, mean that one should give up on the birds, but it does make me wonder whether we are going about saving them in the right way, whether our zeal isn't misplaced as often as not. I remember the purple martin craze of a few years ago. Suddenly every nature and gardening magazine was trum-peting the news that purple martins eat 5,000 mosquitoes in an hour and running ads for martin houses. There was even a purple martin newsletter. It made no difference that mosquitoes aren't a major problem in many communities and that lacking an ade-quate supply the martins, lured by new housing, might starve. Those who already owned martin houses, late-Victorian resi-dences anchored to tall poles, smiled when the rest of us ordered modern houses in kit form. I ordered one of these myself and proceeded to construct a dreadful object: unpainted, it looked like a cheap motel; painted blue and white, it looked like a cheap *Greek* motel and had to be thrown out. Only then did I think to ask the owner of an authentic antique martin house whether in fact the birds ever visited it. She replied sweetly that she hadn't seen a purple martin for years.

The martin mania passed, and I don't know that the birds suf-fered when their temporary popularity waned. Perhaps being brighter than human beings, they weren't tempted by ugly new houses into moving where the natural food supply was inade-quate. But they might have been, and this brings me to the next point: I'm not at all sure that the proliferation of feeders has been a good idea either. Feeding birds induces 'good' feelings, like sending CARE packages to poor countries. It may or may not be helpful to the birds themselves, whose life-cycles aren't an analog of our own. Wild life can't be allowed to become wholly depen-

dent on man—if it does, it ceases to be wildlife and other arrangements have to be made. I can't even be certain that feeding has
helped the immediately endangered species.

Certainly it isn't they who come to the feeders but an idle race
of lazy gastronomes who increasingly pick and choose. No thistle
seed? The goldfinches, who don't care that it costs about $1 a
pound, pass me by. The cardinals, on the other hand, want sunflower. Standard mixtures no longer attract this fastidious clientele, which is far from doing its job of clearing the garden of
insects. Soon they will have lost the habit of foraging for themselves. In short, and as far as I can make out, I am either in the
business of feeding a barbarian horde of cowbirds, starlings, etc.,
or I am spoiling a number of pets; and in either case I am doing
more harm than good.

Just how serious the situation was I hadn't realized until the
recent death of a beloved cat. He had never hunted—like all my
creatures he was too well-fed to bother. But his presence had
obviously inhibited the birds to some extent because the news of
his death all but brought them into the house. Cardinals built a
nest within a few feet of the porch where we constantly sit. Purple
finches actually built another inside a Tunisian birdcage that
hangs on the porch itself. The weeks that followed were nerve-
wracking. We couldn't cut the hedge or mow the lawn; a long-
standing arrangement to paint the house had to be put off. Nobody
dared sit on the porch—it made the parent finches nervous. The
launching of the baby cardinals was agony enough, but they finally made it. Not the finches, who liked their wire mosque so
well they refused to leave it. They even learned to use the swings
and retreated piteously into the dome when their parents tried to
coax them out. Naturally I fed them, seeing that the parents
sensibly wouldn't. And it was then I saw where the St.-Francis-of-
Assisi complex was leading. I stopped putting worms on their
threshold, and one afternoon the cage was empty. Just in time.
Another week, and the little finches would have tamed themselves, knocked at the door every morning, become my pets and
dependents forever.

BLUES

Nature's favorite color is a washed-out magenta, the original shade (and the one their hybrids will revert to if they go to seed) of petunias, garden phlox, sweet peas, nicotiana, foxgloves and so many others that Thalassa Cruso says it is known in her family as Garden-of-Eden, on the premise that all flowers must have started out that color. Some gardeners like Garden-of-Eden too, but the preferred color of the unsophisticated is firehouse red, the winner among tulips, zinnias, dahlias, salvia, impatiens, begonias, etc., by a wide margin. Orange and yellow come next, then pink, with blue and white, both comparatively rare in nature, last on the list—a spectrum that runs from hot to cold.

It follows that blue and white are the choices of the discriminating, and your real garden snob will go so far as to cast whole gardens in one or the other. White has perhaps the higher status. White flowers have always had an aura of luxury and expense, partly because so many of them are imported from warmer climates and must be grown under glass. In the eighteenth century, which put a much higher value on scent than we do, the fact that they were also heavily perfumed made white flowers such as the gardenia and the tuberose favorites with collectors. But white is also a distinctively modern color, or un-color, because of its cool neutrality. It will even take the curse off otherwise unacceptable objects, including flowers. Syrie Maugham's all-white rooms, famous in the 1920's and 1930's, were full of rococo pieces pickled and rubbed with white paint, a form of vandalism that imparted instant chic. White gardens came into fashion during the same period and for some of the same reasons. Though flowers were still massively grown in borders, doubts arose as to whether they were really in good taste. To have them all white met the objection, and still does. Even a white gladiolus may get by—just —while one in any other color is beyond the pale.

The blues are a little different—not chic exactly, though Edith Wharton's all-blue garden at her Pavillion Colombe outside Paris was the ultimate in elegance. But they also have overtones of class distinction, and this may be as good a place as any to admit that there

is such a thing in gardening. When, for example, I say that gladiolas
are beyond the pale, I am not making a strictly aesthetic judgment.
What I crassly mean is that they are non-U, that objectionable if
handy phrase coined *not* by Nancy Mitford but by a rather pompous professor who mined her books for upper-class speech
patterns and later expanded the definition to include other things
such as clothes and food—but not flowers, an odd omission in
garden-loving England, where they bear the marks of caste just as
fatally as 'notepaper' and 'putting the milk in first.' So do they
here, though no class-conscious English person would admit it,
everything 'transatlantic' being non-U by definition. Never mind.
We, too, have U and non-U gardens, with the same taboos: gladiolas, scarlet salvia, wax begonias, red-hot pokers, orange marigolds,
and many more it would be tedious to enumerate are all non-U,
too obviously, perhaps, to merit mention.

Subtler points of U and non-U are raised by the fancier cre-
ations of the hybridists, which force choices between simple
flowers and elaborate ones, true and false colors. Non-U, after all,
doesn't inevitably mean plebeian. A cottage garden can't be non-
U; a suburban one stuffed with the latest hybrids can, and no one
has described it better than Mitford in *The Pursuit of Love*. It is
the Surrey property of Sir Leicester Kroesig, a bourgeois banker.
'You could hardly see any beautiful, pale, bright, yellow-green of
spring, every tree appeared to be entirely covered with a waving
mass of pink or mauve tissue paper. The daffodils were so thick on
the ground that they too obscured the green, they were new varieties of terrifying size, either dead white or dark yellow, thick and
fleshy; they did not look at all like the fragile friends of one's
childhood. The whole effect was of a scene for musical comedy.'
Almost worse is Sir Leicester's water-garden 'full of enormous
pink forget-me-nots and dark-brown irises.'

Though more sumptuous than anything we can normally manage, Sir Leicester's garden is nevertheless the essence of non-U
because everything in it is a kind of euphemism, a genteel refine-
ment on the real thing exactly analogous to 'passed on' for 'died'
or 'gown' for 'dress.' This type of non-U-ness did not come to
gardens before the nineteenth century, when the importers of
exotics and the hybridists got seriously to work. It dates from
the craze for bedding-out (see ANNUALS), a style that by itself
was non-U and so considered at the time by people of taste because it reeked of middle-class pretension. Before that, the means

were lacking—as we see in Jane Austen. 'My brother Mr. Suckling's seat' near Bristol would clearly have resembled Sir Leicester's had Mr. Suckling had access to modern azaleas, gladiolas
and iris, and it was only because he didn't that his grounds could
be said to put Mrs. Elkin 'so exactly in mind of' Mr. Woodhouse's
with their forest trees and modestly flowering shrubs.

No doubt about it, for all the marvels they have produced, it is
the hybridists and their accomplices, the importers of exotic
plants, who, however unwittingly, have introduced previously
unheard-of vulgarisms to the garden world. A hybridist can take a
simple flower and double or triple the petals, ruffle them, curl
them. He can make an aster look like a chrysanthemum, a tulip
like a peony, a marigold like a carnation, ad infinitum—a galaxy
of 'glads,' 'snaps,' and 'mums' that might be indistinguishable if
they didn't come in such odd sizes and colors. The hybridist can
turn the colossus into a pigmy and vice versa. Above all, he can
mess up the normal color range of a plant so that it no longer
sends a familiar message to the eye. Burpee for years ran a contest
offering $10,000 to anyone who raised a white marigold. They
never explained why a flower with gold in its name would be more
desirable in white. They didn't have to, not to an audience trained
to prefer, and to pay more for, any departure from the natural:
chartreuse narcissus, mauve daylilies, pink forget-me-nots and
those bi-colors inflicted wherever possible.

Notice that blue doesn't appear on this list. That isn't for want
of trying. The search is on for a blue rose, a blue daylily, no doubt
a blue anything that isn't that color in nature, and so far these
efforts have failed. If I understand the scanty references I find to
the subject that is because blue plant pigment is unusually hard to
manipulate. Apropos daylilies, for instance, *Wyman* explains:
'Blue, since it occurs in the daylily as a sap-soluble pigment, will
be difficult—perhaps impossible to segregate. Lilacs, purples,
orchids, mauves we have; and working with them we may eventually get near blues, but pure blues probably never.'

I haven't enough knowledge to follow this. If anything, I would
imagine a sap-soluble pigment to be easier to isolate than some
other kind. Neither do I understand another account (in *Time-
Life*'s *Roses*) of how a hybridizer tried to produce a blue rose:
'Using sophisticated techniques of chemical analysis, Mrs. Whisler selected the crossbred lavender hybrid teas in order to produce
offspring having optimum amounts of cyanidin, the pigment that

imparts purple or magenta tones, and flavone, the pigment that gives light yellow tones.' Now why in the world would she do that? I know nothing of sophisticated techniques of chemical analysis but quite a lot about ordinary paint, and the two must differ enormously if purple and yellow could be expected to make blue. (For what it is worth, they didn't make a blue rose, which is still in the future, and I hope will stay there.)

Cyanidin is bothersome too. It isn't in my dictionaries for a start. Cyano-, however, is, and it refers to blue (from the Greek *kyanos*, dark blue) not purple, which must be cyanidin plus red. Cyanidin itself is surely the primary pigment that gives us true-blue flowers like delphiniums. Obviously, it is present in others in mixed or diluted form and can be intensified by crossbreeding, but not isolated. It can't be manufactured by man, at least not in the plant world. (Chemicals are another matter. Indigo, the principal source of blue dye for centuries, was wiped out as a commercial crop almost overnight with the invention of aniline dyes.) I am guessing, but if I am right, the rarity of true blue in nature would be accounted for, along with what is to me of equal importance, its resistance to corruption.

I must declare an interest. Whatever the reasons (and I don't think anyone knows or has studied why people respond to colors as they do—snobbery aside, there are unplumbed depths in the psyche that affect whole nations: why do the liberty-loving choose blue and white for their flags, while those who opt for tyrants invariably prefer red and black?) I love blue more than any other color. I am inordinately attracted to any blue substance: to minerals like turquoise and lapis lazuli, to sapphires and aquamarines; to cobalt skies and blue-black seas; Moslem tiles—and to a blue flower whether or not it has any other merit.

Take anchusa, the Italian bugloss, a hairy perennial that looks like an outsize borage (which it is) and does little credit to the well-groomed border. But an anchusa in bloom is like a Christmas tree with lights so intensely azure they shine out clear across a garden, and I always keep at least one. I harbor the royal blue perennial cornflowers (*Centaurea montana*) for the same reason and in spite of their floppy, undistinguished foliage; and over some opposition (my mother can't abide their prickly, bristly appearance), the steel-blue globe thistle (*Echinops*), whose unopened buds are little balls covered with spikes, miniatures of those weapons one sees in the medieval armory. I doubt if I would care for the veronicas, which are somewhat nondescript and require to be massed to make an effect, if they didn't come in a variety of stained-glass window blues (the pinks and whites leave me cold); and I wouldn't tolerate the invasive, floppy *Tradescantia virginiana* (spiderwort) if it weren't for the cultivar Blue Stone. (Save the tradescantias for rough spots where you want a little color—they don't belong in a border.)

All the above have the advantage of being tough as well as blue. They are perennials you can plant and more or less forget. What they lack is the elegance that doesn't necessarily go with hardiness. For that combination among the blues I look first to the campanulas, especially *C. persicifolia*, the peach-leaved bellflower that will produce flush after flush of enchanting bloom on the wiry stems if you have the patience to go out every morning and remove the faded flowers. These campanulas need only to have their basal rosettes divided every so often to last practically forever, and they are my favorites, though fancier, doubled varieties exist. (*C. glomerata*, dark purple, is one, and to my mind the flowers are too heavy for the stalks.) The same plant in little is *C. carpatica*, and I like it too. Both are to be had in white as well.

Platycodons (blue, white, and a dim pink) are next. Closed, they are lanterns, and they open into stars. Platycodons, too, will be with you forever if you remember where they are and don't wield a careless trowel in early spring. They vanish over winter and don't emerge until mid-May, camouflaged as baby asparagus, and if these easily overlooked shoots are damaged they are done for. Otherwise, they come up in the same place year after year, don't encroach on their neighbors, must not be divided. (Many gardeners get the idea that all perennials should be split up after a few years, often with fatal results. If the clump doesn't increase in size, leave it alone. I lost the best flaxes I ever had, and the only ones to last longer than two years, because some demon whispered that the time had come to separate them; and since that day I have learned to look twice at the structure and growth habits of plants before I start moving them around. In general, those that want dividing will have already started the process for themselves, forming obviously distinct offsets. Those that don't do this, or go to ground leaving no trace, should be left to their own devices —unless, of course, they are bulbs or rhizomes, like iris, which must always be divided.)

Other blue perennials, as handsome as they are durable, that shouldn't be tampered with once established, are the monkshoods and *Baptisia australis*, the false indigo. Monkshoods (*Aconitum*) are tall, elegant plants with glossy, deeply incised foliage and helmeted flowers. Most bloom in the fall, like shade and have a slightly sinister air, perhaps because one knows they are poisonous. 'Very dangerous if eaten or if their juices get into scratches,' one authority advises. To my knowledge, neither animal nor child has ever nibbled on my thirty-five-year-old clumps and my hands, perpetually scratched like those of most gardeners, have survived unscathed the staking, tying, cutting down of the stalks. But it is a thing to know, and I pass it on. The baptisia poses no such problem. It can be a great big perennial, the size of a small shrub, and it is covered with pea-like flowers that are the true indigo blue. (Though called false, the baptisia must be related to the true indigo, which it resembles, because the stems will, I read, produce a weak blue dye.) These and one or two other stand-bys—Virginia bluebells, the powder-blue *Phlox divaricata*, both semi-wildings; Stokes's asters, fringed like sea-anemones—complete the list of blue perennials in residence here. Now for the trouble-makers, those I can't grow for the life of me.

The giant delphiniums come first. I don't mean the garland larkspurs (Belladonna and Bellamosum, light and dark blue respectively, are the classics), nor the Chinese species, nor Connecticut Yankee, developed by the photographer Edward Steichen. All these are of moderate height with loosely organized flowers like big larkspurs, very pretty and easy to grow—if I couldn't succeed with a flower called Connecticut Yankee, I really would die of shame—and given my contempt for the grosser hybrids, they should do me nicely. Alas, where delphiniums are concerned, good taste flies out the window. I want the biggest and showiest, those rulers of the race whose densely packed spires can reach to six feet, the glory of the English herbaceous border. I can do without the pinks and purples. The myriad blues are what I want, all the sapphires and azures of a Chartres window, and an occasional white.

It is hopeless. Delphiniums like a cool damp climate, neither too hot nor too cold, and a sweet soil, what the English call a chalk garden. (Does anyone remember the play of that name and the entrance of Gladys Cooper in a floppy hat, limp dress, garden basket of the type called a Sussex trug over her arm—or have I invented the trug?—deathlessly beautiful at age seventy? Eighty? When I think of delphiniums, that apparition comes back to me.)

I supply the lime they need, surround their tender shoots with ashes to keep off slugs, water them tenderly. I tie the stalks individually to slim bamboo poles. The commoner types respond handsomely, but not the giants. They bloom once and never again. I tell myself the climate is at fault, and to an extent that is true. The giant delphiniums thrive along the Maine coast and in the Pacific northwest, home of the Pacific hybrids that even the English now carry in their catalogues, for they are the world's best. Here, better gardeners than I am treat them as biennials and start them early under glass.

I can't do that and excused myself accordingly—until a few years ago when I pulled up to a derelict gas pump on a nearby back road, magnetized by the sight of five-foot delphiniums (and columbines nearly as large) growing in a grassy little pasture that showed no sign of having been cultivated. Queried, the rustic who ran the pump allowed that he raised them both from seed he got from an English firm called Thompson & Morgan. Had I heard of it? I had. At that time it had no American outlet, and I was rather smug about having got hold of a catalogue. Their delphinium seed (Blackmore & Langdon hybrids, the equivalent of our Pacific giants) hadn't done badly either. It was and is the most viable I have tried and once produced a respectable stand that lasted all of three years, a record, but nothing like these beauties in bloom among the weeds. How *he* had got hold of a catalogue was impossible to ask without implying an insulting incredulity. All I could do was humbly ask to buy a few plants, which naturally died on me, and to speculate that the real right way to cultivate giant delphiniums is to scatter the seed in an unplowed field.

Then there is the dustily blue *Catananche caerulea*: Cupid's dart, a daisy with a purple splotch and petals trimmed with pinking shears. Catananches aren't much to look at individually. They should be grown in large clumps drifting through a border, as I first saw them in an Oxford college garden—a garden that also had two white peacocks trailing their fans across a faultless lawn. The lawn and the peacocks are beyond me to imitate. The catananches ought not to be. They aren't rare plants, yet I can't grow them in sufficient quantity to make those blue clouds, or make them last. They tolerate the seed bed; they won't endure transplanting to the perennial beds, and that is that.

Still, they can't be classified as total disasters. I reserve that category for, first, *Meconopsis betonicifolia*, the fabled Himalayan poppy, the color of a summer sky, with golden anthers—and my abominable snowman. It grows in England but I have never seen it—not the tiniest shoot having come up from repeated sowings. (Nurseries don't carry it: poppies of this type are notoriously difficult to transplant.) I would give anything for a glimpse of it, even in somebody else's garden. The fact that nobody I know or have heard of grows it ought to console me. *Wyman* says this poppy 'always makes a great impression on American tourists visiting England, for it is practically unknown in the U.S.,' and I would bet that it is practically unknown in the Himalayas, too, these days, given the record of third-world countries in stripping their forests and wilderness lands, a record considerably worse than our own. What I can't understand is why, if it is practically unknown in the U.S., the seeds are sold by a number of companies. Somebody, somewhere, is cultivating this elusive blue papaver. It is clear I never will.

Another total failure is the gentians. One thinks of these as wild flowers, but some are in cultivation and can be found at nurseries, and since the wild gentians are all on the endangered-species list, growing them in the garden may be the only way to preserve them. I can't do it. There was a moment when I had four little *G. septemfidae* in the seed bed, a whole year old. These aren't the most exciting of the gentians, not to be compared with the exquisite fringed gentian (*G. crinita*) that is now almost extinct. But I am not fussy and was looking forward to transplanting my little specimens to a spot under the apple tree. Some unknown force put an end to that hope, and I didn't see them again.

Meanwhile I have embarked on yet another, probably doomed project. It is now my ambition to grow agapanthus, the so-called lily-of-the-nile, not a lily and with no connection to the Nile. (It comes from South Africa.) The flowers are blue or white, and it used to be considered a pot plant only, the tubers to be stored indoors over winter. Now, however, a hardy strain has been developed (*A. orientalis*) which we are promised will grow outdoors, with some protection, where temperatures don't fall below zero. Absent for some years from Wayside's catalogue, these were offered again in 1980 and I ordered the blue, which now sit in the perennial bed. They didn't bloom the first summer and don't have the air of looking forward to their winter season. Neither do I. Something tells me they won't make it. In that case I will try something else. There is no shortage of frustrating blue perennials.

I might have another go at the maddening little shrub called caryopteris, a kind of spirea that bursts into a cobalt-blue bloom at summer's end, a time when other blue flowers are absent or hard to come by. *C.* × *clandonensis*, Heavenly Blue, is the variety to order, and reorder. Three have been given homes here and quickly made their exit to a better world. According to *Wyman*, in a curiously worded sentence, caryopteris 'may be killed back by severe winters and, if not, a severe pruning in early spring will usually force it to produce better flowers.' Which seems to mean that being killed back is good for them. Mine haven't taken this view, and as for pruning them, they haven't given me the opportunity. Once killed back, they have chosen to leave it at that.

COMPOST

When fully 'cooked,' it looks like the blackest, richest soil in the world—or a devil's food cake. But it isn't soil at all, and in the earlier stages of decomposition you see, impacted like the layers of an archaeological site, what it is made of. This will vary from garden to garden. In mine, leaves and grass clippings are the chief ingredients—then cabbage stumps, pea vines, hydrangea heads, apples, hedge clippings, spent annuals, carrot tops, and I am sometimes afraid of coming on the fragile skeleton of a bird or mouse, though I never have—all the debris, in short, that the unconverted pay good money to have raked up, bagged, and carted away to the dump or removed by the garbage men. The compost heaps devour them all and return them in a form that is priceless while costing nothing.

You can't buy compost. Neither can a healthy, well-conducted garden do without it. Even if you can't bring yourself to believe in it as fertilizer and use it only in conjunction with chemicals, you still can't do without it, for the very life of the soil itself depends on it. Without the microorganisms at work in compost, soil would literally be dead. Nature supplies the model in field and forest, whose base is in a perpetual cycle of decay and renewal—a vast program of soil building that a compost heap merely imitates. The process can be speeded up by the addition of animal manures, which will enrich the mixture as well; some materials also 'burn' faster than others; and shredding helps. But sooner or later any pile of organic matter will reduce itself to a rich dark humus that is the finest soil conditioner available. It imparts an incomparable tilth (sections of my flower and vegetable plots can be dug with bare hands), protects plants equally from drought and freezing, is the ideal environment for earthworms (without which a good garden cannot do either—see EARTHWORMS). Together with cow manure—fresh when I can get it, dehydrated in 50-pound bags when I can't—seaweed and a little bonemeal, it is also the only fertilizer I have used for thirty years, and the results are impressive if I do say so.

All this has taken time, and faith. When I learned about composting after the war, it was a hobby for cranks, and neighbors refused to believe the heaps didn't attract rats. (They don't.) Today most gardeners have some idea of how to construct them, and composting machines are available—rotating drums said to produce the stuff in fourteen days. There are also shredders to break up branches and heavier materials like corn shucks, which in the ordinary way take years to decompose. Now that 'organic' has become a catch word, composting has even acquired a kind of mythical status. That is nonsense. It is a practice as old as agriculture, and no civilization has survived for long that hasn't found a way to recycle its vegetable and animal wastes.

The Mayas are a case in point. Yearly they burned over their cornfields, grown in cleared spaces in the jungle, and yearly planted new ones because they had found no other way to enrich the old. When the distance between city and food source became too great, the cities were abandoned—or so goes the most plausible explanation for their swift decline. In Asia, on the other hand, the composting of vegetable, animal and even human wastes (China's famous 'night soil') has been practiced for thousands of years, making it possible to support populations many times greater than those of pre-Columbian America. Composting was, in fact, general throughout the world until the development of chemical fertilizers, which farmers were brought to believe were all that was necessary to replenish the soil. Especially was this true in advanced America, where some old-fashioned gardeners let their trash piles decay in order to acquire humus for a few favored plants but the vast majority relied on chemicals. I certainly did when I planted our wartime victory garden. Clearly though I remembered the smoking piles of straw and manure on our Hungarian estate, I supposed, rightly, that such methods were outmoded in America and knowing nothing of the virtues of mulch allowed the chemicals to be poured on. The family paid handsomely, too, to have the leaves raked up and removed each fall. It pains me now to think of it.

Not until 1945 or thereabouts did I learn that we were guilty of something like original sin. Someone sent me a copy of a magazine called *Organic Gardening & Farming*. It was and is (the *Farming* has since been dropped) an inelegant little publication printed on cheap stock, with photographs strictly of the hand-held Kodak variety and a down-home prose style. It changed my life nevertheless and is the only magazine I have continuously subscribed to for thirty-five years. The editor and publisher was J. I. Rodale, whose bearded countenance glared forth from the editorial page like that of an Old Testament prophet in those days (since his death it has been supplanted by the more benign one of his son), and his message was stamped on every page. Like all great messages, it was simple, and to those of us hearing it for the first time, a blinding revelation. Soil, he told us, isn't a substance to hold up plants in order that they may be fed with artificial fertilizers, and we who treated it as such were violating the cycle of nature. We must give back what we took away. Moreover we must stop using man-made poisons to deal with pests if toxic residues weren't to build up to intolerable heights. By relying on chemicals we were contaminating the food we ate, the air we breathed, the earth and the waters under the earth.

Any instantaneous conversion implies an already existing bias, even if one is unaware of it. To swallow Rodale without question, one had already to be indisposed toward the modern world and to have an instinctive mistrust of scientific progress. It didn't hurt either to have some experience of civilizations older than our own and thus not to feel the misplaced American contempt for the way things are done in 'backward' countries. Anyway, I was obviously prepared to accept him lock, stock and barrel—though this was a good fifteen years before the publication of Rachel Carson's *Silent Spring*, twenty before the banning of DDT, and thirty before the use of defoliants in Vietnam whose atrocious consequences we are hearing about for the first time. No American lake or river had yet been found deadly to wild or human life. No area of the country could then have been called, as parts of northern New Jersey now are, with gallows humor, 'cancer alley.' Rodale didn't just look like a Jeremiah. He was one, and for a long while he suffered the consequences, ridicule being the least, the threat of prosecution the worst. Both the Federal Trade Commission and the American Medical Association gave him trouble at various periods, and the chemical companies would have been glad to see him disappear. But time has been on his side. What they tried to condemn as quackery has too often turned out to be, literally, dead right, and today even the United States Department of Agriculture, for years anything but his friend, is sponsoring projects he pioneered.

This isn't to say that he didn't have in him a vein of nuttiness, which manifested itself in various ways—in crackpot theories about language; in his morality plays about health, which he put on at his own expense at a theater in New York's Bowery; and in a sense of humor that owed not a little to Baron Münchausen. But these, you felt, were the oddities of the self-taught and the self-made. Jerome Irving Rodale was a son of the old New York ghetto and by his own admission was plagued from childhood with its multiple neuroses. Thus the sickly boy became a fitness freak; the undereducated young man, a voracious but indiscriminate reader. He craved success, and achieved it, first as a chartered accountant, then as the manufacturer of electric-wiring devices, finally as a publisher. But the fanatic who would have gone down, guns blazing, in the service of a good cause can never have been far beneath the surface. He wasn't really a businessman, still less an intellectual. He was a visionary, and in 1940 he found his vision.

It came to him in a book called *An Agricultural Testament*, by Sir Albert Howard. Sir Albert had been an agronomist in British government service in India, and is now considered to have been the founder of modern organic farming—which could be described as a hybrid of western science and eastern agricultural wisdom based on poverty. For Sir Albert had what was rare in the early part of this century, a respect for 'native' methods and needs. He noticed, for example, that plant and animal diseases were more prevalent on chemically farmed government lands than on those of Indian peasants too poor to buy artificial fertilizer. On the other hand, the peasants' yields were low in spite of their intelligent rotation of crops, which helped to maintain a surprising degree of fertility. These observations came together in his decision to improve on local methods by devising a way to recycle the nutrients available in plant wastes on the spot. The result was the Indore system of composting, so called after the Indian state where he worked, and the original model for the scientifically layered heap we know. Sir Albert was of course primarily concerned with the economics of poverty in an undeveloped country, but he came to believe that the problems he encountered would soon have a world-wide application. Most important of all, he was convinced that chemical fertilizers, insecticides and drugs were the worst of all possible answers, the result of a dangerously mistaken view that animal, vegetable and human life are separable entities.

All this, which isn't as simple as I have made it, was set forth in *An Agricultural Testament*, and it seems to have sunk without a trace, at least in America, where Rodale may have been its only reader—and how he chanced to come upon it I never found out. He wasn't a farmer or even a gardener, though he had by that time migrated to the small Pennsylvania town where his electrical firm had its headquarters. Nevertheless, as he once told me, 'It hit me like a ton of brick. For the first time, I realized that food affects health, and that chemical fertilizers are dangerous to people, animals and the soil. I realized that our lives wouldn't be complete without a farm. No longer could I eat store-bought vegetables and meat. A powerful impetus surged over us, and within a few weeks my wife and I had become the proud owners of one of the worst pieces of land in the country.'

What followed was the prototype of countless similar stories told and retold in the pages of *Organic Gardening*—a sort of cross between the comic misadventures of S. J. Perelman on *his* Pennsylvania farm and morality tales with a happy ending. (I sometimes wished I could bring the two men together; they had more in common than might have been readily apparent to either.) Everything was wrong: the soil ruined by generations of chemical farmers, the animals sick, even the barn rats crazed from eating sprayed grain. But the Rodales (unlike the Perelmans) persevered and at last had their reward in a beautiful harvest of corn. Rodale had his second epiphany: 'If this was what a couple of amateurs could do, what could experienced soil men accomplish with the organic method? I felt I had to share this experience with the rest of the country. It wouldn't be fair to know this and say nothing about it.' *It wouldn't be fair*. . . . The essence of the man was in that endearing sentence. He had to share everything he knew, or believed, or that had happened to him. Like Freud, he was often his own case history. And so the experienced soil men were found, and the magazine that would expound the theory begun. As it happened, he already owned a small press, so there was no delay, and the first issue of the magazine appeared in 1942.

It was the preliminary trickle of a flood. Books, newsletters, other magazines (*Prevention* is the best known), brochures poured from the Rodale Press as his areas of concern broadened to include food additives, fluoridation, artificial vitamins, plastic, refined sugar, hormones in animal feed and God knows what else. I can't claim to have followed him down all these avenues. My favorites were and still are *Organic Gardening* and *The Encyclopedia of Organic Gardening*, my bible. I don't subscribe to *Prevention*, which is dedicated to health, mostly because I haven't the backbone to follow its precepts. I smoke, drink coffee and alcohol, use refined sugar to make jelly, buy eggs at the store, don't like most health foods, am perfectly aware that commercially raised chickens are death but eat them anyway because no local source supplies organically raised meats. And so on. I'm not a convert Rodale would take much pride in.

But I have been faithful in my fashion and look back on my visit to his farm as one of the more inspiriting events in my life. It happened in the early 1960's after my request for an interview. I had been commissioned to write an article about him, but that was an excuse. I had long wanted to set eyes on him and the farm, which I took to be a latter-day offshoot of those nineteenth-century experiments in living off the land, something like Bronson Alcott's Fruitlands, all unbolted bread and water and vegetarianism but without the metaphysics, and my first sight of Rodale seemed to confirm the impression that he belonged in another century. With his neatly trimmed beard, three-piece city suit and overcoat, he was an incongruously formal figure against the backdrop of rich Pennsylvania farmland. He might have been a visiting preacher, and one looked for the buggy he had just stepped out of. That impression, however, was incorrect. He may have been a visionary but he lived in the present, and he knew how things worked. The farm worked. You could see that at a glance. The compost piles, standing here and there in the fields like huge prehistoric structures, were awesome, obviously the last word in composting technology. The cattle were sleek; the chickens in the chicken houses, organically fed and living over specially designed pits of compost and topsoil, not only looked healthy, their premises were free of the usual chicken-house stink—and the one we had roasted for supper was the nearest thing to a *poulet de Bresse* I have eaten in this country, the breakfast egg the next morning was of a quality I had forgotten. No nonsense here about high thinking and bad food.

Still, it wouldn't have been the farm I was expecting if that had been all there was to it. There had to be a touch or two of fantasy, of magic, and sure enough . . . Why, for instance, were the trees in the orchard twined with copper wires like bonsai in training? Why were cans of water buried among the cabbage heads? Well, that was part of an experiment with static electricity, which perhaps has a vivifying effect on plants. We had seen snapshots in the magazine of beans growing under wire and a control crop grown without, and manifestly the wired beans were taller and more productive. So the question was whether metal has the power to attract static electricity, which could then be expected to help the growth of trees and cabbages as well as beans. (This is my memory at least, and I find that as usual it has oversimplified. Electroculture is more fully if to me still bafflingly discussed in *The Encyclopedia of Organic Gardening*.)

Field trials were of course the farm's main business, for not only was Rodale curious to know all there was to know, he had much to prove to skeptics—about the superior food value of organically grown crops, about the non-toxic control of insects, and a lot else. Like his mentor Sir Albert Howard, he had his laboratory in the field and didn't believe in abstract research. That remains true of the Rodale operations, which have been enlarged in recent years. The Organic Gardening and Farming Research Center is now a 300-acre farm some distance from the old place and may not have the same charm (I haven't visited it), though the projects sound just as fascinating. In the last couple of years, for instance, they have been concentrating on the giant amaranth as a possible grain source for home gardens; and as you might expect the amaranth is an ancient food crop grown in remote and romantic parts of the world—Nepal, Mexico, Africa, whence seed has been fetched for trials. Today, the Research Center has 308 varieties of this plant, which is very beautiful, under cultivation. We readers are waiting to see how it all turns out, just as we followed the fortunes of electrocuted beans and are now learning how to construct solar greenhouses and wood-burning furnaces.

J. I. Rodale died of heart failure in 1971 as he was about to be interviewed by Dick Cavett. I had been worried about this appearance: Would he make a good impression, or come across as a bearded old crank? It was almost as though a member of one's family were suddenly going to be hauled into the spotlight, and one wasn't sure he could cope. Perhaps he wasn't sure either. At any rate, he collapsed. He was seventy-three. Adele Davis's death at a much earlier age caused considerable loss of faith in her theories and there were those who felt that Rodale should have lasted into his high nineties to prove his. Which of course is nonsense. Had he lived otherwise, he might have died much sooner.

Be that as it may, he was a loss. His son Robert, who bears a close physical resemblance to him even to the beard, is an able successor and professionally speaking does a better job than his father did. The magazines are far better edited than they were, and there are fewer detours into sheer zaniness. The younger Rodale is less likely than the old to cast doubt on the movement by his eccentricities, and if called into court would probably make a more convincing witness. But I miss the old boy who first laid it on the line for us all those years ago, who fought the good fight with Jewish jokes and mind-boggling schemes (one I recall was the use of playing cards to illustrate certain points about health)—and I know his son does too. But he has his memorial, a couple of million of them, surely, by now, in the form of all those compost heaps ripening on farms and in gardens where compost heaps never were before, where the very word 'compost' was unknown until he taught us what it meant.

--- ❦ ---

DAHLIAS

Looking at my dahlias one summer day, a friend whose taste runs to the small and impeccable said sadly, 'You do like big, conspicuous flowers, don't you?' She meant vulgar, and I am used to that. It hasn't escaped me that mine is the only Wasp garden in town to contain dahlias, and not the discreet little singles either. Some are as blowzy as half-dressed Renoir girls; others are like spiky sea-creatures, water-lilies, or the spirals in a crystal paperweight; and they do shoot up to prodigious heights. But to me they are sumptuous, not vulgar, and I love their colors, their willingness to bloom until the frost kills them and, yes, their assertiveness. I *do* like big flowers when they are also beautiful.

Dahlias are, of course, tropicals. They come from Mexico, and most books, including the *R.H.S.*, say they were introduced to the Madrid Botanical Garden in 1798, whence they made their way to France and England. Early garden dahlias in England were derived from seed sent by Lady Holland, wife of the British ambassador to Spain, in 1804; and the Empress Josephine grew them at Malmaison. Most of which is true as far as it goes, but one may wonder why it took so long for a plant first seen by Cortes in 1519 to reach Europe, and the answer is that we really don't know exactly when the dahlia, or a host of other New World flowers, was first imported to Spain; but it was certainly well before 1789.

There is a reason for this obscurity. Spain, wishing to protect the flora in her New World possessions, and incidentally aware that her real riches might turn out to be vegetable rather than mineral, imposed in 1566 a ban on all exploration by foreign plant-hunters and forbade publication of any information on the natural resources of Spanish America. But the ban didn't apply to the importation of plants to Spain itself, and they arrived on every boat. Nasturtiums were growing in the Seville garden of Nicholas Monardes (a botanist for whom bee balm is named) by 1569; marigolds came even earlier—they were aboard the first ships returning with the news of Cortes' conquest in 1520, and dahlias may have been in that shipment too. Many of these plants grew in monastery gardens. There has never been a more knowledgeable group of botanists and horticulturists than the Spanish fathers in the New World. It is largely thanks to them that Spain's American colonies were a flourishing garden at a time when England's were mere specks on the map, constantly threatened with starvation. (Contrast the success of the Spanish settlement at St. Augustine with the dismal failure of Raleigh's on Roanoke Island.) Not only did they discover the potato, the pineapple, tobacco, tomatoes, maize, etc., they paid their debt to Amerindian agriculture by introducing wheat, peaches, grapes, olives, figs, lettuce, oranges, pears, barley, onions, and countless other crops to the New World that, in Anglo-Saxon myth, they ravished. They gave more than they got, but that is another story. My point here is that one can't really speak of 'discoveries' by other Europeans of plants that the Spaniards must have known about for centuries.

Take the fuchsia. The first non-Spaniard to observe and name it was a French priest, Charles Plumier, who located it in Santo Domingo in 1703. It was then rediscovered—twice in Chile, the second time by an English sea captain who took his specimen home to England, where it was growing in 1800; yet again in Guatemala, and lastly in Morelia, Mexico, in 1898. Now it is true that not all these were the same varieties. What is impossible is that no Spaniard had known of their existence before 1703. The city of Morelia was founded in 1541. It isn't conceivable that the brilliantly conspicuous fuchsia went unnoticed by some inquisitive Spanish friar for the next three hundred years. We know about the English sea captain's fuchsia growing at Wapping on Thames because that is part of our world. What was growing on a similar window sill in Andalusia we have no idea.

An English history of Spanish gardens, both before and after the Conquest, remains to be written. In the meantime, all we know is what can be seen through the cracks that appeared in the famous embargo. Cracks there were, of course—no ban of that sort can ever be airtight, and this one wasn't either. Not only did an occasional Plumier slip through, Spanish botanists themselves (and I'm not clear about how they got away with this) published enough information to give their European colleagues a fair idea of what was growing in their colonies. The Jesuit missionary José de Acosta, who was in Latin America from 1570 to 1587, described many of its flora in his *Natural and Moral History of the Indies*. The Monardes who grew nasturtiums published the first real herbal on New World plants between 1565 and 1571; and there were many others, all eagerly translated.

French, Dutch and English incursions into Spain's possessions brought still more information, and in several cases the plants themselves. (Drake's raid on the Florida coast in 1568 procured him samples of the potato, which he eventually took to England; marigolds and nasturtiums were growing in French royal gardens by the end of the seventeenth century.) Nothing, after all, is easier than smuggling seeds and bulbs, and where piracy failed, diplomats with their immunity to baggage inspection were most helpful. In 1750, the German ambassador to Mexico sent flower seed to his botanist friend, Gottfried Zinn, for whom the flowers were eventually named. And dahlias, too, were smuggled. So says Claire S. Haughton in *Green Immigrants* (1978), a book full of interesting if sometimes confusing research. According to her, a French ambassador to Mexico was inadvertently responsible for introducing dahlias to France, I gather (she doesn't give the date) a century or more before the time usually assigned. It was inadvertent because his real aim was to ship specimens of the cochineal louse, the producer of a valuable dye on which Spain then had a monopoly. No naturalist, the poor man knew only that the louse fed on a plant but not which one, and possibly confused by the similarity between the word cochineal and the Aztec name for the dahlia, *cocoxochitl*, he sent his bugs attached to dahlia plants. In fact, the cochineal feeds exclusively on a certain cactus, and his were dead on arrival in Paris. But the dahlias were alive and were sent to the Jardin des Plantes, where they did so well they were given away to French gardeners and a few years later were being exported to England.

That wasn't all. A Dutch importer got his hands on some dahlia tubers in 1782; and finally the Swedish botanist for whom they were named, Anders Dahl, somehow procured enough specimens to have produced several hybrids before his death in 1789. The significance of that date now emerges. It didn't mark the introduction of the dahlia to Europe, where the *cocoxochitl* was already known, but rather an attempt by the Spanish government to lay official claim to it. The king accordingly held a celebration in its honor at the Madrid Botanical Garden (in 1789), and wishing at the same time to identify himself with modern science, renamed it, not out of the blue as most accounts leave one to infer, but after the botanist most closely associated with its development. That, roughly, is Haughton's account. Nobody else mentions the celebration. Frances Perry (*Flowers of the World*, 1973), sticking by 1789 as the date of introduction, says that Vincente Cervantes, Superintendent of the Botanic Garden at Mexico City, sent dahlia seed to Abbé Cavanilles of Madrid, and that it was the abbé who named the flower in honor of Dahl. Haughton, too, mentions Cavanilles, but not as an abbé and not in connection with dahlias. *She* says he was a well known collector of exotics in whose gardens grew, among other Mexican plants, the cosmos. But at this stage it becomes tiresome to try to get the story straight. In spite of confusions in her text, I am prepared to take Haughton's word for it that the dahlia reached Europe well before 1789.

Why isn't this made clear in encyclopedias? Partly, I believe, because of a built-in bias in most Anglo-Saxon sources against Latins in general and Spaniards in particular. Most of us were brought up in the belief that the wicked Spaniards raped the New World while the virtuous English brought light and civilization— a dubious theory not difficult to disprove but present even in horticultural histories, where the Spanish contribution is regularly downgraded or dismissed: pirates like Drake and Hawkins are heroes for having stolen plants like the potato from Spanish colonies, while the very names of the Spaniards who propagated them are unknown. Other examples could be cited of these prejudices, but a particularly egregious one appears in F. R. Cowell's *The Garden as Fine Art* (1978), where he makes this preposterous claim: 'The fine gardens [the Aztecs] had created in Mexico amazed their Spanish conquerors, who, however, had no more interest in them than they had shown toward the splendid gardens of the Moors in their own land. Nothing like the ancient Mexican gardens had ever existed further north where the British first came as settlers. Unlike the Spaniards, they brought with them that love of gardens which some generations of their forebears had begun to foster in England . . .'

Scarcely a word of this is accurate. Like Cowell, we take for granted English preëminence in horticulture, forgetting that it is of relatively recent date. Before the nineteenth century, the Spaniards, the French, the Dutch led the field in the discovery and propagation of plants. (In passing, one might note that it was a Spanish queen, Catherine of Aragon, who reintroduced the peach —and cherries and plums—to an England devastated by the Wars of the Roses.) In the sixteenth century, the Spaniards, who had in fact absorbed all the Moors could teach them, were the most advanced agriculturists in Europe and far from showing no interest in Mexican gardens, were positively obsessed with them. Reports from the Indies were more concerned with flowers and fruits than with any other subject, including gold—beginning with those of Columbus himself, who regretted he hadn't brought a botanist along on the first voyage and thereafter wrote repeatedly of the botanical wonders he saw. That the Council of the Indies should have taken steps to preserve the vegetation of the New World by imposing the ban should speak for itself—though it will, of course, be put down to commercial greed, as if the English, the Dutch and every other European power hadn't been as eager to lay hands on

New World products, and far less worried about their wanton exploitation.

But even if one hasn't read the histories, the chronicles of Bernal Díaz and Bartolomé de las Casas and others, one can still look at the physical evidence the Spaniards left behind them. Whatever their sins may have been, no Europeans did more to beautify the countries they conquered. Every Spanish–American city was laid out with an eye to public and private gardens—more than you can say for ours. Even the unspeakable Pizarro planned his new Peruvian capital to include spaces for gardens, with water conduits to serve them. Beautiful gardens were everywhere in Latin America; but one might name two famous ones in Mexico: that of Don Manuel de Ibara near Tacuba, and the Borda gardens in Cuernavaca, diminished now but said to rival the Generalife in their day. Nor should Americans forget the orange and olive groves, the vineyards and patio gardens of California, all of Spanish origin. It boils down to what one means by love of gardens. No Latin could have written 'A garden is a lovesome thing, God wot!' —that sort of sentiment is foreign to them. We, on the other hand, distrust their inability to identify flowers by name, their love for the straight line and the pruned tree, and above all their desire to put land to good use. Somewhere in Trollope, and I can't remember which novel, there is a description of a Tuscan property to which the unhappy English heroine is obliged to retire, her misery greatly increased by the dreariness of terraces planted in olives and grapes, and vegetables actually quite near the house. Trollope hasn't a good word to say for this earthly paradise, and many Spanish gardens would naturally be dismissed on the same ground. The Dominican convent at San Jacinto near Mexico City, with its fifteen acres of shady walks under orange and lemon trees, its pomegranates, figs and grapes as well as native Mexican fruits, would be less a garden than a commercial enterprise. (That the English colonists were not blind to the economic value of plants is shown by the establishment of the Trustee's Garden at Savannah in 1733, which was entirely devoted to plants of possible commercial utility and in fact the first of its kind in the world; but that wouldn't count in the indictment against Spain.)

Iberian horticulture might appear to have no connection with a New England village, but it happens that I have examples all around me. Our Portuguese fishing families with their grape arbors, their vegetables interplanted with tall old roses are in that (alas, fading) tradition, and dahlias are one of their specialties—some of them brought long ago from the Azores to blaze like bonfires against the picket fences. I identify with these exuberant patches, closer to my heart than any number of carefully chosen evergreens and ground covers set in wood chips, and won't allow that their owners are less talented gardeners than Anglo-Saxon members of the garden club. It is my Portuguese neighbor who advises me about dahlias, she who tells me to ignore the conventional wisdom and plant them early or there will be no flowers before August. Plant them deeply (say, ten inches), and they can go in well before the last possible frost in May because their shoots won't yet be above ground by then.

Again, it was my neighbor who solved the maddening puzzle of how to divide (or not to divide) dahlia tubers. Books tell you to cut off each one, keeping a piece of the old stalk it was attached to—or the tuber will come up 'blind,' i.e., no flowers. She, and now I, say it can't be done. A big clump will have as many as fifteen tubers inextricably entangled and not more than three or four of them will be attached to the stalk in any way apparent to the naked eye. Furthermore, you don't *want* fifteen separate tubers, each of which will produce a single rather spindly plant, and all of them of the same variety. So the procedure is as follows: when you dig the clumps up for storage in the fall, leave them intact. (I store mine in plastic bags filled with vermiculite, a substance I loathe but which is far better for this purpose than the old newspapers, peat moss, or aluminum foil that used to be all we had.) In spring when you take them out a certain amount of drying will have occurred, and a massive clump gently shaken will separate itself into several parts. Plant these—or, if no separation occurs without the use of force, simply replant the whole clump. It will grow into an immense plant. But what is wrong with that? Experts pinch out the weaker stems, and the side buds; they also cut the stalks back. I don't. I don't find that cutting back deters the tall varieties from eventually reaching the height they intended to be in the first place, and I'm not interested in 'exhibition blooms.' I harvest dahlias continuously for the house, and that is all the pruning they get.

One never runs out of dahlia stock but does get bored with the endless multiplication of the same cultivars. There are two ways to buy new ones: mail order or off the shelf at a garden center, and oddly enough I have done better with the latter. Many mail-order houses send out a single tuber coated with wax and charge $2.50 and up for it. At best, these produce a skimpy plant and often they come to nothing. At garden centers you can often find unwaxed clumps from Holland, packed in peat moss and costing a modest $1.98. A color photograph is clipped to the packet, and it is accurate. What you see is what you get, complete with instructions for planting. These, to my mind, are the best dahlias on the market and an amazing bargain.

The intelligent thing to do would be to save those labels for cross-indexing with those you attach to the dahlias when you store them. On the other hand, it probably won't make much difference if you do. I have never found a satisfactory way to identify dahlias in storage. Wooden or plastic labels tied to the stalk work their way loose as the clump dries out. Adhesive tape sticks but the ink smears and fades. I can therefore count on a certain number of mistakes when they are replanted: A five-footer will be at the front of the bed instead of the back, a pink be discovered among the yellows. It doesn't matter as much as you might think. Dahlia colors are pure, and if you stay away from the fire-engine reds, they go well together and with other flowers. I am no hand at color schemes anyway. Obviously, one tries to avoid the worst (which for me was an old scarlet poppy next to which mauve foxgloves invariably self-sowed themselves), but I don't think it's necessary to plan a herbaceous border down to the last forget-me-not. By choosing the colors I like I generally find they get on with each other, and the occasional surprise is as likely to be a pleasant one as the reverse. Dahlias, however, do look best in groups, like all flowers, and not standing up like lonely sentinels.

Now for the caveat: Dahlias have to be staked, no matter what size they are. Their stalks are hollow, almost like bamboo, and very brittle, and no matter how deeply you plant the clumps there isn't much by way of anchorage for them. With the arrival of the equinoctial storms, a stand of them will go over like felled trees, and there is no more impossible job than to right them once that has happened. They must therefore be lashed to tall, heavy masts —and these will look hideous if, as one is advised to do, they are driven in early, even before planting, to avoid damaging the tubers. I take that risk. I start with small stakes and only hammer in the large ones toward the end, when the plants are tall enough to hide them. And I can't say any appreciable harm has been done. The dahlias are the last thing in the garden to remind me of sum-

mer, and the last gathering is as fresh and lovely as the first. After
the killing frost, sometime in late October, when I go out and see
them hanging in blackened rags, I lose interest in what is left.
What are a few bedraggled chrysanthemums beside them?

--- ∽ ---

DAYLILIES
(*Hemerocallis*)

The yeomen of the garden, daylilies are unbelievably sturdy and
accommodating. Sun or shade, wet soil or dry, anything suits
them. They don't attract pests and are never sick. Moreover they
are edible, and in Asia where they originated, a veritable pharma-
copoeia. The product called gum-jum or gum-tsoy, sold in China-
towns, is daylily blossoms steamed and dried and used like okra to
thicken soups. (Fresh, they can be dipped in batter and fried.) In
late spring, the tender heart of the plant can be blanched like
asparagus or eaten raw, and the raw young roots are said to be
excellent. Since they are also used as a diuretic (not to mention a
cure for piles, dropsy, jaundice and other ailments), I have hesi-
tated to try them. But there is something engaging about a plant
with so many dimensions, so bent on giving good value.

Daylily species are found in the tropics and have been seen in
Lapland. In America, early colonists planted them around farmhouses and in cemeteries, whence they leapfrogged over walls and
established themselves along roadsides. *H. flava*, the sweet-scented
lemon lily, and *H. fulva*, burnt orange, were the commonest types
in this country, and gardens laid out before 1900 nearly always
had a stand or two. Ours had a bank of *H. fulva* forty feet long and
still does, because I am reluctant to replace it with new hybrid
varieties. A gardener in business for any length of time has regularly to decide whether he wants to keep up with the latest in
plants or live with the older varieties he is fond of, and it can be
difficult. A garden entirely stocked with the newest, showiest hybrids is as depressing as a woman with a face-lift: the past is
erased at the expense of character. But neither is anything gained
by clinging to second-rate specimens when newer and more beau-

tiful ones are available. With daylilies, however, the breeders have surely gone too far. More than 15,000 varieties exist, with several hundred new ones being registered every year, and as usual when this is done to a flower, the type is utterly corrupted. We now have doubles, triples, miniatures, polychromes, bicolors—and a leathery new texture. Ninety-nine percent of the new varieties I wouldn't have at any price. Daylilies colored orchid, cream, peach, make me slightly sick, and the names are awful too: I would blush to admit I was growing Precious One, Disneyland, or Bitsy. Nor am I impressed that I can now have one or another kind of daylily blooming from May to frost. I don't want any perennial dominating my borders to that extent. A border is among other things a calendar of the seasons, and I don't look for columbines in August or chrysanthemums in July. Daylilies come in midsummer as far as I am concerned, and that is another reason why the bank of *H. fulva* won't be replaced.

This isn't to say that I altogether exclude modern daylilies from the garden. They have undeniable advantages. The flowers are larger and the blooming period somewhat longer, and now and again I come across one I can't resist. When that happens, I don't throw away the old clump but plant it elsewhere in a less conspicuous place, because the decision may be reversed, as occurred about five years ago. Carried away, not for the first time, by a plant from a distinguished cultural background, I ordered an expensive new daylily and, not for the first time, found it to be an elaboration of the original form that was subtly, fatally wrong in almost every particular—too ruffled, the texture coarsened, the color impure. It made me pine for the virginal lemon lily it replaced, and fortunately the remedy was at hand. The lemon lily is back where it was, and the newcomer in exile near the compost heaps.

———— ❧ ————

EARTHWORMS

The way people go on about them, you would think earthworms were a regular garden pest. Gardening columns constantly run letters asking how to 'control' them in lawns and flowerpots, and rarely do these queries receive the proper reply: Don't. They are wholly beneficial, and the garden without them is well on its way to becoming a desert. Earthworms help to create topsoil; they also burrow as far down as six feet, aerating the soil and breaking up hardpans. Every bit of soil ingested by them comes out many times enriched with minerals—as much nitrogenous fertilizer as fifty tons per acre in good organic earth.

That, if anything, is the difficulty. The gardener with soil full of earthworms can bless himself, for they are a sign of good tilth and fertility. But they don't go willingly about their useful work in poor, hard ground where they are most needed. It's another case of them as has, gets. Earthworms can be ordered by mail, and when I was an early convert to organic gardening, I sent for a batch in hopes they would set about improving my soil then and there. I never saw them again. To breed earthworms, as it were, you must provide the rich, organic environment they like, and if you have that, you already have them. They appear automatically in mulches, compost heaps, etc., but they won't colonize barren soil and they are very sensitive to chemicals.

What then of the 'unsightly' worm castings I read of on lawns? I can only say that one must be fastidious indeed to object to what looks like black, granulated soil, and in any case I have never noticed them on the lawn—a very large expanse teeming with worms, some of them so big they have caused alarm in those mowing it for the first time. In damp weather, the vibrations of the machine sometimes force them to the surface, and force me to explain that no, they aren't harmful, not a menace but a Good Thing. Nor can I see why they should be a Bad Thing in a flower-pot. Thalassa Cruso, of all people, speaks of protecting pots set outdoors for the summer from 'foraging worms' and at summer's end would have one submerge the pots in buckets of water over-night to destroy any worms that may have got into them. She doesn't explain what can possibly be wrong with a worm or two spending the winter in a pot and fertilizing it; and I personally welcome them if they happen to stray into my homemade potting soil or otherwise find their way into containers.

Still, I think I know what is behind the prejudice against them. Though I have no fear of earthworms, I do have a morbid horror of snakes. The smallest garter snake sends me shrieking for help; and the information that many of them are useful predators leaves me more than cold. I can therefore imagine that one might have the same reaction to earthworms, and be indifferent to the news that they are essential to the health of the soil. I can only say that if one is *not* the victim of an uncontrollable phobia, one should make every effort to encourage them.

———————— ❧ ————————

ENDIVE

Endive is a chicory and chicory is endive, depending on where you live, and the confusion can lead to ordering the wrong seed. So: If you want the ruffled green winter salad with a blanched heart, that is *Cichorium endivia*, in catalogues usually labeled endive. If you want the fat blond shoot that costs a fortune and is so good braised or as a salad, that is *Cichorium Intybus*, otherwise Belgian endive or *witloof* (but in most encyclopedias under chicory). The first I don't think justifies itself in the home garden; it is just as good bought at a reliable market. The second, if you value it as I do and object to paying the price, is worth the considerable trouble of forcing it.

In theory, you could go out and dig up a supply of *Cichorium Intybus*. It is that plant with blue daisy-like flowers you see by every roadside in August, and it is an escapee, brought here originally by Europeans, who roast and grind the root as a substitute for or an additive to coffee. Otherwise, you sow the seed in June, thin the seedlings to about eight inches apart and let everything go until the end of October, when it is time to begin the rather messy business called forcing. You dig up the roots, rinse and trim them neatly, and cut off all but an inch of the leaves. The next step used to be to plunge them into a deep box filled with damp sand, somewhere in a warm, dark cellar. The roots, trying to replace their lost leaves, then send up a pale, thick bud through the sand —the same as those tenderly packed in tissue paper in the market. They won't perhaps be as perfectly formed—they tend to be skimpier and looser-leaved—as the commercial product, but they are every bit as delicious either in a salad or sautéed in butter (with a squeeze of lemon and a touch of sugar).

That is the old-fashioned way. A friend has now told me hers, which I haven't tried but which sounds much easier and cleaner than the sandbox. She fills a small plastic garbage pail with vermiculite, inserts the roots in that, and to provide the necessary darkness covers the pail with black polyethylene. Otherwise, the procedure is the same. When the tips of the new shoots can be seen they are ready to be pulled up, and the root cut off (it won't try again) and replaced with a fresh one. In mild climates, the roots can stay in the ground until you are ready to blanch them, half a dozen or so at a time. But where the ground freezes early they must be dug all at once and stored in a bag in a cool, dark place. They won't sprout until they are replanted and given moisture but they shouldn't be allowed to dry out. Manage things right, and you can have a supply all through the darkest and dreariest winter months, and smile pityingly at those who are paying through the nose for this de luxe vegetable.

Honesty compels me to add that there is another method, and I'm sorry to report that it comes from France, where standards must be falling rapidly. It is called hygroponic, and the growing medium is chemically fertilized water. Solely in the interests of research, I have tasted hygroponically grown tomatoes and cucumbers and can state that they are vile. Nor will I believe they are anything but poison to the human body. In the continuing dispute between organic gardeners and the agricultural establishment, the chief bone of contention is whether or not the source of fertilizer makes a difference to the nutritional value of food crops. The organic people say it does and have laboratory tests to prove it. The chemically oriented say it doesn't and have tests to prove *their* thesis. To me, it stands to reason they are wrong, but even if they aren't, there can be, to an educated palate, no argument about the difference in flavor—and of all chemically fertilized vegetables, those grown hygroponically are the worst. I feel sure the endive thus raised is no exception, though I haven't and wouldn't try it. (Anyone interested, however, can write the J. A. Demonchaux Co., 827 North Kansas, Topeka, Kan. 66608 for the special seed required and directions.)

EVERGREENS

Roughly, there are two kinds: conifers with needles or soft coral-line sprays, and the fleshy-leaved types like mountain laurel. Climate draws another line for northern gardeners. Not for us the sacred Mediterranean triad of cypress, stone pine and olive. We can only dream of banks of camellias luxuriating in the shade of live oaks. We must do without the citruses, sweet bay and myrtle, oleanders and hedges of rosemary. All we have is rhododendrons, mountain laurel, yews, some andromedas and hollies and the familiar boreal conifers. Many of these are very beautiful. My complaint is against our national preference for those that look like Christmas trees. This conical image endlessly imprinted on the retina makes me sigh for an oak, and I sometimes think the country will smother in spruce and fir, arborvitae and hemlock. Evergreen foundation planting is everywhere the substitute for the privacy of walls and fences, and where I live some of our best architecture is hidden by dark towers planted a generation or two ago, evidently with no premonition of what their eventual size would be. Today's choices are equally banal, though dwarfer in habit. Not lilacs in the New England dooryard bloom: Those are Pfitzer junipers.

The Victorians are responsible, as usual. It was they who introduced all this evergreenery into landscaping. The English eighteenth-century designers, inspired by Claude Lorrain and Salvator Rosa, hung the native oaks and beeches like scenery in a theater, in lines or wedges. Conifers weren't present in these compositions, and their later introduction, like that of rhododendrons and azaleas, was an error of taste that has been perpetuated. Evergreens don't mix well with hardwoods, handsome though they are in avenues or in solitary splendor. Neither should they be spotted at hazard on a lawn. They are best grouped with their own kind, and not too closely. Over-dense planting is the second commonest mistake I see around me: trees grown lopsided because deprived of light, with half their branches bare. Nurseries should label their specimens in large letters: THIS FIR WILL BE THIRTY FEET HIGH AND TEN FEET WIDE IN FIFTEEN YEARS. This is doubly important since, unlike hardwoods, most evergreens are or should be clothed in branches from top to bottom, and they need space as well as light.

Winter is naturally the season of concern, what to do about a garden that is snowbound for something like three months of the year. We must have evergreens, even if we plant them for the wrong reasons. There is, for example, the curious notion that they cheer a place up. In the words of A. J. Downing, who introduced landscaping to nineteenth-century America, they 'give an appearance of verdure and life' that 'cheats winter of half its dreariness.' Well, some do and some don't, and the kinds I mostly observe do not. I know of few more lowering sights than the Norway spruces, hung with mourning rags, that encumber my village. There is nothing intrinsically uplifting about our popular conifers. American arborvitae and the misnamed red cedar (really *Juniperus virginiana*—only three true cedars grow in the United States, and none is a native) turn rusty as old clothes when the cold hits them. Irish yew, like a frozen black waterfall in its fastigiate form, is a magnificent evergreen, and one of the gloomiest, a frequent choice in cemeteries. The darkness that makes evergreens so welcome in sunlit countries has the opposite effect in the North.

But if Downing was wrong about the cheer, he was right that a garden without evergreens is a wasteland in winter. The question is which ones to grow and how to arrange them, and in spite of oppressive overplanting, this seems to me an almost totally neglected branch of American gardening. How often does one see photographs of gardens taken in winter in the pages of magazines or books? It is assumed, and rightly, that they aren't worth looking at in that season, though it does occupy a quarter of the year. I attribute this to the American reaction to snow. Except in skiiers and a few eccentrics like myself, it arouses something like panic. It follows that the moment the snow does fly, gardens are closed down, more than closed—abandoned. Some people do make a point of buying living Christmas trees and later planting them in memoriam—a custom I deplore because it merely adds to the excess of evergreens already on the scene. In fact, we have never tried to devise a winter aesthetic, and the failure is the more striking in that the modern landscape movement has otherwise been so strongly influenced by the Japanese, who are masters of the genre.

But then the Japanese adore snow. It is an eternal theme in their art and literature, has even a spiritual value. When asked to define Nō drama, its other worldliness, stillness and profundity, the greatest of Nō masters summoned these Zen images: 'Snow covers the thousand mountains—why does one peak remain unwhitened?' And: 'Snow piled in a silver bowl.' Readers of *The Tale of Genji* will remember innumerable episodes where a snowfall plays a key part in the emotional state of the characters—just as it does in Kawabata's modern novel, *The Snow Country*, almost a thousand years later. Far from resenting the snow that descends on his islands, the Japanese is deeply moved by the transfiguring effect on landscape and plants. And one must say that nature has blessed him: Japanese evergreens are extraordinary. They include the majestic cryptomeria, a relative of the sequoia; hinoki and sawara false cypress; the Nikko fir; *T. cuspidata* and other yews; exquisite pines, hollies, evergreen azaleas and ground covers.

With these to work with, it isn't surprising that the snow-laden Japanese garden is a wonderland. Nor is it an accident. Much of Japanese pruning is done to enhance the appearance of trees and shrubs under snow, notably the technique called cloud-pruning, in which large portions of foliage are stripped away to expose the branches, while that at the tips is shaped into layers or tufts. In winter, these tufts are like cushions for snow to rest on, and they transform the shrub from a shapeless lump into the dramatic forms depicted in the paintings and prints: ink strokes on a white ground.

Now the strange thing is that the Japanese way with evergreens, and the evergreens themselves, aren't unknown in this country. Even cloud-pruning is practiced; but you have to go West, where the snow doesn't fall, to see it. One knows, in part, why this should be. Not only has the Japanese impact on landscape gardening been greater in California than anywhere else, the Oriental hand with the shears is also available in that fortunate land. One has only to study the photographs (in, for example, *Time-Life*'s *Pruning and Grafting*) to detect the offstage presence of a skilled Japanese gardener, or someone trained in his tradition. In New England, we have no access to those techniques short of learning them for ourselves. It is also true that some of the shrubs and trees in California gardens aren't hardy here. Most of the Japanese ones, however, are—and even unpruned ought to stimulate the imagination of landscape architects more than they do. Instead, we have the familiar rock pile, shelving away from bleak house and planted with—yes, those Pfitzer junipers, those dwarf rhododendrons and azaleas, those Mugo pines. Versions of this formula are all over the northeast and all are mistranslations of the original, as dreary in winter as in summer. Yet all the Japanese evergreens I have named are to be found in American nurseries. That they are so seldom used can only be attributed to the widening gap between landscape architects and horticulturists now being fostered in universities (see WOMAN'S PLACE) or the invincible puritanism of the Harvard school of landscape architecture. Either way, the designer has failed to take advantage of the riches available to create a winter aesthetic that could successfully imitate, let alone supplant with some original contribution, the Japanese vision.

Still, that vision isn't for everybody. It isn't for me, with my white clapboard house built just after the Revolution, and my garden dominated by a Congregational church. I may as well admit that I have done poorly with evergreens—at first rejecting them because the garden was a summer one, then when I realized it wasn't, that we would in fact spend many winters here, falling victim to the Downing fallacy with its promise of cheer. Even so, I chose as few as possible. A weeping white pine went in by the summer house; a *Chamaecyparis obtusa* and two Japanese yews were interplanted with Chinese dogwood and a *Viburnum plicatum Mariesii* (a shrub whose blooms march by twos on top of the branches, creating the illusion of snow having fallen on it—it is, of course, a native of Japan and I rather imagine was bred to accentuate this characteristic). A hemlock hedge I already had, and three Taniyosho pines were planted in its vicinity. I violated no rules. It ought to work: it doesn't, and the arrival of snow, ironically, shows why. Each of these evergreens is, in its way, choice; but with everything else in the garden edited out, they are too widely dispersed to make common cause, and on a field of white look pointless.

Alternatives, I now see, were open to me. Since my garden is a series of rooms, I could have given at least one of them green walls and upholstered it with poufs and ottomans of yew and holly and weeping hemlock. (But that would have meant getting rid of the flowering shrubs.) Or I could have made more hedges, giving the place an evergreen skeleton. Formal European gardens, though not specifically designed for winter, are, so to speak, weatherproof, and acquire a romantic dimension when their evergreen architecture is outlined in white, their fountains dripping with icicles. Nothing so grand for me, of course, but a little more formality— box clipped low around the flower beds—would have helped. Unfortunately, I gave up on box rather too soon. I knew it could be grown here. Tough old specimens are to be seen next to decaying farmhouses and some of us found them in our village gardens when we bought our houses—gnarled and out of shape. Pruning didn't suit them. No matter how carefully tackled, the cut sections invariably died. Discouraged, I removed two mangled specimens; and new young plants didn't do well either. Probably they were the wrong kind. The variety called Newport Blue is, I am assured, hardy here; and Wayside has another, Green Velvet, bred in Ontario and guaranteed to stand harsher climates than this one. I can see it clipped into balls or little pyramids, to mark the corners of the flower beds, and I may try it, for the acrid scent of box on a hot day is something I miss.

What I would *not* do is introduce evergreens that aren't in fact green, such as I increasingly see offered in catalogues. I am disturbed by plants in colors other than those I expect, in seasons when I don't expect them: red maples and copper beeches that make summer look like autumn, crimson barberry hedges. Blue-needled spruces and junipers aren't for me, nor the false cypresses and arborvitae with yellow-gold tips now prominent in de luxe catalogues. I can't justify my prejudice—who can when it comes to gardening, and particularly to color? Ninety percent of America's gardeners disagree with me about evergreens in general and probably about their color as well. I can't help that. A garden is a private world or it is nothing, and the gardener must be allowed his vagaries.

———————— ❧ ————————

FAILURES

. . . For I do believe that flowers have feelings, and that those feelings extend to the human being who tends them . . . By no other theory can I explain, for example, my own total failure to grow alstroemerias, the lovely Peruvian lilies that flower in July. On the packet—or rather the bulb bag—it tells you that 'they resent lime.' Not a speck of lime did they get. It wasn't lime they resented, it was me. Again, it said that they 'succeed best in half shade.' They got it, but they didn't succeed; my own shadow had fallen across them. In desperation I bought them in pots, and planted them already established. But they died down and never came up again. 'Death,' they obviously said to themselves, 'is better than the thought of seeing *that* face again.'

BEVERLEY NICHOLS
Garden Open Tomorrow

Sooner or later every gardener must face the fact that certain things are going to die on him. It is a temptation to be anthropomorphic about plants, to suspect that they do it to annoy. One knows, after all, that they lead lives of their own: plant the lily bulb in the center of the bed and watch it come up under a brick near the edge; pull up a sick little bush and throw it on the compost heap, and ten to one, it will obstinately revive. Usually, though, gardening failures, like airplane crashes, are the result of 'human error,' of not reading the directions or paying attention.

It may be something as simple as absent-mindedly liming the hydrangea, or as subtle as not noticing that a streetlight shines all night on the chrysanthemum bed—chrysanthemum bloom is triggered by long dark nights and a persistent light may confuse them. A dog may regularly visit a bush that is turning yellow. The gardener must keep his eye peeled, as much for the things that do well as those that do badly. The two are related. The acid soil that favors the iris is bad for the peonies, and trying to grow them together doesn't work. You could learn this from a book but also from simple observation. People who blame their failures on 'not having a green thumb' (and they are legion) usually haven't done their homework. There is of course no such thing as a green thumb. Gardening is a vocation like any other—a calling, if you like, but not a gift from heaven. One acquires the necessary skills and knowledge to do it successfully, or one doesn't. The ancients gardened without guidance from books, by eye and by hand, and while I am a devotee of gardening books and love to study and quarrel with them, I don't think they are a substitute for practical experience, any more than cookbooks are.

One must, to begin with, acquire a mental map of the terrain, know where falls the shadow, where shines the sun—and when. For several seasons I made the elementary mistake of planting shrub roses in early spring, in locations that were full of sun at that time. Three months later, I would discover that the July sun vanished behind the street elms by two in the afternoon, and that the roses did poorly as a result. One learns these things eventually, but it takes time, which is why the gardener should hold his hand for at least a year before making any permanent arrangements. Until a twelve-month cycle has revolved, he won't know where are the low spots that collect moisture and freeze hard in winter, where the dessicating west wind does its evil work, or the opposite: Where is the cosy corner in which the tender seedlings can most safely be trusted to winter over?

There is no substitute for observation, and it must be never-ending. Overnight, the enemy leaves his campfires burning and steals a march. The hedge looks all right, doesn't it? Pass a hand over the surface and a cloud of—what, white fly?—ascends. Perhaps a shower of reddened needles falls to earth. The hedge is *not* all right; you might have noticed this weeks ago and, if like me you don't care to spray, done the organic and just as effective thing and turned a blast of water from the hose on it. Predators of all kinds move with supernatural speed in summer. One day the tomato vines are the picture of health. Go away for the weekend, and when you return they look as though rats had been at them. It isn't rats, it's the tomato worm who wears so wonderful a green-and-black camouflage that you may stare at the plant for half an hour without seeing him. (When you do, fetch the scissors and cut him in half, a disgusting business but much safer than spraying— see PESTS AND DISEASES.) Other troubles may be more insidious, take longer to diagnose. Often, for instance, we don't realize the effect of a tree on its surroundings—how much water it absorbs, how far the roots extend—and are correspondingly disappointed when ground covers or other plants fail to survive even at what seems a safe distance.

Nevertheless, not all failures are self-imposed, the result of ignorance, carelessness or inexperience. It takes a while to grasp that a garden isn't a testing ground for character and to stop asking, what did I do wrong? Maybe nothing. Some plantsmen abet guilt feelings—and incidentally try to protect themselves—with warnings that their product has been inspected and mailed to you in perfect condition. The rest, they imply, is up to you. No matter that it arrives looking like a wad of wet moss, no way to tell which end is up, or a dried-up stick in a bag: if nothing comes of it, the fault is yours. Not so. There is a great deal wrong with the way many plants are grown and shipped today. Half-a-dozen years ago, the nurseries in my neighborhood grew their own stock and were responsible for it. Mail-order houses were equally scrupulous, and the best still are. But more and more the average garden center is relying on mass production for its overgrown annuals, unpinched and about to bloom; perennials that might have been baked in clay; and those shrubs whose burlapped roots look and feel like cannonballs. Of course you are a fool to buy these, and in that sense the resulting failure is on your own head. But there may be nothing else readily to hand, and a dozen reasons why there is no time to scour the catalogues and wait for weeks for plants that may be no better than the garden-center ones when they do arrive. Seed, too, is unreliable in spite of vacuum packs and dating, and if it is properly sown and tended and does not germinate or produce healthy plants, it is occasion not for hand-wringing and self-reproach but for an angry letter to the source. I love Beverley Nichols for having the same trouble I do. But it could also be that his alstromerias were a bad lot.

FENNEL

Finocchio in Italian, it looks like a swollen celery stalk with a feathered crest and when raw is scented with anise. Braising dilutes this flavor to a faint whiff but it is still a vegetable that not everyone likes. Italian markets carry it around Thanksgiving: it is then huge and can be tough. Grown in the garden it is quite different—smaller, more delicate, requiring half the cooking time of the market kind. Sliced in a salad it is delicious. I find it difficult to grow, perhaps because my climate really isn't right for it. In its Mediterranean home, it is a winter/spring crop like artichokes (in Italy, the young leaves of both are often fried and served together in a *fritto misto*), which means a long, cool, not freezing, period of growth. In the northern United States, fennel must be brought to maturity before frost, and since it makes most of its growth in hot summer weather that can be a problem: it may bolt. On the other hand, if planted too late, it won't get a chance to mature before freezing. One must take the risk.

The seed should be sown in June. When the seedlings are about three inches high, transplant them to a deeply dug and enriched furrow, setting them about six inches apart. As they grow, the soil must be drawn up around them, as with leeks, to blanch them. Let the stalks be exposed as little as possible and when you run out of earth, pile on salt hay or straw. They need plenty of water and a coolish location to do well, but around the beginning of October they should be ready to pull. This is quite a job. They send down a formidable taproot and a pitchfork may be needed to dislodge them.

----- ❦ -----

FROST

Probable frost dates for a given locality can be learned from gardening journals, newspapers or friends. Weathermen forecast approaching frosts, usually specifying 'low-lying areas.' But the only absolutely reliable information will come from a next-door neighbor. I live on a small peninsula at the end of Long Island Sound, where the temperatures are moderated by the influence of the sea. No more than a mile inland, still within view of the water, frost will strike several days earlier (in the autumn) or later (in the spring) than it does in my garden. Nor does frost behave as one might expect: A wind-blown hilltop is less susceptible than a sheltered hollow where the air settles. Frost dates also vary from year to year. Here, May 5 has for the past twenty years been a safe day for setting out tender vegetables. (I know because I keep records.) But on May 12, 1977, an unannounced wet snowfall sent distracted gardeners in search of bushel baskets, plastic bags, anything that could be tossed over just-planted pepper bushes, tomatoes and eggplant. The painter at work in my kitchen downed tools without apology and departed—he had three dozen tomato plants to save.

Accurate prediction of spring frosts is much more important to the gardener than knowing when to expect the blackening of his dahlias in the fall. By October, nothing much is left to worry about. The summer annuals are nearing their end or have already been pulled up. The autumn perennials don't mind the early frosts, and potted plants that have been summering out-of-doors should have been taken in long ago. It is a peaceful moment. Signs of decay, of imminent death, come as a relief after a fruitful season, and the sinister words 'killing frost' hold no terrors for me. It will all begin again, soon enough.

In spring it is different: A killing frost devastates the heart as well as the garden. Little plants, whether raised on the window sill or bought at alarming prices at a nursery have, one feels, a right to life. Unlike the tacky-looking remnants of summer's end, they are full of promise. To see them killed is painful and, practically speaking, a disaster too, because every single one will have to be replaced. Time, care and money have all been wasted. Patience is the only way out. Take careful note of the last likely frost date, then wait another week before planting. Remember that it is a fallacy that plants set out early have the advantage. Experienced gardeners know that when the nights are still cold they will stand like sentinels in their places, unmoving until the weather warms up. Why then is it so often the experienced gardener who takes chances? Maybe to prove his superiority. It seems wrong, unfair, that his garden should produce no earlier than that of his clumsy and indifferent neighbor. But unless he resorts to hot and cold frames or invests in cloches, his results will be the same as anyone else's. The seasons can't be rushed, or halted.

———————— ❧ ————————

FRUIT

Five or six dwarf fruit trees, plus two espaliers, are all my garden will accommodate. At the moment, the order of precedence is: one sour cherry (thrice grafted with three varieties for cross-pollination); one quince; one apricot; one peach; one pear, one plum. Others have come and gone: a nectarine, planted too deeply, which caused it to turn into a standard—as dwarfs will if you fail to keep the basal graft above ground; an ever-nonbearing pear; another apricot, destroyed by borers; also two varieties of hazelnut, carefully chosen to cross-pollinate, which they never did. This year's harvest was a small bowl of peaches and enough quinces (somewhat damaged by the curculio worm) to make four jars of exquisite jelly, three of which and not without an inner struggle I gave away for Christmas—one of them to a friend who thanked me profusely for a biography of Mariano Fortuny, though how these two items could have got mixed up under her Christmas tree I hadn't the fortitude to inquire. It may, however, be my last gift of quince jelly, for how can I decently explain that, coming from my garden, it is practically worth its weight in gold, let alone that of a lavishly illustrated coffee-table book?

The truth is that I am no hand at raising fruit and seriously doubt that many home gardeners are. The birds get the cherries, and don't imagine that covering the trees with netting will help. Inevitably a bird will somehow get inside the netting, flutter in despair, have to be freed, etc. And meanwhile the squirrel is testing the peaches. He does this the moment a blush appears on their cheeks, while they are still quite green. A blushing peach isn't necessarily a ripe peach, but he doesn't know that. He picks one, nibbles it, then casts it away in disgust; and the only cure for this would be to trap or shoot him. The pears he leaves alone—they are even harder. Pears, you see, don't ripen on the tree. You are supposed to pluck them at a certain point and carry them into the house, where you wrap them tenderly in tissue or newspaper and let them mellow in a cool, dark place. Mine don't mellow: they rot. The quinces, as noted, are always damaged and some years are too few to bother with. As for the apricots, I believe I have harvested no more than five or six in as many years. A late frost will finish them and if that doesn't do it, a dry summer will. They simply drop off the tree before they are ripe and the sight of them lying in the grass is depressing.

I don't doubt that a professional would know the cure for these ills. Spraying might help but I don't see how, even if I were willing to do it. Not even sprays are claimed to be very effective against borers. For them the recommended method of destruction is usually to insert a wire into the entrance of their tunnel and poke it up until the creature is impaled. But by that time it is probably too late. The care and maintenance of fruit trees is a subject in itself, and I am aware of most of the methods involved. Some I object to because they mean the use of poisons; others are just too much trouble. That I go on ordering fruit trees represents, as was said of second marriages, the triumph of optimism over experience, and I persist in believing that somehow, someday, a bowl of ripe, home-grown fruit will come to rest on the kitchen table. I know in my heart that it won't, but meanwhile I go on watering and mulching and pruning the little trees, and they do look pretty when they bloom in spring. Next year, I may get a withered plum or two and that would be a novelty. But it's too early to tell.

◇

GARLIC
(*Allium sativum*)

There is a Provençal soup whose principal ingredient is a whole head of garlic, and in Greece a dish of lamb baked with several dozen cloves until they dissolve and form a liaison with the meat. Neither tastes outstandingly of garlic, first, because the cloves are young and fresh, and second, because they are left whole. Only crushed old garlic has the sulphurous stink Anglo-Saxons associate with it, that made it taboo at American tables in my youth. Now the pendulum has swung too far the other way. Inexperienced cooks put garlic in dishes where it doesn't belong—a *bolognese* sauce, for instance. Contrary to legend, Italians do *not* put garlic in salads, not even rubbing it on a bread crust and swabbing the bowl with this. That is a French habit. Garlic is a staple of peasant dishes in southern Europe and in some of the cuisines of China; in no case should it be aged or stale; and that is why I find it worthwhile to grow. Garden garlic is mild and sweet, totally different from the commercial product, of which the worst is packed in a little plastic-covered box. (So-called garlic salt is beneath discussion.)

Like shallots, garlic can be grown indefinitely from a single purchase at the market of a half-a-dozen heads. Break them up and plant the individual cloves about five inches apart (each will form a new head), and in about five months, there will be a generous crop. You can do this in early May, harvesting in October—or the other way around: Planted in October, garlic will winter over and make big, fat heads by the following August. You know they are ready when the green tops begin to wither and topple over. That is absolutely all there is to growing garlic.

The heads are best stored in a string bag in a cool place, but, of course, what everyone wants is a braid to hang in the kitchen. I wish I could say I have mastered this trick. I value the old skills and am humiliated when I prove to be clumsy at them. My garlic braids aren't exactly a triumph, but here, anyway, is one way to do it: Cut a yard or two of heavy, ropy twine and tie a loop in the middle. Working on a flat surface and starting at the loop, lay the garlic heads, the smallest at the top, on either side of the doubled length of twine and begin to plait the leaves—left, right, left, right, as with hair—using the twine always as the third strand. Keep this up until all the bulbs are incorporated, then tie a knot at the bottom. Pick up the loop and the whole thing *should* fall gracefully in place, ready to be hung on a hook. It may not look very professional (it helps if the garlic is clean and the hairy bottoms are cut off) but 'gourmet' shops and catalogues charge anywhere from $15 to $30 for such braids, and the garlic isn't as fresh. If the braids turn out well, one naturally wants to show them off in a prominent place, and in that case somewhere other than a hot kitchen should be found, and the garlic used up fairly quickly. Garlic in its prime is a seasonal vegetable like any other, and once it has aged there isn't much difference between the garden and the store-bought. So do have at least one orgy of it right after the first harvest. Ford Madox Ford's story (in *Provence*) of the young woman who stuffed a roasting chicken with a kilo of garlic—Ford calls this dish a *poulet Béarnaise*—and having eaten it, was miraculously cured of bad garlic breath, is almost certainly apocryphal. The notion that the body if sufficiently loaded with garlic will adjust itself and cease to give off the fumes is widespread, and I have had at least one friend who subscribed to it, fondly believing himself to be living evidence of its truth. He was a charming man and a wonderful pianist, so I never had the heart to tell him how wrong he was. Doctors are beginning to think some of the ancient medical claims for garlic may have a basis in fact, but this particular legend is unlikely to be scientifically sustained. If the garlic you eat is young and sufficiently cooked, the reek will be much less. You will still be advertising what you had for dinner. Never mind. In the garlic season it is well worth it.

GOOSEBERRIES
AND CURRANTS
(*Ribes*)

Some minds lock gears beyond repair when confronted with directions. Take this:

Cut the plants back to six to eight inches above the ground. During the first winter, cut the original stubs and all but the strongest canes to ground level; during the second winter, cut out all but the original six canes plus the three strongest canes of the current year; during the third winter, prune out all but the three strongest canes of that year's growth plus three of the six canes of the first year's growth. Each winter thereafter, cut out the three oldest canes and all but three of the current season's growth; thus each plant will produce fruit on one-, two-, and three-year old canes.

Anybody who can understand that is on the way to growing gooseberries. I could as readily put together a combustion engine. In the first place, how have those original six canes survived if I cut them to the ground? And why six? My gooseberries don't produce that many, and if they did I couldn't distinguish between the oldest and the second oldest canes. Wood, other than the current year's growth, looks pretty much the same on berry bushes. Should I mark them, as my poet friend did the beans I asked him to plant one year? I came home to find labels in his fine, superliterary hand: 'Bush beans, first edition.' 'Lima beans, second edition' . . . I picture the gooseberries thus festooned and decide to go my usual slack, unprofessional way. Berry bushes are the devil to prune, and I do the gooseberries and currants by the easiest method I know: Let them rip until production starts to slack off, then have at them, cutting out all but the canes that are manifestly that year's growth. The bushes thrive and give every sign of lasting forever.

On the other hand, the berries themselves aren't first-water, and it isn't my fault. Americans, I am informed by *Wyman* and other sources, are put off by the trouble of picking and preparing these fruits, which are 'out of style.' And the truth of the statement is confirmed by the wretched selections in the catalogues. For years I have tried to lay hands on the fat, hairy, green English gooseberry, *uva-crispa*. If anyone is growing them in this country, I wish they would let me know. All I can find is Pixwell, whose name is a bad joke. Pixwell is small, spiny, and doesn't pick well at all. Neither will it make anything resembling a British gooseberry tart. Currant offerings are confined to Red Lake. Try to find a white or black currant bush. I suspect that we are being discouraged from growing any kind of *Ribes*, because of their propensity to harbor a blister rust damaging to white pines. In principle, both currants and gooseberries are forbidden fruit wherever the white pine grows—which happens to be all over the East. But who enforces the law, if it is a law? Nurseries don't acknowledge it and will ship anywhere. Yet I'm told I should consult my county extension agent before ordering.

This shadowy personage fascinates me. He appears constantly in gardening articles. Want to dig a pond? Consult your county extension agent about local conditions. Frost dates? He can tell you what they are in your neighborhood. He is credited with knowing everything there is to know, but in my county he must be hiding out or using an alias. Under no conceivable heading is he to be found in the phone book. And in this case, I'm not sorry. I very much doubt if I would follow his advice if he told me not to grow currants or gooseberries. Imperfect as they are, they aren't sold in markets, and if I want the jellies and fools they make, I have no alternative to growing them at home. Furthermore, as between the berries and the pines, I have the feeling I am being manipulated by the lumber companies. I read with disgust that the European black currant (pathetically described as an 'unarmed shrub' in the *R.H.S.*) is being eradicated by federal and state agencies wherever it is found adjacent to white pines. Small wonder that American-made crème de cassis is undrinkable.

Not much imagination goes into hedges or the way we grow them, at least not in the North, where it's mostly the same old ever-greens: yew, arborvitae, hemlock, etc. Yew is the handsomest by far, and English (or Irish, they are the same *Taxus baccata* with subspecies) the most famous—with, it seems, an undeserved repu-tation for slow growth. An English source asserts that yew will reach maturity in ten years, and that many of those yew gardens visiting Americans take to be contemporary with the Tudor manor house they belong to, aren't. The topiary garden at Compton Wynyates was laid out in 1895, and has looked much as it does today for fifty years. The difference, as usual, must be one of climate, because over here English yew seems to take forever to grow a couple of feet, and to make a brioche with a button-top would need a century. Furthermore, it isn't reliably hardy much farther north than New York City.

We prefer the Japanese yew (*T. cuspidata*) or the cross be-tween the two (*T. × media*) and their cultivars. There is a lot of confusion about these, however, and many complaints about mis-taken identifications and names with no botanical standing. So it would be well to come to a thorough understanding with your nurseryman about exactly what you are getting. Any Japanese yew will be hardy anywhere just short of the Canadian border, but its growth habit may give you an unwelcome surprise. It may have the columnar form or grow laterally; reach ten feet, or half that. (*T. cuspidata densa* has been known to be four feet high but twenty feet across; the upright *T. × media* Hicksii two or three times as tall as it is wide.)

But why must it always be a yew or a hemlock or something equally familiar? I have been stuck with a hemlock hedge (not planted by me) for forty years, and have never liked it. It looks better now than it used to, because a year or so ago I left it unpruned—and the long, feathery sprays were quite lovely. It is now snipped rather than pruned, but it remains a banal choice. It could have been a holly hedge—not on the scale of John Evelyn's, which was four hundred feet long and nine feet high. That, by the way, was badly damaged by Peter the Great's merry men during their stay at Sayes Court. It amused these barbarians to ram it with wheelbarrows, which at least showed how tough they were. A holly hedge is a formidable barrier and might even be painful to the careless pruner—though not more so than one made of barberry. (English holly, however, is only marginally hardy this far north; the American, *I. opaca*, practically identical in appearance, is the one I would use.) Holly to most people means the sprig that sits atop the Christmas pudding. But the genus *Ilex* to which it belongs has other species with entirely different foliage. The Japanese holly (*I. crenata*), looks like box from a slight distance, is just as elegant and for a cold climate a far better choice. Another handsome Oriental holly is *I. pedunculosa*. This one looks like laurel but is a welcome change from that, to me, rather lugubrious and overplanted shrub.

Other broad-leaved evergreens that might not come immediately to mind for hedges can in fact be trained to make them. Two varieties of *Euonymus fortunei* would be worth trying. The well-known Sarcoxie, usually planted as an individual shrub, is naturally inclined to mass and spread and keeps its glossy leaves all winter. The lesser known *vegetus*, which is half a vine, is even better looking and has scarlet fruits besides. According to *Wyman*, this Chinese species shares with ivy the odd characteristic of drastically changing its foliage when mature. One seventy-five-year-old plant of *E. fortunei reticulatus* was found to have no less than ten distinct types of foliage of varying sizes, some with rootlets. (I have also found holdfasts on my Sarcoxie, though it isn't listed as a vine or being grown as one.) Whether this would be a disadvantage or not I can't say. To me, it wouldn't, but it is something to know about. Lastly, I would suggest to anyone who can grow *Mahonia Acquifolium*, the so-called Oregon grape-holly, which isn't a holly, that it would make a beautiful hedge—green in summer, mahogany color in winter, with yellow flowers and fruit like a blueberry in season. Were I to judge from the wind-burned specimens I have barely dragged through a winter, I would say it is hopeless for New England. But directly across the street is galling proof to the contrary. My neighbor's large, glistening mahonia is protected from west winds by her house, and that is probably why it survives and mine don't. But there may be another reason, *Wyman* says: 'The right clone can be grown in the full sun without winter foliage burn, but many clones cannot. So . . .

it behooves nurserymen to propagate asexually from the right, glossy-leaved clones.' As presumably it behooves (a fine, assertive word that) the gardener to ascertain (how?) that the mahonia he has ordered was correctly propagated. I didn't.

In this country we tend to think that a hedge must be all of the same material and that evergreen. Europeans are more flexible. In the fuchsia garden at Hidcote (see TWO GARDENERS) are the so-called tapestry hedges which are made of green and variegated holly, yew, box and copper beech—a combination also used at Longleat by Russell Page. The drawback to these would surely be the blanks left by the deciduous beech in winter, and how this is dealt with I can't find out. Maybe it doesn't matter. And in case you are wondering what beech is doing in a hedge at all, the answer is, first, that European beech is wider than it is tall, which makes it more adaptable to hedging than the American species (taller than it is wide); and, second, that Europeans, habitually and with pruning and training more savage than anything American gardeners are willing to contemplate, turn what we think of as trees into hedges—or tall, formal screens. Hornbeams and syca-mores as well as beech are used (pin oaks and the Siberian elm aren't excluded either), and while it is true that they can grow to prodigious size—a famous beech hedge at Stobhill Castle in Scot-land, planted in 1746, is now eighty-five feet high—they can be kept within bounds by gardeners not afraid of the knife. I have seen beech hedges in France not more than twelve feet high and three feet wide. But of course they aren't evergreen, and that brings up the question of what one asks of a hedge.

If it is to be the substitute for a wall, it must be evergreen. In other situations, ease of maintenance, beauty of foliage or flowers ought to be considered more than they are. Species of *Elaeagnus*, the Russian olive, make lovely, silvery hedges. So does the equally rugged *Prinsepia sinensis* from Manchuria, with tiny leaves and yellow flowers much subtler than the forsythia's, but admittedly hard to locate. Or consider the buckthorn (*Rhamnus Frangula*) which aside from not being evergreen has every virtue. The vari-ety Tallhedge will grow in sun or shade, even in the filthy air of cities, is hardy, has flowers rather like privet followed by white berries pleasing to birds, doesn't go naked at the knees like so many hedge plants—and you needn't lay a hand to it. It has the property of looking sheared though it isn't. (Clip the top only if you want to keep it under fifteen feet.) Why it isn't in every catalogue I can't imagine, but such are the mysteries of supply and demand. Nearly all catalogues have some version of the barberry, a thorny, nasty-tempered genus I'm not fond of. That is perhaps because *B. vulgaris*, the European barberry brought here in colonial times, is now a local pest. Birds evidently planted it in various crevices of our walls, and no power on earth can root it out. I read that it is on the U.S.D.A.'s black list as a carrier of the destructive wheat rust (as are other barberries). Would they would send an agent to rid me of mine, which unfortunately seem to be in robust health. But though I am prejudiced against them, I must admit that some of the less common barberries have their charm. You might run across *B. verruculosa* (Weston Nurseries of Hopkinton, Massachusetts, carries it; see CATALOGUES), with lustrous foliage, green on top, white beneath that turns a dusky bronze in winter—or *B. Gilgiana*, which is deciduous but in autumn is a bonfire of scarlet foliage and clustered berries. There are others, none easy to find. Most nurseries for reasons obscure to me prefer to carry some version of *B. Thunbergii*, especially the dwarf Red Pygmy. I loathe Red Pygmy—and am only slightly less hostile to the other members of this deciduous Japanese species.

Most of these are in the category of formal hedges, and it is curious that Americans, so reluctant to apply the shears to plants in general, should prefer the shaved hedge. You don't see many loose, flowering hedgerows in this country. The exception is forsythia, so grossly overplanted that the discriminating gardener must strike it from his list. Other flowering shrubs that take to hedging—Chinese lilacs; hawthorns; spiraeas ($\times$ *Vanhouttei* or *prunifolia*); hydrangeas (several but *arborescens* is best); mockoranges; even some of the viburnums and dogwoods—we tend to plant as individual specimens and let it go at that. Space may have something to do with it. People imagine that a flowering hedge will take up more room, which needn't be true.

A more cogent reason is the want of familiarity with how to manage them. Europe has a thousand-year tradition of the hedge as boundary line between properties: the English hedgerow goes back to the Saxon village whose barrier reef was called the *haga* after the Saxon word for the hawthorn's fruit. To the Normans, hedge was *haye*, and the man in charge of them became the hayward. These hedgerows are fast disappearing, to the dismay of English conservationists (and perhaps of French ones too, because the same thing is happening there), and the drive is on to save the

old—while planting new ones in the interests of ecology as well
as beauty.

We might profitably do the same. But the hedger's art isn't easily acquired. Hawthorns, the classic material, are tough, and if you
would have yourself a private 'Méséglise way' you must be re-
signed to having it less perfectly formed than Proust's original.
You can, however, produce a reasonable facsimile provided you
can face the ruthless treatment such hedges require, at least in
their infancy. *C. laevigata* (sometimes *Oxycantha*) is the lovely
white or pink European species—though you might do better with
our native *C. crus-galli*, hardy as far north as Canada. But whichever you choose, they will arrive from the nursery as little trees
four to five feet high. You must now make up your mind to cut
them back to six to twelve inches from the ground. (You are, in
fact, advised to do this with all deciduous shrubs and trees intended for hedging.) Do this as soon as they are planted, and it
will force side shoots to grow from what would otherwise be a
naked trunk forever. Leave them alone for a year, after which they
will probably have to be pruned quite heavily again. By the third
year, you can usually resort to normal trimming. With flowering
hedges this is done according to the same rules that apply to the
plants when they are grown as shrubs: Those that flower in spring
must be attended to right after the blossoms fade. The midsummer
bloomers can be cut in the fall or early the following spring. In
other words, the former treatment would apply to Chinese lilacs,
the latter to hydrangeas. (*H. arborescens*, the old snowball, can
even be cut to the ground in spring, though I wouldn't. My Portuguese neighbor, who has a near-hedge of *H. macrophylla* of a
mysterious dark-purple color, cuts that back eight to ten inches in
April, which I take to be about right.)

I haven't spoken of privet, held in such contempt that the
garden-proud will have nothing to do with it. Officially, I despise
it myself and would never make a hedge of it. But in one of those
unrevised boskets common in old gardens, filled up long ago with
bushes that for want of a bright idea of how to replace them (not
to speak of plain laziness) have been left to their fate, I have some
privets. Having no particular policy about pruning them, I get
someone to hack at them every five years or so; and in the intervals
I can't help noticing that when they flower in August, they smell
as divinely as anything in the garden. Not everybody agrees. The
same people who draw back from the scent of Asiatic lilies claim

to be suffocated by privet in bloom. That is their problem. Mine is that some way should be found to incorporate a shrub so vigorous, indestructible and deliciously scented into a garden without losing all claims to status or originality. There may be one: The best way to grow privet, which won't flower if continuously pruned as a hedge, is as a wind-screen—and if you want to see how lovely that can be, visit eastern Long Island, where they serve as the equivalent of the English hedgerow, albeit unpruned and untended, and probably also doomed, since they divide the vanishing potato fields and mark the sandy roads to the sea. In this form many people don't recognize them as ordinary old privet and certainly would not if you made an avenue of them some fifteen feet high—though not, of course, on Long Island. But in gardening a difference of fifty or a hundred miles, a departure from custom, however slight, can produce the illusion of novelty.

---◇---

HELP

McC. is a Scot, a tall, lean, saturnine fellow born just short of seventy years ago near Aberdeen, and he comes from a long line of estate gardeners. The Scotch genius for horticulture has been recognized for centuries and in many countries, and McC. is a worthy successor to that tradition. He rose rapidly to the top of his profession, and after his emigration to America was head gardener to three Long Island millionaires, each sorry to part with him. I haven't quite understood how he came to pick our village for his retirement—'caught my fancy' is all he will say—and still less why he decided to give me some of his time. Boredom perhaps (he is quite rich and certainly doesn't need the money), or a touch of nostalgia. He once said my garden reminded him of home, by which, of course, he meant the cottage gardens of the villages, not the ordered splendors of the castle garden his father managed and where he grew up.

Anyway, I am grateful, because what McC. doesn't know about horticulture isn't worth bothering about. He carries a knife, curved like a crane's bill and sharpened to a deadly edge, and this he whips out to prune a dwarf fruit tree in minutes ('Mind you don't leave a stump; cut your branch right to the bone'); and a hedge clipped by McC., by hand, the top sloping inward, seems to know it has been barbered by an expert who doesn't tolerate gaps or snaggled branches. Things grow for McC., too, as if they recognized his authority. A seedling or a shrub planted by him sits there as if fixed by a nail, and you know it won't blow over or dare to wilt. He could graft if he had the opportunity—the technique of producing standard roses isn't beyond him—and could grow camellias and melons for me in winter if I had a greenhouse. (*He* has one, a small Lord & Burnham model.) He knows how to train grapevines and berry bushes and make them productive, and how to seduce a rose into covering the summer house. Finally, he is reliable. If he says he will drop by at ten o'clock, he drops by at ten o'clock, wearing an old suede jacket, his pruning knife in his pocket.

There is only one trouble with McC. He doesn't exist outside my fevered imagination.

Well-trained gardeners who like their work must live in America, but not around here and not in my price range. When I look back on the long procession of incompetents, dumbbells and eccentrics, young and old, foreign and domestic, who have worked for me, I wonder how I and the garden have survived their ministrations. I recall, for example, Mr. R., a well-known figure in town because in spite of his shabby get-up he is said to be very rich, with large plantations in Brazil—or it may be the Cape Verde Islands. You see him moving at a rapid hobble along the street, on his way to some garden or other, usually belonging to a newcomer because we old-timers know that he brings death and destruction with him. Those he has worked for discuss him with tears in their eyes. The summer he gardened for me he killed two cherry trees, uprooted a plantation of Dutch iris and imparted crooked lines to the perennial beds from which they have never fully recovered. I worked in New York in those days, and when I came up for weekends my first wish was naturally to see the garden—a wish strongly opposed by the family, who offered me drinks, produced piles of mail, announced that we had to leave immediately for a dinner twenty miles away, anything to keep me from a tour of inspection. It was, they explained, Mr. R.'s canny habit to get his job done between five and six A.M., long before anyone was around to stop him. By breakfast time, the little heaps of plants he had pulled up were already past saving, the cement already setting between the bricks laid in the wrong place. Nothing one could say or do made any impression. I fired him in a blazing passion, but when we meet, which is often, he beams upon me and invariably passes a pleasant remark about the weather.

He was followed by A., who was, as they say, right off the boat. He spoke only Portuguese. I addressed him in Spanish, which he seemed to understand. Or I thought he did until I found him mowing the grass strip in front of the house, the grass-catcher not on the mower, which was blasting a steady stream of damp cuttings onto the façade. When this was pointed out, he smiled dreamily and moved into the street, the mower still going. I watched him cover a half-block of naked asphalt before I led him gently to the back door and paid him off.

He, as I remember it, was followed by Mr. H., of impeccable Yankee lineage—no language trouble there, and he was handy too, could make or mend anything; and the most remarkable painter I ever knew: Any object painted by him, including the house, stayed pristine for a decade. But Mr. H. had two problems. He weighed close to four hundred pounds, and he was mad, certifiably so, poor man, for he had done time. It showed in his stream-of-consciousness talk—which flowed on and on without pause or relevance and was distracting until one learned to tune out—and in a tendency to paranoid outbursts, which one also learned to ignore. His weight caused him to adopt some peculiar methods as well. He weeded, for example, in the reclining position of those stout riverine gods on Roman fountains, and dug in the same attitude, using a small trowel. I remember him attacking in this manner three large, well-rooted shrubs I wanted removed. It took a week. Mr. H. stayed with me for five or six years, getting fatter and crazier every year, until he retired at his own request, fuming over some fancied slight.

It occurs to me that I attract the mentally unbalanced. Or perhaps their therapists have advised them to take up outdoor work? There was the beautiful young Italian, a veritable Donatello with black curly hair and a bronze torso we saw a lot of because he liked to bare it while he worked. He arrived in a Cadillac of immense size, did little work but talked a lot about trips he intended to make, businesses he meant to start, and often asked to use the telephone. He was eventually arrested for having tried to murder his mistress, and though he was given a suspended sentence it seemed better not to have him around.

Yet another case, that of B. B., was an authentic tragedy. This nice man, who seemed perfectly normal, was the father of children and what is quite rare, made a point of saying how much he liked gardening. He killed himself a few weeks after he had agreed to see me through a summer. It was such a shock I wracked my brains trying to remember some missing clue to his state of mind. We had put in some roses and fruit trees together, and in these shared chores one learns, or senses, quite a lot about the other person—something of his sympathies and his attitude toward life —and yet no inkling of his despair had reached me. If anything I had the impression he was enjoying himself.

I was guilty of a common fallacy: We all, I think, tend to imagine that the people who work for us take the same satisfaction we do in a happy effect achieved, a heavy chore got through. Rarely is it so. Why should B. B. have looked forward to taking care of *my* garden, planting *my* fruit trees? To him, it was just a part-time job, a way to earn some extra cash for a few months. Had he been a professional, it might have been different. In that case his career-ist's pride would have been involved. But B. B. was a machinist, not a nurseryman or an arborist; and that has been true of all my helpers. They all belong to the ranks of the temporarily unemployed or they are moonlighting. Not one of them has ever had the slightest knowledge of horticulture, or ever acquired it—not even my dear A.V., with me for five years, who truly did love the garden, loved, that is, dressing it up to look its best, especially when company was expected, and did mysteriously acquire a passion for building compost heaps, but never learned to identify a single flower, bush or tree or any of the techniques connected with growing them. And, as he often told me, the men at 'the shop' thought he was nuts to get such a kick out of working here.

Gardening is so little esteemed in this country that I can't imagine where or how someone who wanted to study it as a profession would go for instruction. It's a vicious circle. Those who, like me, need help can't find it and so are forced to cut down on their plantings, abandon the flowers or the vegetables or both, thus diminishing the potential job market for those who might choose to earn a living at it. There is a gap here, and some of the young have undertaken to fill it—at exorbitant rates. They are innocent of the most elementary techniques, barely know a rose from a cabbage, or even how to mow a lawn properly. Their tools are a rotary mower, an electric hedge cutter and a pickup truck. At best, they are the maturing flower children of the 1960's, still wearing their beards and pigtails; at worst, grasping little entrepreneurs who know just enough to demand $18 an hour. So for me it has to be the lunatic fringe, and now and again I am lucky—as with A. V., whose only noticeable eccentricity was a tendency to fall off ladders and out of trees. Right now, I am in a hopeful phase. My current helper is a young man sound in wind, limb, and as far as I know, mind, and a whiz at getting through the work. But he is also a talented sculptor, and his pieces are beginning to sell so well that I foresee the day when he will think twice about raking up twenty bushels of apples.

<hr />

HERBS

When I was a child, herbs were practically unknown in middle-class American kitchens. Fresh parsley and chives, dried sage and thyme were the only ones I remember. (Add mint for juleps in the South, and in New Orleans, filé—made of powdered sassafras leaves.) Even people who traveled and knew about foreign food didn't ask the family cook to prepare *poulet à l'estragon* when they came home; she would probably have departed forthwith if they had. For other reasons, she did in fact depart from many households sometime after World War II, and that was what started a lot of us on the road to culinary sophistication. A rocky one it was. Not only was the kitchen itself discovered to be a rather uncomfortable and forbidding place—no copper pans and pretty tiles in those days, no food processors—the good plain dishes that had come out of it were much harder to prepare than one had thought.

One solution was something called a casserole, by which was meant a stew dressed up with herbs and wine, therefore foreign and an acceptable substitute for roasts that required timing and vegetables cooked *à point*. Wrong on all counts. Casserole isn't the

French name for a stew but for a cooking vessel; and Europeans
don't douse everything in seasonings and alcohol. I still shudder to
remember some of those concoctions, reeking of oregano and bay,
acidulated with California red. The herbs, of course, were dried,
not at all the equivalent of the fresh, but we didn't know that.
Fresh herbs were never seen in markets; plants were hard to find,
and catalogues didn't carry the long lists of seed they do today.
We learned the hard way.

   All that seems very long ago, now that the cooking revolution
has transformed American kitchens, introduced Chinese parsley to
supermarkets and made gastronomes of us all. When I planted my
first tarragon in the early 1950's, I could claim to be one of the
avant-garde. Today, my herb beds are, I realize, woefully passé.
Because I don't cook Oriental food, I have no pak-choi, cumin,
mitsuba, fenugreek or coriander. Not yet having joined the ranks
of those who weave and dye their own cloth, I do without woad,
bedstraw, *Anthemis tinctoria.* I would rather buy cough medicine
than attempt to brew it from horehound; my aversion to health
food (as opposed to food that is healthy) eliminates Russian comfrey and amaranth. In short, my list of herbs is conventional and
within manageable bounds—almost. My corner of New England
happens to be well endowed with herb farms and my will power
easily sapped by the sight of plants for sale. Surely a gold-leaved
marjoram wouldn't be amiss? What about a *Lavandula viris* from
the Canary Islands? And inevitably the car fills up with plants that
will turn out to be too large, too small, or simply not as interesting
as their history and provenance have made them sound. There is, I
find, that drawback to herbs. No other class of plant bears such a
weight of myth and symbolism, and it can be oversold. For me
there comes a time when it isn't enough to know that a plant was
sacred to Jupiter, used to ward off snakes, a symbol of loyalty or
mentioned by Theophrastus, when all it looks like is a not very
exciting wild flower/weed.

   The truth is I am ambivalent about herbs—or should I say
about herbalists? Gardeners who raise herbs for their botanical
interest, without quaintness or sentimentality, I respect and sometimes envy. It is the cultist I dread, the person who can't look at a
rue without murmuring that it is herb of grace o' Sundays, or a
hyssop without dragging in the Biblical references. And the pity is
that this person is all too frequently the author of slim volumes of
herbal lore, illustrated with medieval woodcuts. The dean of the

school must be Henry Beston, whose *Herbs and the Earth*, first published in 1935, is now a classic and still selling briskly in paperback. Typical is this description of his garden in Maine:

Here are Hyssop and Basil, a corner shrub of Southernwood, a clump of kitchen Sage, Pot Marjoram and Lavender (that European-minded plant), Virgil's Cerinthe with its yellow blossoms, Spike Vervain (to the classical peoples the most sacred of all growing things), a plant or two of the Biblical 'Hyssop' which is Marjoram (*Origanum Maru*) sent me by a scholar in Palestine, a good clump of Costmary and its botanical relative Camphor Balsam, Lovage and Woundwort, Valerian and Comfrey, a noble plant of Absinthe Wormwood, and even, O happy rarity, that preeminent plant of folklore, the screaming Mandrake Root. The Thymes are by themselves, and to one side. . . . stands that ancient potency, a bank of Rue. A border facing north I give over to a white Astilbe and a very unpretending show of white and yellow annuals.

I chose this passage because it is full of key words—'noble,' 'ancient,' 'sacred,' the requisite classical and folkloric allusions, and the self-conscious charm (why are his annuals unpretending?) that marks the genre. Today's writers may be less stately than Beston, but they also can be too arch by half. I quote from *Gardener's Magic and Other Old Wives' Tales*, by Brigid Boland (1977): 'Thus to use camellia to cure cataract all you need to do is to pick it before sunrise, telling it that you need it "for the white growth of the eyes": but for senecio to be effective against toothache you must dig up the root without using iron, touch the tooth with it three times, and then replant it at once; luckily this can be done in daylight, so that it is not necessary for both patient and gardener to be up in the small hours.' Here it is the tone rather than the actual words (though 'luckily' is offensive) that I mind. Are we to laugh at the folly of our ancestors who knew no better? Though it is true that plants were for thousands of years men's only medicines, I can think of more amusing phenomena. On the other hand, neither am I ready to subscribe to the alternative: that our forebears knew more than we do about healing the sick.

The latter is a relatively recent development, the outcome of the discovery of 'natural living,' and manifests itself in a continuing stream of publications purporting to transmit the native wisdom of peasants and primitives. Unlike Boland, the authors mean to be taken seriously. An example is *The Concise Herbal Encyclopedia* by Donald Law, published in 1973. Law is a mine of information on the ancient history of herbs, and if he had left it at that, his book would have a certain value. But he also believes in astrology and is given to such statements as that 'in the Nevada desert, where atomic tests were made, is a simple herb from which American scientists have developed an antidote to radiation sickness!' (What that miraculous herb is, he doesn't say.) His recipes imply that herbs will cure anything from cancer to madness. No harm may have been done by this book and others like it, but I wonder. I understand the premise. I even share it: Modern medicine isn't what it's cracked up to be, and we are often overdosed with dangerous drugs. But surely the appropriate response isn't a retreat into medievalism. Whatever its pernicious aspects, modern medicine keeps a lot more people going than herbs did and if it comes to that, doesn't by any means exclude natural substances. It does rule out, I think rightly, the contemporary witches and warlocks who dabble in herbs and find it profitable to market antique prescriptions to the credulous.

Meanwhile, there are the actual herbs, and left to themselves they do little to foster sentimentality. They are sober, unspectacular plants, and though they have been in our service for so long, the least susceptible to domestication. If they were animals, one would be warned against trying to tame them. They can't be grown under conditions differing in any important respect from those they are accustomed to in the wild—which for most of them means the arid, stony, sweet soil of the Mediterranean littoral. Fertilizer is the last thing they need, though a little compost is acceptable. They can't exist without water but prefer too little to too much. Above all, they detest indoor life. Pictures in decorating magazines invariably show potted herbs in kitchens. Experienced gardeners (and cooks) know that these are scenery imported for the occasion and that nobody but a greenhorn would invest in those kits that promise a wilderness of aromatics on the window sill. Annual herbs want to be baked in the summer sun, not the heat of a stove. The perennials require a period of hibernating cold before they recoup for another season. With rare exceptions, neither will endure more than a few weeks in a winter kitchen.

Herbs are recalcitrant in other ways. Many of them won't come true from seed and to be faithful to type (or properly identifiable to their owners) should be grown from cuttings taken from a plant of undoubted lineage. Some, like the thymes, hybridize themselves even under controlled conditions, confusing the botanists, who every so often change their minds and decide to rearrange a whole genus. The increasing popularity of herbs doesn't help, on the contrary. Those who raise them for the commercial market aren't as conscientious as the owners of small herb farms who do business on a limited scale and whose prices, in general, are higher. They, too, can make mistakes, but they are usually honest ones and subject to correction. Plants sold at garden centers or, God forbid, at supermarkets, can be outrageously mislabeled, and the salespeople seldom have the faintest idea what they are handling.

I have learned, too, not to rely on cookbooks, herbal or otherwise, to guide me in the purchase of plants. Herbalists aren't always cooks, or vice versa. Thus, Julia Child on bay: American bay, she says, is stronger than the French, and one should look for the French. In fact, there aren't two kinds. True bay is *Laurus nobilis* wherever found. But there is on the American market at least one product *sold* as bay that isn't even a relative. The label calls it 'California bay laurel,' and the botanical name is *Umbellularia californica*. Until recently, I, too, was under the impression that this was a particularly pungent bay. I owe my enlightenment to the owner of a local nursery, who further informs me that *Umbellularia californica* is mildly poisonous if eaten in quantity and really shouldn't be marketed. And I have been told of other false bays lurking on the grocery shelves. Similarly, Marcella Hazan talks about oregano and marjoram as if they were distinct plants. They aren't exactly, and I don't think the oregano she knows in Italy is the *Origanum vulgare* always sold here as Italian oregano. But see below for further caveats and suggestions:

THYME

Not only are the thymes an enormous family, the *R.H.S.* notes that they are 'notoriously difficult to classify and identify and, as the specific limits are often not well defined and local races and variants are very numerous, accounts by different botanists often disagree widely. . . .' That is putting it gently. Thymes listed in one encyclopedia may not appear in another, or be given another name. And if the authorities can't get together, still less can the catalogues and nurserymen, who not infrequently resort to such vague descriptions as 'dwarf,' 'creeping,' (all thymes are one or the other or both), French, German, English, 'winter,' 'hairy' (terms that are botanically meaningless) or, tossing in the sponge, simply 'a small perennial, used in seasoning.' What kind of seasoning? Thymes can smell like caraway, pine, camphor, lavender, or turpentine, and these assuredly would be fatal to a *bouquet garni*.

What one needs first of all to know is that thymes are roughly of three types: the creepers that form carpets (*Thymus Serpyllum*, shepherd's or wild thyme, is the prototype but also *T. Drucei*, both commonly called mother-of-thyme); those that are like little shrubs and are chiefly for the rock garden (some of the scented thymes belong to this category as do many others grown for their form or their flowers); and, lastly and most important to the cook, *Thymus vulgaris*, the true culinary herb. Even that isn't as simple as it sounds. I buy culinary thymes with monotonous regularity because I rarely succeed in pulling them through a winter, and though not as observant as one should be, I have noticed that I don't always get the same plant. Variants of *Thymus vulgaris* include the so-called French, with tiny leaves, and the broader-leaved English. I doubt if I could tell the difference when it comes to flavor, but I now ask for the English because it seems to be slightly hardier. At other times, I am fairly sure I have been sold what is called winter (sometimes German) thyme. This is *Thymus hyemalis* and could be mistaken for *vulgaris*. The important difference is the inferior aroma. However, *T. citriodorus*, a cross of *vulgaris*, unquestionably is a culinary herb, provided you want the taste of lemon.

The thymes are a good example of why one really must have some grasp of Latin names for plants. The checking and cross-checking may be a bore to the uncommitted. Equally is it a bore to discover in mid-July that a plant isn't what you thought. I myself would now never send away for an herb except from a source I knew well. My advice is to buy in person, if that is possible, and to be prepared to make a nuisance of yourself if your questions aren't satisfactorily answered. By the same token, don't order seed from catalogues that don't give Latin names. Even then, you may be stung. (See below.)

TARRAGON

The trap to be avoided with tarragon is in buying seed. What you will get is Russian tarragon (*Artemisia Redowski*), a rampant weed with no aromatic properties whatever. True or French tarragon is *A. Dracunculus* and is propagated by division, layering or cuttings. This raises the hen-egg issue: Where did the aboriginal tarragon come from? I don't know, only that tarragon of all herbs must be purchased in plant form and not grown from seed, no matter how reliable the purveyor may be. Park, for example, one of the best, offers seeds of something they call Russian tarragon and further identify as *A. Dracunculus*. Since it can't be both, I guess the first definition to be correct. Tarragon plants sold at a good nursery probably are true tarragon but I wouldn't give them the benefit of the doubt without pinching and sniffing. A strong essence of pernod with a whiff of camphor should assail the nostrils. False tarragon has no identifiable smell.

The leaves ought to be another guide but may not be, owing to a midsummer phenomenon, an abrupt achievement of maturity which, overnight, hardens a succulent willow-green plant with flat, limp, mildly flavored leaves into a woody little shrub whose leaves are thin as needles, dark, and intensely aromatic. What is mystifying is that they are the same leaves—not replacements— and that it all happens so fast. In any case, it is in the early stages that true tarragon is hardest to distinguish from false—that is, at about the time the herb beds need replenishing. Later in the year, the difference will be clearer, but by then you can have a flourishing patch of *A. Redowski*. So the final test must be the tongue and nose.

Fresh tarragon, however, neither tastes nor smells quite like the dried and is altered by cooking. So if you haven't eaten it raw before, be prepared for the sharp reminder that it is a wormwood. I find it too strong for salad, but I do incorporate it into a chicken-liver pâté, and, of course, it is the only garnish for *oeufs en gelée*. Don't attempt to grow it indoors, or indeed out-of-doors in a mild climate, because it needs a period of dormancy brought on by cold. On the other hand, a brutal winter can kill it. I mulch my tarragons with large flat stones around the roots, and thus cared

for they have lasted more than twenty years. Tarragon freezes
well.

LOVAGE

People who have lovage are wonderfully generous about giving
hunks of it away, and once you have acquired it, you see why. Full
grown, it is five feet tall, self-sows liberally if the birds don't get
the seed first, doesn't mind shade, is unkillable. Nobody needs as
much lovage as, inevitably in a year or two, he has. It is true that
it smells and tastes like celery, but it can't be eaten like celery—
the flavor is too strong and the stalks are tough. A few leaves
added to a soup or stew are sufficient to impart a celery flavor, and
I prefer it to celery in a *court bouillon*. A friend of mine devours
the leaves raw on sliced tomatoes in a sandwich. I keep it because
I have it (it was, of course, a present), but given the amount I
use in relation to the colossal size, I can't call it an essential herb.

SORREL

When I first planted sorrel the Connecticut Yankee who worked
for me was incredulous. That, he said with disgust, is sourgrass
and what do you want with it? He was right. Wild sorrel, called
sourgrass, sourweed and other pejoratives indicative of its oxalic
acid content, *is* a weed all over the Northeast and Canada, and the
arrowhead leaves are the same shape as those of the cultivated
varieties, only smaller. What I was growing was *Rumex scutatus*,
known to food snobs as French sorrel for no better reason than
that the French eat it and we don't. It goes into *potage à l'oseille*,
and at the restaurant of the Troisgros brothers at Roanne I had it
in a creamy sauce for salmon—an idea I have adapted to shad as
well. The French also prepare it as a vegetable. The first step in all
these is to melt the leaves in butter, a process that can panic the
cook into thinking there isn't nearly enough. Sorrel reduces more
drastically even than spinach, but the flavor is so intense that a
little goes a long way. Half a dozen plants should be enough for
any household, and if not there will soon be more. Sorrel goes to
seed in midsummer, sending up tough stalks that must be cut to
the ground if little plants aren't to spring up all over the place. (It
isn't good to eat during this period; wait for the new leaves to
appear at the base.) Since sorrel is a perennial, some people like to

keep it in a separate bed rather than among the vegetables, and it would be easier to control that way. It's a question of space. My patch is in the kitchen garden—proving, by the way, that sorrel isn't, as one is often told, a sign of acid soil. My soil isn't acid, but it is rich and moist, which I take to be sorrel's main requirements.

ROSEMARY

A perennial in warm climates, rosemary makes hedges like lavender. Not in New England, and after years of frustration I grow it as a houseplant that summers outdoors. It is the only culinary herb that will do this for me, and the secret is the pot. I used to put the plants in the ground, dig them up, pot them and bring them indoors in the fall, take them out and replant them in spring, etc.—a procedure they loathed. The digging and re-digging upsets them, as well as reminding them that they really need a period of mild cold such as they have in southern Italy. Anchored in a pot, they seem to forget this requirement and will return peaceably to a warm kitchen window. In this fashion, I have maintained a rosemary for five or six years and unintentionally turned it into a bonsai. The roots must be strangling, but as the foliage is kept pruned by the constant demands I make on it, a balance is achieved. (Taking note, I now do the same thing to myrtle, scented geraniums and lemon verbena, all made into miniature standards that live permanently in pots.) I stuff pork as well as lamb roasts with rosemary and lay sprigs of it across fish to be grilled. They sparkle and sputter alarmingly and drip a burning resin that does wonders for blue- and swordfish.

A word of warning about rosemary in kitchens: I have an electric stove. A gas one can kill a plant in short order. I learned this when I left a handsome specimen with a friend. He placed it near his gas range and presently mailed me a postcard. 'R.I.P.,' it said, 'one rosemary bush.' I haven't researched the matter, but I wouldn't be surprised if other herbs reacted in the same way to gas. Anyone who has had similar demises might look into it.

SAGE

The sages are many and include the medicinal herb clary, pineapple sage (a beautiful plant not hardy in the North), salvia, and many more. Cooking sage is *Salvia officinalis* and the only herb to be usable twelve months of the year in the garden. The leaves, pebbled like a little gray lizard's skin, cling to the bush all winter even when coated with ice, and when thawed release a summery aroma. The bush itself is tough—with age it develops the gnarled look of an ancient tree and needs only to be lopped back severely in late spring. It recovers at once, sends out new growth and, eventually, blue flowers. Sage hasn't the prestige of tarragon. I don't recall it in *haute cuisine*. But Italians like it with veal and game, and in Tuscany I learned to cut it up over dishes made with dried beans. In Tuscany, too, I tasted a nibble that turned out to be sage leaves dipped in a light flour-and-water batter and fried in oil. These are gobbled up when served with drinks, and if you like surprises, you can be reasonably sure of creating one. People rarely guess what these crusty tidbits are.

DILL

One sowing may suffice for a lifetime, for dill—an annual—can reseed itself in perpetuity and yield two crops a year. Then again, it may not. For a long while I had to plant it each spring, producing sad little crops that burned out early. Then suddenly I had dill three feet tall, flowering into golden umbels that scattered seed all over the kitchen garden, and a cycle was established. Some germinates in the fall, making bushy plants quite different from the feathery early crop. The foliage is thicker, almost like a fern's, and they last well beyond the first frost but don't bloom. The rest of the seed apparently hibernates beneath the heavy autumn mulch and somehow fights its way back to life the following spring, to emerge as conventionally fluffy dill and produce more seed. I would boast of this success if I knew how to repeat it. All herbs are independent, not to say cussed, in their determination to have their own way, and dill more so than most. You can't transplant it—therefore, don't buy seedlings—and when picked for herbal bouquets, it may live for days or collapse without warning. As to what conditions it likes, I assume that since it is associated with the cooking of northern and eastern Europe, it is native to those regions and to be treated differently from the Mediterranean lovers of heat and thin soil. I know it likes cool weather and so should be seeded early (it bolts and is useless in midsummer except for the flower heads, but if these are harvested for pickles, a second crop won't, of course, be forthcoming). I further believe that un-like most herbs dill thrives on the moist coolness of mulch. That, at any rate, is what I give it and is worth a try for anyone who is troubled with prematurely blasted plants.

Dill is another herb that freezes well, especially the fall crop with bulkier foliage. I freeze the stalks in bunches, and when I need a tablespoon or two, remove the whole thing and clip from the end, exactly as I would with a bunch of the fresh. If dill is chopped up before it is frozen, it becomes unmanageable. I read about chopping and freezing herbs into ice cubes and can't imag-ine a messier business. One reason I don't freeze many is that they go limp when they thaw, rendering them useless in salads. Add to that having to salvage the fragile leaves from a pool of water, and I would rather do without.

OREGANO

There is no such thing as oregano pure and simple. What there is is the genus *Origanum*, and it includes the marjorams as well as the plant called oregano. Start at the beginning: The herb com-monly known as sweet, garden or knotted marjoram is *O. majorana* and/or *Majorana hortensis*; pot marjoram is *O. Onites*; winter marjoram, *O. heracleoticum*. (I omit dittany of Crete, *O. Dic-tammus*—not to be confused with the garden perennial a.k.a. fraxinella or burning bush—because it isn't a good culinary herb, and because it is usually sold as dittany, and you can forget that it is an *Origanum*.) Only *O. Majorana* is hardy in the northern United States. Lastly, there is *O. vulgare* or wild marjoram, a hardy perennial that grows all over Europe and is now naturalized in this country, where it is sold as the Italian herb that gives pungency to pizza, spaghetti sauces, etc., i.e., oregano. The hitch is that to me and several of my friends, *O. vulgare*, far from having a robust flavor, has proved disappointingly dim and characterless. There must, we feel, be a mistake somewhere.

Oregano is certainly what Italians call the spicy herb popular in the cooking of the *mezzogiorno*, but that is no guarantee that the herb in question is *O. vulgare*—traditionally a medicinal rather than a culinary herb and so described in older encyclopedias. It could just as well be one of *vulgare*'s subspecies (*aureum* or *viride* for example), or another oregano altogether. (Research at several nurseries last summer turned up plants labeled as follows: 'dark green oregano,' probably meant to be *viride*, 'Greek oregano,' conceivably dittany, which is sometimes called Cretan dittany, and 'Oregano Coleus amboicensus,' which is unknown to science. No salesperson could say what any of these was supposed to be.) But I am inclined to think that Italian oregano is actually *O. Onites*, the pot marjoram, believed by some authorities to be a subspecies of *vulgare*. Confusion between the two has long existed. Writing on pot marjoram, Beston says to 'call it in Latin what you will,' and goes on to speculate that 'it may be *Origanum Onites*, an old perennial plant from the Caucasus, or a horticultural variety of the wild Marjoram of Europe and the British Isles, *Origanum Vulgaris* (sic).' This, however, isn't very helpful to northern gardeners, because to him the two cannot be interchangeable: *Onites* is a tender little shrub, which wouldn't matter in Italy but would here, while *vulgare* is fully hardy.

Time-Life's *Herbs*, meanwhile, throws another monkey wrench with the statement that the dried oregano sold commercially in this country is usually a Mexican variety (not identified) of wild marjoram that neither tastes nor smells like the true home-grown variety—though whether this refers only to the dry form isn't clear. Be that as it may, *Herbs* goes along with other American sources and names *O. vulgare* as the Italian herb for cooking. I will continue to insist that it isn't, and the next time I go to Italy will try to unravel the facts of the matter. It is, anyway, certain that *vulgare* is the only hardy oregano. Whether that advantage makes it worthwhile to grow must be up to the cook. To this cook, it doesn't. The only member of the species I grow is sweet marjoram (*O. Majorana*), *Onites* being virtually unobtainable. (Neither, of course, is hardy.)

CHERVIL

A little herb so refined and elegant it could be mistaken for a rare fern until it is sniffed. Then you know why it is one of the classic quartet of *fines herbes*: chervil, tarragon, parsley, and chives. The flavor is similar to tarragon's, though fainter, and in a salad I omit the tarragon and let the chervil provide the whiff of anise. An annual, it will self-sow as enthusiastically as dill, browning off just as dill does when the weather heats up, and making a second crop in the fall. In my vegetable garden it has commandeered a corner to itself, not a convenient one, naturally, but I don't interfere, knowing it would die on me if I did.

PARSLEY

No food snob today will use anything but the flat-leaved Italian variety, which they have been assured by Marcella Hazan, among others, is superior in flavor to the curly-leaved. Well, I don't agree. I use Italian parsley when instructed to do so in a recipe, and not otherwise. I much prefer the curly kind, which is also more versatile. Unlike the Italian, it can be frizzled to accompany fish or croquettes; grated in a Mouli made in France for the purpose; and heaped on a platter as decoration. I grow enormous quantities of it, mixing in a few plants of the Italian variety for those occasions when I need it—mostly to save face.

Parsley is a biennial and will flower and set seed the second year. The inexperienced think its survival portends another crop, and are doomed to disappointment. Once the seed heads appear, the plants are finished. (The seeds, to be sure, will make plants the following summer, but in the meantime you will be without garden-grown parsley. It is therefore necessary to begin anew each spring, preferably not with seedlings, which are expensive and don't transplant very well. (The lower leaves are apt to turn yellow, and the whole plant takes time to regain its equilibrium.) Seed, however, is notoriously hard to germinate, and books recommend soaking it overnight to loosen the tough outer casing. My advice is: don't. The wet gelatinous mass sticks to the fingers and is impossible to sow evenly. Thalassa Cruso has solved this problem once and for all: you hoe a shallow trench and sow the seed. Then step into the kitchen and set a kettle of water to boil. The instant it does, seize it, dash back to the garden and dribble the scalding water down the row. Cover lightly with soil. A uniform row nearly always results.

Parsley is as miserable in the kitchen as most herbs. Limp, etoliated and not enough for a family, a pot of it isn't worth the effort when any good grocer has crisper, greener bunches to sell. It has a long season in the garden too—I have picked it as late as December, even under a light covering of snow.

BAY

Laurus nobilis, the laurel of antiquity, Petrarch's crown; alias the standard shrub with the round head and its feet in a square white box that does sentry duty outside European hotels and restaurants; alias the leaf that with parsley and thyme makes up a *bouquet garni*. What bay is not is one of several shrubs and trees often called laurel that may be *Prunus Laurocerasus, P. lusitanica, L. canariensis, Kalmia latifolia* (our mountain laurel, whose leaves are poisonous), *Aucuba japonica*, or *Umbellularia californica*. Bay isn't hardy in the American north but can be treated as a house plant, though not in a hot kitchen. In summer outdoors it needs to be shaded from the noonday sun; in winter, grown in a sunny room with temperatures cool enough to approximate the Mediterranean climate at that season. In its native soil, a bay tree can grow sixty feet tall; in the American South, twenty or thirty is more like it, and in a pot it is kept within bounds by clipping. Potted bay is anything but a rampant grower. Always rooted from cuttings, it can take as much as a year to catch on and may never do so. A bay cutting given me by a friend six months ago is still sitting under a plastic tent, trying to make up its mind. Another, which has rooted, sends forth a leaf now and again, like someone putting up a finger to test the wind, retiring for weeks before it sends out another. At this rate, I won't have anything resembling a presentable shrub for years, and a friend who owns one confirms that this is likely. Is it worth the wait? If the aim is to have fresh bay leaves for cooking, certainly not. There isn't that much difference between one plucked from a plant and one from a store-bought jar—provided the latter is *Laurus nobilis* and not a substitute as noted earlier. Growing a bay tree is a fancy, something one undertakes for romantic reasons, and because it is, as they say, a 'challenge.'

LAVENDER

Around my rose beds are some sixty lavenders, all ordered and planted at the same time, all sold me as 'true English lavender.' Even as I dug them in I saw the little plants differed from one another, but I put this down to their immaturity. I was wrong. The passage of time confirmed that I had several varieties and was once more adrift in the sea of herbal confusion. Some had blue-green foliage, others grey; one plant had leaves like needles; its neighbor's were broader and flatter; the colors varied from white to deep purple and the heights from one to three feet. Had I been swindled? Why were they so different? Did it matter?

I decided it didn't. A hedge of lavender is a hedge of lavender and always enchanting when in bloom. To demand that it be composed of identical plants is perhaps to descend to finickiness. But the puzzle of their origin nagged, driving me to encyclopedias and what is often far more enlightening, to asking questions of gardeners better informed than myself. From these I was encouraged to learn that I am not simply an idiot in my inability to understand the lavenders—which comprise some twenty species, making it inaccurate to speak of 'true' lavender. True in what sense? Any species that has been identified ought to qualify; but what most of us are after is common or garden lavender, and knowing gardening encyclopedias as I do, I wasn't surprised to find that it has four different names, depending on which source you use. Most American dictionaries call it *Lavandula officinalis*, *L. Spica*, or *L. vera*. The *R.H.S.* opts for *L. Spica*. Not so *Hortus III*, which considers them all to be *L. angustifolia* or one of its subspecies. Right away you have a premonition of the trial that awaits when you order or buy lavender plants—let alone the seed, of which more in a moment. Any of the above may be called 'true English lavender,' or just 'true lavender.' But there are cultivars as well, of which the best known are Hidcote, deep-violet flowers, about one foot; Munstead, mauve flowers, fifteen inches; Twickel purple, three feet; Grey Lady, deep lavender, two feet. There are also white lavenders (*alba*) but I know of no named cultivar.

You should now further understand what isn't made sufficiently clear in the literature: Lavender does not come true from seed, making it possible to sow a packet legitimately labeled *L. officinalis* (and/or *spica*, *vera*, etc.) and end up with a mixed litter like mine. Technically, this would clear a nurseryman from charges of bad faith when a batch of plants turned out not to be uniform—except that a really scrupulous one wouldn't raise his plants from seed. He would grow them from cuttings taken from parents whose ancestry was known to him. Only in that way could he label his offerings specifically and correctly. Or so I am told.

But if my own researches are any guide, he would still have his work cut out for him.

Suppose he is growing a lavender he believes to be 'French.' In *Time-Life* that is *L. stoechas* (also known as 'Spanish' lavender but never mind that). *Hortus III* concurs, but also calls a very different lavender 'French': *L. dentata* (in *Time-Life* 'fringed'— as the name indicates). The *R.H.S.* assigns no nationality either to *stoechas* or *dentata*. The single 'French' lavender there is Nana Compacta, a cultivar of *L. Spica*—alias *angustifolia* in *Hortus III*, which also lists Nana but doesn't call it 'French.' Is that clear to everybody? It isn't to me, and wouldn't be worth pursuing if it weren't for the important question of hardiness.

Lavenders vary considerably in this respect and where I live it is of more than passing interest to know which can stand the winters and which can't. Let us say I want a 'French' lavender: If it is either *L. dentata* or *L. stoechas* I must abandon the idea because both can be grown outdoors only in the lower South. But if it is a cultivar of *spica* and/or *angustifolia*, I am safe. How to find a way out of the maze? Catalogues are no help. Few of them sell lavender plants and when they do the descriptions are—I suspect deliberately—vague and all-embracing. Two that I have before me, put out by small but sophisticated New England nurseries I won't name because they are otherwise pretty good, are fair samples. One offers both 'French' and 'English' lavender without further definition—no Latin names, no varieties. The other lists *L. Spica* and *L. vera* as separate species, which they haven't been considered for many years. There must be a way to get hold of lavender plants correctly identified, but neither I nor (more to the point) my herbalist friends have found it. They agree that the situation is chaotic and getting worse, but there seems to be nowhere to go from here. The lavenders are a lottery, but at least there is no such thing as an ugly one.

BASIL

Surely nobody needs to be told how to grow the king of annual herbs, the tomato's best friend, and now that Americans have discovered *pesto*, an herb to be found in every proud cook's garden.

Basil, thank God, has no taxonomic problems, and a child can grow it successfully. The only difficulty is to have enough, and a flat or two of seedlings isn't. Not if you love *pesto*, and especially not if you intend to freeze it. Better to sow seed, several short rows in succession so that the plants won't all reach maturity at once. Basil flowers should be cut off to keep the plant producing, but if you have overestimated the supply, let a part of the row come into bloom and the bees will thank you. (Of course, it would be nicer if they were your own bees so you could have basil honey; but one must think, too, of the common weal.)

Actually, my enthusiasm for frozen *pesto* has waned, and I grow less basil than I did when it seemed a miracle that one could have this treat in the dead of winter. Treat it may be, but it is only the shade of its summer self. Basil, a true tropical that is blackened by a touch of frost in the garden, is saved in the freezer by the olive oil. But something happens to it that doesn't to hardier herbs like tarragon. The heart goes out of it—and I think also out of basil subjected to prolonged heat. (I am speaking of the fresh, the dried I never use.) I therefore see no point in adding it to a tomato sauce that is going to be cooked longer than the five minutes required for a *primavera*, say, in which the basil is barely wilted. So it's the old story: The real thrill lies not in eating the ghosts of herbs and vegetables out of season but in enduring the ennui of winter and letting it sharpen the appetite for the *primeurs* when at long last they arrive. Nothing can replace the shock of pleasure given by a small mountain of fresh basil in the summer kitchen, waiting to be crushed with mortar and pestle if one is a tradition- alist, by the Cuisinart if not. I find the aroma so intoxicating I would turn it into a perfume if I knew how. (And my favorite apothecaries, Caswell-Massey of New York, apparently cater to people who do just that. They sell oil of basil for a princely $18.50 the half ounce, more than that commanded by oil of freesia or night-scented stock.)

There are several sorts of basil, but the common or sweet (*Ocimum Basilicum*) does very well. Some Europeans feel that the smaller-leaved *O. minimum* or pot-basil has a superior flavor. I don't think there is anything to choose between them unless one wants basil in a pot, in which case *minimum* is neater and prettier. (But forget about growing basil in the winter kitchen; if white fly doesn't attack it, it will lose its savor anyway.) Purple basil is a new introduction (1962)—curiously, because the breeders who work on mauve daylilies and triply frilled snapdragons almost never turn their attention to herbs, and a new variety produced by man is practically unheard of. Dark Purple was bred at the University of Connecticut and has the unique distinction of being the only herb ever awarded the All-America medal. These facts, I felt, put me under obligation to plant it, and caused me some guilt at having to confess that I don't care for it—neither the funereal color nor the taste. As for purple *pesto*, who could face it?

MINT

Were I to involve myself with the mints I don't doubt I would be plunged into the chaos that engulfs the thymes, the oreganos and the lavenders. I have only to glance at *Hortus III*, where I read that 'although over 600 species have been named, the conservative view is that these are mainly variants or hybrids of about 25 well-defined species, most of which readily hybridize among themselves. . . .' I then note that *M. rotundifolia*, apple mint in *Wyman* and *Time-Life*, is a misnomer for *M. suaveolens*—and I see the waters closing over me. I won't go another step. The mint bed will remain anonymous. It has only two permanent occupants—a curly mint given me years ago, and another that smells of citron. The first I assume to be the cultivar Crispata of *M. spicata* or maybe the crispa variety of *M. aquatica*; the second fits no description I have but might be . . . never mind. I am determined not to find out. Sometimes, it is true, I have thought of revising the bed and planting a choice selection of named varieties, and to this end have introduced a plant or two of pennyroyal (*M. Pulegium*), *M. piperita* (peppermint) or some other variety picked up at an herb farm. Most of them have been strangled by the fiercely territorial incumbents. I let them fight it out.

Every garden should have one area that can safely be neglected, and a mint bed is the ideal choice. My unknown mints, fenced in with old boards, get no attention beyond a shovelful of compost now and then. They never have a shadow of a pest or a blight. Once a summer I get down on my knees and trace the stolons that have escaped the fence, ripping them from their moorings and throwing them on the compost heap. As gardening jobs go, this one is a delight. The heavenly smell invades every pore, and if I

were the size of a cat I would roll luxuriously in the pile of dis-
cards. I don't know what else to do with them. Mint, like lovage, is
an excessive herb that one can't begin to use up. A snip or two in a
drink, another chopped up to go with the early peas or potatoes,
mint tea if you like it. None of these makes a dent in a flourishing
mint bed. Nevertheless, it is a thing to have. I can't really imagine
a garden without one.

------------ ◇ ------------

HYBRIDS

Mius is gaining skill in hybridizing certain flowers; and I have finally
succeeded in convincing him that, in the beds of seedlings thus obtained,
the least robust varieties often give the most beautiful flowers. But
it is only with great difficulty that I can get him to set aside the
common, vigorous varieties that can get along without his attentions,
in order to favour those that are harder to cultivate and require his care.

If, among her artists, Greece does not count a single Spartan, is this
not because Sparta threw her puny children into pits?

ANDRÉ GIDE
The Journals of André Gide
Translated by Justin O'Brian

It isn't often that I find myself in sympathy with Gide, but when
he writes about his garden I find in him a fellow-spirit. Though he
could obviously afford a professional gardener, he did a lot of the
work himself and suffered the same exasperations as the rest of us,
particularly in this matter of the survival of the unfittest. Elsewhere: 'Each year, upon returning to my garden again, the same
dismay: disappearance of the rare species and varieties; triumph
of the common and mediocre ones.' And he notes that 'When my
cat catches a bird it is invariably, rather than a sparrow, a
warbler.'

We all, of course, notice the same thing, which is why I am
hopelessly puzzled by the expression 'hybrid vigor,' frequently
encountered in catalogues and garden books. I understand that
hybrids may be bred for greater beauty, higher yields, even resistance to certain diseases. But history, and particularly recent his-

tory, does not show that they have greater vigor or durability. On the contrary, and as Gide says, it is the common, unimproved varieties that survive—not the hybrids. And older hybrids are tougher than new ones: In my garden are two stands of pink phlox that are thirty-five years old. They start to bloom at the end of June and continue into September. The newer, flashier phloxes with larger flower trusses bloom six weeks later, and are far more subject to powdery mildew into the bargain. Everybody knows, too, that the antique roses live forever, while the hybrid teas wither away in a few years, unless they freeze to death first. Without hybrids, the vegetable world would be a far less beautiful place than it is, and a less productive one too; but that isn't the whole story. The intense plant-breeding techniques of the last seventy years may be producing too many Athenians while disdaining the Spartans, and that could be a very bad idea.

The problem isn't one to worry gardeners (yet) but in world agriculture a threat is developing and we should be aware of it. The fact is that we are running out of a resource as vital as petroleum. The technical name for it is germ plasm and it means the genetic plant material whose biological diversity the hybridist could, until recently, draw on to a practically limitless extent. But the genetic base of our major food crops is narrowing steadily. An analogy might be the royal family that, having pursued a policy of perpetual intermarriage, winds up with many of its members afflicted with hereditary blindness, hemophilia or congenital idiocy. According to a recent study, most modern agriculture has come to be based on fewer than thirty plant species, and some of the consequences are already visible. Genetic diversity is agriculture's first line of defense against pests, diseases and adverse climatic conditions. Endless fields of genetically identical hybrid crops are on the contrary an invitation to disaster—disasters such as the wheat stem rust of 1954 and the southern corn blight of 1970, in which thousands of acres were destroyed.

The remedy, to revert to human terms, is 'new blood,' in this case local and native varieties both wild and cultivated. But reservoirs of these are drying up as more and more farmers abandon the hardier ancestral strains and turn to hybrid varieties. And particularly is this true in what we condescendingly call the third world, until lately an important source of many different kinds of native seeds. Those are now in the process of disappearing as farmers are encouraged to turn to the more productive hybrids offered them by foreign seed stations. In the 1960's we heard a lot about the green revolution, miracle rice, etc. The green revolution may yet turn into a green nightmare; for not only do the new hybrids lack the resilience of the older native strains with their built-in adaptation to local conditions, they depend for their success on chemical fertilizers and pesticides—which, aside from other disadvantages, are for the most part manufactured by western conglomerates that are in turn dependent on that other scarce resource: oil.

The National Academy of Science, recognizing the danger, has already outlined a program for collecting and storing the seeds of wild species, a splendid move but one rather akin to collecting endangered animals in zoos where they may or may not (like the pandas in the Washington Zoo) be able to breed and perpetuate themselves. Stories of 5,000-year-old corn sprouting after its discovery in Egyptian tombs notwithstanding, few seeds last forever and such a procedure can't go far toward safeguarding world supplies of germ plasm. That can best be done, as with animals, by conservation of native habitats—or by farmers and gardeners growing and saving the seed of localized, open-pollinated varieties both old and new. (Congress is, at this writing, wrestling with legislation to protect the breeders of open-pollinated vegetables by the extension of patents, a move some people are afraid will eventually allow a few large seed companies to determine what we home gardeners can grow—but that is another, if closely related, question—see SEED.) Meanwhile, the home gardener can take some small steps in the right direction.

An article in the May 1980 issue of *Organic Gardening* (whose author will recognize how heavily I have borrowed from his research) suggests the following: Don't limit your seed orders to big companies; spread them among smaller, preferably local suppliers, and grow at least one new variety each year. Plant the so-called heirloom varieties when you can find them—and if you have them already, save the seed and replant it. Don't concentrate on the new hybrids offered each year (which anyway you can't reproduce, owing to the fact that hybrid seed doesn't come 'true') but rather look for open-pollinated types (which do).

In these ways we can help to conserve a vital resource, and of course the advice is exactly contrary to what Gide had in mind. Half a century ago, it would have been preposterous to suggest that the development of hybrids was in any way undesirable; and to most gardeners and farmers it still is. As Harold Loden, vice-president of the American Seed Trade Association, recently asked: 'Why would a farmer want to plant less than the best?' Why indeed? We have heard the question before from a candidate who made it to the White House. Ask a man why he wants less than the best, and he automatically answers that he doesn't; but experience indicates that the question should be rephrased: Best for whom, and for how long? Politics aside, the farmer may find himself seriously misled when he automatically chooses the hybrid seed that companies thrust upon him through advertising and other pressures, and so may the gardener. Rather, they should both ask themselves where this increased specialization is leading. (One wonders what Gide would have had to say about the Common Catalogue, a set of rules that controls what varieties can be grown in France and other Common Market countries—laws that would forbid him to sow the seeds of plants whose wind-borne pollen might cross-breed with protected varieties growing in nearby gardens or fields.) We live in a world where the Athenian-Spartan dichotomy no longer applies, where the exquisitely developed and nurtured hybrid, bred to exist under circumstances not less than ideal, is a luxury we can't afford. The time may come, is perhaps already here, when the old, tough, common varieties, the Spartans of the vegetable kingdom, will be needed to save the plant world, and us, from extinction.

Meanwhile, if you are lucky enough to possess the seeds of a cucumber strain grown by a great-uncle, *bonne chance*. And hang on to those ancestral beans.

---------- ❧ ----------

INVITATIONS

By planting flowers one invites butterflies . . . by planting pines one invites the wind . . . by planting bananas one invites the rain, and by planting willow trees one invites cicadas.

CHAO CH'ANG
Quoted in *Gardens of China* by Osvald Sirén

I V Y
(*Hedera helix*)

English ivy we call it, but no city has more of it than Paris. It is everywhere, clambering over walls, substituting for grass in the parks and private gardens; in the Faubourg St. Germain it mounts to the tops of forest trees, where little owls nest in the branches. I have always admired Paris ivy, but never examined it closely until a recent visit—when I had occasion to walk daily past the wall that guards the Italian Embassy on the side of the cul-de-sac called the Cité de Varenne. High as a fortress, the wall was dense with ivy that I noticed had an unfamiliar leaf: glossy as black onyx and sharply pointed. I took it for a French variety unobtainable in the United States, and resolved to have some. Snipping cuttings was easy (few people pass that way), and smuggling illegal plant material from abroad is a bad old habit of mine. (See POTATOES.) I had no trouble getting my cuttings back to Connecticut where, however, they refused to take. So I wrote off the French ivy, until later that summer my eye chanced to fall on the ivy growing at the top of the retaining wall above my vegetable garden. Could it be? It was. The dark overhanging clumps were identical with the French, and they seemed to be covered with a faint haze of bloom that attracted bees. The ivy lower down was the usual kind with five-lobed leaves, and that must be why I had been blind to the change at the top. What had happened?

Alas for ignorance. The phenomenon, I have since learned, is natural, though not in New England. When *Hedera helix* climbs high enough and reaches maturity, which takes about thirty years, the leaves undergo a transformation and the vines bloom, then set seed in clusters of tiny blue berries. In benign climates, this happens as a matter of course. The occurrence is rare only where winters regularly kill the vines back. In New England you must have a particularly favorable location for English ivy to outgrow the juvenile form, and unwittingly I had provided it on a south-facing stone wall.

As for the French cuttings, an amateur like myself hadn't much chance of rooting them successfully. Unlike the juvenile sprays a child can propagate in a glass of water, mature ivy strikes with difficulty, like all old wood. European horticulturists know what to do, and from a mature cutting can produce little standard trees requiring a minimum of pruning—or a topiary mound—since mature ivy tends to clump and to stop climbing. These were more popular fifty years ago than they are today, but examples can still be seen in formal plantings abroad. American nurserymen aren't, as far as I know, interested in the time-consuming business of producing them. They offer only juvenile ivy, which sprouts in all directions and can't be trained in the same way. Nor will ivy grown for a ground cover attain maturity. The vines have to climb, as far as they want to go.

Many people hate the look of ivy, or any vine, clambering into trees. They feel it gives an abandoned air to a property, and there is the vague idea that the vines somehow harm the trees. I doubt if they do, and if they did I would run the risk. I am always trying to induce vines to climb trees. A little studied negligence is becoming to a garden: it blurs the edges—always supposing there are edges to blur. Painters love gardens on the fringe of neglect. We owe the landscapes of Watteau, and after him Boucher, Oudry, Fragonard, Hubert Robert and many others to the bankruptcy of the French government in the years immediately before and after the death of the Sun King. Thanks to his extravagance, the royal gardens could no longer be maintained as they had been. Balustrades and staircases sank into moss, trees grew up and were overcome by vines, statues were masked in ivy, until—in time—these neglected dream gardens became the ideal, paving the way for Rousseau's romantic visions of untrammeled nature. From the sixteenth century onward, the voluptuous untidiness of Italian gardens has been part of their charm to painters—and everybody else. We gardeners needn't kill ourselves in the name of order. Some plants should be allowed their way, and one of them is ivy. It makes sense to plant it beneath a tree that may die before the vine comes into its prime. If we had done this with our elms, many of them would now be picturesque supports for a vine that among its other virtues is evergreen, and almost immortal.

--- ⌒ ---

JAMES vs. BENSON

Little by little, even with other cares, the slowly but surely working poison of the garden-mania begins to stir in my long-sluggish veins. Tell Harry, as an intimate instance, that by a masterly inspiration I have at one bold stroke swept away all the complications in the quarter on which the studio looks down, uprooting the wilderness of shrubs, relaying paths, extending borders, etc., and made arrangement to throw the lawn, in one lordly sweep, straight up into that angle—a proceeding that greatly increases our apparent extent and dignity: an improvement, in short, quite unspeakable.

HENRY JAMES
Quoted in *Henry James at Home* by H. M. Hyde

'My little plot,' said Miss Mapp. 'Very modest, as you see, three quarters of an acre at the most, but well screened. My flower beds: sweet roses, tortoiseshell butterflies. Rather a nice clematis. My little Eden, I call it, so small but so well beloved.'

'Enchanting!' said Lucia, looking round the garden before mounting the steps up to the garden-room door. There was a very green and well-kept lawn, set in bright flower beds. A trellis at one end separated it from a kitchen garden beyond, and round the rest ran high brick walls, over which peered the roofs of other houses. In one of these walls was cut a curved archway with a della Robbia head above it.

'Shall we just pop across the lawn,' said Miss Mapp, pointing to this, 'and peep in there while Withers brings our tea? . . . My little secret garden . . . When I am in here and shut the door, I musn't be disturbed for anything less than a telegram. A rule of the house; I am very strict about it. The tower of the church keeping watch, as I always say over my little nook, and taking care of me . . . A little paved walk round, you see, flower beds, a pocket handkerchief of a lawn. . . .'

'Oh, Georgie, isn't it too sweet?' cried Lucia. *'Un giardino segreto. Molto bello!'*

E. F. BENSON
Mapp and Lucia

Would you have guessed that the garden in both passages is one and the same? If you are a Jamesian highbrow, probably not. But if you are a Benson addict (and these, it should be said, have included W. H. Auden) you are likely to know that the terrible Miss Mapp's fictional residence was Henry James's real one at Rye in Sussex. It was called Lamb House, and James took a long lease on it in 1897, living there off and on until his death and dictating many of his novels in the garden room—famous to Bensonites as Miss Mapp's (and later Lucia's) favorite vantage point for spying on the village. Neither was disturbed by James's ghost, and it is ironic that they and not he should have made Lamb House (Mallards in the Lucia novels) immortal. This isn't to compare Benson with James but simply to state a fact. Benson leased Lamb House after James's death in 1916 and lived there until his own in 1940—shortly before the garden room was demolished by a German bomb—and in that space of time populated it with characters that made it entirely his own. When Anne Parrish paid him a call, he received her with these words: 'This is Miss Mapp's garden room, and I am Miss Mapp.' Where James was pompous, he was funny. What Luciaphil can forget the war over 'garden produce' —or Mapp's climbing of that church tower in order to catch Lucia, supposed for excellent reasons to be suffering from flu, actually skipping rope in the *giardino segreto*? I am glad to know that James found a happy refuge at Lamb House, but much gladder that it ultimately fell into the hands of E. F. Benson, whose house and garden have given me more pleasure than James's did.

LAWNS

The single greatest source of complaint by the gardening citizenry. Crab grass is a national obsession and I have yet to meet anyone who enjoys mowing. Some people find relaxation in the evening session with the hose but to judge by the burnt-out state of most lawns in midsummer, not many—and the water companies are against us. Either the rates are so high that every drop from the hose is a dollar bill, or there is a shortage and orders go out that watering can be done only between midnight and three A.M. Yet lawns persist. Not only do millions of houses standing at the center of unfenced lots seem to demand a grassy surround, lawns are part of our English horticultural heritage, coded into the racial memory, and it is vain to point out the differences in climate and skilled labor that make anything resembling an English lawn a mirage in two-thirds of the United States. Those sports inherited from the British Isles, where they were played on grass, must still be played on something resembling the original—Astroturf if necessary, a hideous parody. Tennis (now mostly played on clay courts) is the exception. Golf, almost as popular, still involves greens and these are the nearest thing to the true English lawn in this country. The expense of them is staggering: According to *Time-Life*'s volume on lawns and ground covers, the average putting green costs $2,500 to install, $750 a year to weed, mow and fertilize. Most homeowners must settle for something less extravagant, but they still demand the appearance of grass if not the reality. In Texas and Arizona, dichondra is popular. Seen close to, it looks like a ground ivy but it does make a dense turf and at a distance a dichondra lawn could be mistaken for a grass one. There is something curiously colonial in all this. It is as though we were, even now, the temporary rulers of a foreign continent, India say, determined to impose the familiar on an alien environment.

An English sward is flat as a billiard table, striped like moiré silk, green as an emerald, and apparently weedless. It can be a croquet pitch, a bowling green, a tennis court, a promenade for peacocks, the site of afternoon tea parties under mighty oaks. And along with the *tapis vert* of northern France, it is uniquely the product of a damp climate. Bent grasses are the stuff these dream lawns are made of. Fine-textured as velvet, bent grasses thrive in a cool, drizzly atmosphere, where they can be mown close and often (once a day on the center court at Wimbledon), thus forming a dense turf where weeds find it hard to get a foothold—a case of the rich getting richer. Except in the Pacific northwest or on golf greens constantly cared for, the bents don't do well in the United States. Cool-weather grasses in this country are mostly fescues or bluegrass, tough 'all-purpose' plants that can stand our wild variations between heat and cold and, up to a point, our frequent droughts. They never make a bent-grass turf whatever you do. An American lawn closely mown in mid-August looks as though a prairie fire had swept over it; and artificial watering isn't the whole answer either. The evening ritual with the hose can do more harm than good by causing grass roots to rise to the surface and encouraging weeds, and unless it can be given a thorough soaking, a lawn is best left alone during dry spells. It will green up when the weather cools off—which is fine except that it is precisely in midsummer that the eye longs for a thirst-quenching expanse of green. September is too late.

Still, climate isn't everything. Maintenance is at least as important, and English lawns in the days of their glory were cared for in ways beyond the imagination of the American householder. I have seen men on their knees plucking at (invisible) weeds with the care women devote to their eyebrows; and I have read of sod dug up piece by piece and taken to a greenhouse for grooming, weeding, fertilizing—everything but a fine-tooth comb applied to it before it was relaid in the garden. I believe this bit of Edwardiana. His lawn was a fetish to the Englishman, and one of the proofs is that he invented the lawn mower.

Before 1830, lawns everywhere were scythed like a meadow, a sight I happen to be familiar with because that is how lawns were still cut in my part of Hungary a hundred years later. For us, Edwin Budding's invention might not have existed and a couple of dozen men were needed to scythe the expanses of our *jardin anglais* twice a summer. This resulted in pretty hayricks standing about, but the stubble left scarcely resembled a lawn in the English sense; and even in rainy England the same must have been true. Budding, at any rate, had a better idea. An engineer in the textile trade, he noted a resemblance, which might only have occurred to an Englishman, between the pile on fabric and the velvety pile of grass. In the textile mills, pile was cut by a cylinder with spiral blades: Behold, then, the reel mower, constructed on identical lines, introduced in 1831. Improvements have been made since but no adequate substitute yet devised. The reel mower is one of the secrets of a beautiful lawn.

Reel mowers evoke nostalgia: for lost summer mornings when one was awakened by the gentle crescendo and diminuendo of their whirring blades, and the perfume of new-mown grass drifted through an open window. But more than sentiment is involved in the informed gardener's rejection of the angry roar, the horrid fumes of the gasoline-powered rotary mower that most of us are stuck with today. These machines are anything but an improvement on Mr. Budding's invention. Reel mowers clip like fine scissors, rotary mowers more like a saw slashing at the grass and savagely wounding it—good enough if you are reclaiming a piece of prairie and the last thing you need for a domestic lawn. The rotary mower isn't the only villain. There is also a machine for edging that employs nylon whips. All these devices are horrible, not only for the racket and smell they make but for the damage they do. Unless sharpened to a razor edge, the rotary blade kills the tips of the grass, leaving the lawn with a brownish tinge and open to disease. The design is clumsy too, with the grass catcher either to one side where it bangs into shrubs, or in more expensive models awkwardly at the rear between the handles. The logical place for a grass catcher (which by the way is essential—contrary to what some people think, clippings left on the lawn are *not* good for it) is in front, where it is on reel mowers. Finally, only a reel mower will make those delectable stripes.

Motorized reel mowers are expensive and getting them properly serviced is for some reason difficult in this nation of mechanics. Simpler and better is the unpowered model, lighter by many pounds than the cast-iron prewar machine. The problem is to get anyone to use it. My lawn is far too large for me to cope with and I must depend on hired help. To a man, they insist on a gasoline-powered rotary. That power tools are easier to operate is an article of faith no amount of proof to the contrary can dislodge. I estimate that what with balky starters, pauses for mechanical adjustments, filling with fuel, fetching the fuel from the gas station, etc., etc., it takes twice as long to mow the lawn as it used to, and nobody can convince me that pushing and hauling that monster around is easier than operating one of the new lightweight reel mowers would be. I know it isn't. I also know that practicality and common sense don't come into it. Prestige does, and the masculine penchant for playing with machinery. Men *like* squatting over a mower and speculating why 'she' is burning too much oil. Occasionally I win a skirmish in the war against power tools. The electric hedge-cutter was ultimately conceded to be less efficient than the old hand shears. The reintroduction of a motorless reel mower is a lost cause.

What is the alternative to our continuing slavery to this machine, not to mention outrageous water bills and the labor of fertilizing, weeding, and liming a lawn? In the first place, not ground covers—not if the object is lower maintenance. Landscape architects make lavish use of ground covers, which are requisites of modern design—and handsomer in any context than a scrubby area of grass. Care-free they are not. Everything that a lawn requires except mowing must be done for them too, and a lot of it by hand. Admirable as they are for difficult places a mower can't reach—slopes, rocky terrain—on the flat they are of doubtful value, and to the gardener who wants to make free of every part of his private world, impossible. You can't walk or sit on a ground cover—or play games. They put half the garden out of bounds. I therefore have little use for them except under my apple trees, and the problem remains.

Like a lot of people lately, I have been considering a return to older practices. I have thought of replacing grass with sweet-smelling herbs like camomile. Falstaff said that the more it is trod-den on the faster it grows, which must be true: the famous camomile lawn at Buckingham Palace is trampled by thousands of feet at royal garden parties. I have tried camomile, however, and it didn't take—perhaps because the traffic wasn't heavy enough. There is a good deal about stamping and treading in old texts. Albertus Magnus speaks of a lawn 'carefully weeded and tram-pled underfoot' as if this were a good thing; and Bacon, recom-mending burnet, wild thyme and water mints, says, 'Therefore you are to set whole alleys of them, to have the pleasure when you walk or tread.' And indeed they would have to be tramped on pretty continuously to keep them down. The burnets and water mints I know reach three and four feet and seem an extraordinary choice for a walkway. Altogether, I am dubious as to how these herbal floors, so popular in seventeenth-century England, would work out in twentieth-century America. The aroma would be di-vine but I suspect there were good reasons why they eventually gave way to grass.

More tempting is the flowery mead of medieval paintings and *mille-fleurs* tapestries, where wild pinks, primroses, lily-of-the-valley, iris, were packed into green turf. Old manuals—the earliest by Pietro de' Crescenzi, published in 1471—have directions for making these, of a sort. Pietro says to dig the turf in the wild, weed it, scald it in boiling water to keep weeds from germinating, then set it in place and beat it with a wooden mallet, as is done today. Then plant it with flowers and scythe it twice a year. This leaves a good many questions unanswered. In spring, there will have been Boccaccio's 'grass of deepest green, starred with a thousand vari-ous flowers,' the condition we see in the pictures. But what of summer, when the flowers (all spring bloomers you notice) would have gone and the grass become three feet high? Or a little later when, scythed, it would be an unsightly field of stubble? On these points the old gardeners are silent, and in the pictures it is always the first of May, never the last of August.

Many of the same objections would seem to me to apply to the increasingly popular idea today of letting the grass grow and the lawn turn into a meadow, or a prairie—according to whether you live in the East or the West. Moved by ecological concerns, the desire to get rid of gasoline-powered mowers, and surely by simple laziness, a lot of people are going in for what are called 'natural lawns,' which consist of local wild grasses and wild flowers, need no water or fertilizer and provide refuge for birds who will obligingly scatter the wild-flower seeds for you in future years. It all sounds most attractive, until you begin to study the articles on the subject. Then you begin to wonder.

In the first place, the grass you already have apparently won't do. According to Leslie Sauer, a partner in a new firm called Andropogon, which specializes in ecological landscaping, you must open up pockets of soil and plant the seed of wild flowers and native pasture grass mixtures (available at rural feed stores, she says) to help things along. But I am not clear about this matter of the grasses. Mrs. Sauer is quoted in *The New York Times* as saying that the traditional lawn grasses—bluegrass, fescue, perennial rye—are cool-season grasses that go dormant in summer, 'whereas the natural lawn is a warm-season plant community that develops slowly in spring, thrives in summer and fades when the trees change color.' An article in *Organic Gardening* seems to contradict that. It says the grass you have will grow tall and scraggy in the first season of letting a lawn go. Soon, however, various wild flowers will appear, along with 'the stronger native grasses,' which will 'muscle out the weeds.' (Neither source comments on how one would tell a weed from a wild flower in this context.) Then it adds: 'The trouble with most native cool-season meadow grasses is that they turn brown during the summer before greening up again in the fall.' Where this leaves one, I don't know.

In any case, it isn't the end of the difficulties. As *Organic Gardening* points out, a meadow left completely alone will turn into a forest. Woody species must therefore be kept in check—by cutting. As you can't do that with an ordinary lawn mower, you are told either to rent a sit-down machine for the (probably) twice-annual mowing—or to use a scythe. Now scything is an exercise that might easily kill the average suburban homeowner who already has trouble with a power mower. It is strenuous to a degree, as everyone knows who has read the chapter in *Anna Karenina* where Levin joins the peasants at their work, and an art into the bargain. The man who balks at the mechanical mowing of a lawn isn't, believe me, going to take to a scythe. So it's back to a huge, evil-smelling machine at least twice a year. In the East, that is. In the West, where the natural lawn is a prairie, *Organic Gardening* notes that the 'authentic and best way' to maintain it is by burning, which fights weeds, and when the ashes have settled, gives the plants a dose of fertilizer in the form of potash, phosphorus and calcium. Be sure, it adds, to check with your local fire department to find out if burning is legal. The average gardener needn't, I think, bother with that precaution. How could burning be legal, and if it were, who in his right mind would run the risk? So it's the mower or the scythe again, and it turns out that a little weeding will be necessary too. Ragweed and Canada thistles will have to be pulled, and one should keep an eye out for poison ivy. And to these hazards I would add another, never spoken of by the proponents of natural lawns. They create a habitat for wildlife: raccoons, possums and squirrels are mentioned, all of which I already have; and a family in Texas reports an armadillo it gives them great pleasure to watch. But if I had a natural lawn, especially in the West, I would be watching for something else: snakes. That I am dealing with a grass snake or a king cobra makes no difference to me, and the mere possibility that one was lurking in my natural lawn would be enough to make me cut it down and return to the tiresome disciplines of turf.

So what with one thing and another, I would reject a natural lawn even if it made sense in a garden like mine and wouldn't look (as I see in photographs, it *does* look) as though one were too slatternly to keep a garden decent. It's all very well to talk about ecology. My garden is alive with birds and small animals (minus snakes) as it is. I don't need more. I only regret that my attitude places me on the side of the law. Letting the grass grow beyond a certain point is illegal in most communities, and in some of them the town has the right to invade your property, mow the lawn, and charge you for it into the bargain. Where does such regulation stop? I am also forbidden to raise chickens or bees or a little pot for my own use. Might it not equally be found that my vegetable garden violated community standards in some way? I find such infringements of individual rights intolerable and so, as a matter of fact, have the courts when would-be growers of natural lawns have tested the principle. *Organic Gardening* itself succeeded in having a local ordinance that forced the mowing of lawns overturned. I was happy to read that. The fact that I don't myself want a hayfield in the backyard is beside the point.

Alternatives are few, but there is one I would commend to lawn-lovers in the North: that old favorite, white clover (*Trifolium repens*). Clover lawns aren't new and time was when all good grass mixtures included clover seed. Clover will grow almost anywhere that isn't too dry or too hot, isn't particular about soil (which it benefits by adding nitrogen), makes a dense, weed-resistant carpet that cuts mowing by half, greens up early. The white haze of blossom, lovely in itself, is much visited by honey-bees. In short, it seems to have every advantage over grass. Yet clover lawns are now exceedingly rare—out of fashion according to *Time-Life*, which goes on to explain that clover is 'notorious' for staining clothes. That was news to me, but it isn't the determining factor. The real reason you don't see clover any more is that it is killed by broad-leaved herbicides. That, too, was news to me, and I suspect to most people who don't use herbicides. It also explains why clover seed is now hard to find and frightfully expensive. Once again, a good thing is quietly pushed off the market for reasons that have nothing to do with the consumer's interests. One can't call it a conspiracy exactly, but the effect is the same. The average gardener simply doesn't know the advantages of clover, and if he does is discouraged by the price from buying the seed.

I discovered the virtues of clover by accident, when it began to appear in the lawn some years ago. Soon, the green tide had spread, and now I do all I can to encourage it, even to braving the high price of the seed. I am in hopes that one of these days it will take over the lawn completely. Meanwhile, I am observing the posteriors of croquet players who tend to lounge on the lawn between turns: No sign of green stains so far, and I conclude that clover's reputation for staining clothes must date from the far-off days when white flannel trousers and organdy dresses were worn at garden parties. It has no effect on blue jeans.

LILIES

The nineteenth and early twentieth centuries were the golden age of plant collectors: David Douglas who brought the Douglas fir, the Monterey pine and many other conifers to England; John Jeffrey who followed Douglas to the American West; E. H. Wilson who gave us the Chinese dogwood, the Regale lily and the dazzling Davidia or dove tree that in bloom seems to be aflutter with white birds; Reginald Farrer, George Forrest and dozens of others who changed the face of our gardens. Plant collecting was a dangerous business then. Douglas was torn to pieces by a wild bull in Hawaii; Farrar met his end in Upper Burma; Jeffrey vanished into the California gold rush; Forrest died of heart failure on his seventh expedition to Yünnan. And since that time the floral storehouses of western Asia have become if anything more difficult to penetrate. We hear no more of famous botanist-explorers or newly discovered specimens for the garden. Today it is the hybridizers who revolutionize our plantings, and of these none has wrought more changes than the American lily breeders in the last thirty years. We can now be said to dominate this field, though the lilies themselves have come from every part of the earth.

Well I remember my first lily plantings after the war, when only the better known species and a few hybrids were available. Madonna lilies came mostly from France and were often afflicted with virus, as were the gold-banded *Auratum platyphyllums* from Japan. Even Regales did poorly for me (in all honesty, they still do). Then, beginning in the 1950's, came the revolution that has made American hybrids the finest in the horticultural world: the Mid-Century Asiatics like the nasturtium-red Enchantment, a June bloomer; the amazing Aurelian hybrids, shaped like trumpets which follow in July: Black Dragon, Green Magic, Golden Splendor, Pink Perfection—each more beautiful than the last; and finally the August lilies that almost cross the boundary line of decency. Anywhere from three to six feet tall, they open a scape of seven, ten, sometimes fifteen or more flowers modeled on starfish. Crosses between *L. auratum* and *L. speciosum*, they magnify the characteristics of each. Those that take their color from *L. speci-*

osum rubrum are suffused with every nuance of crimson and ruby, flecked with maroon; many of the whites are marked with the gold ray that distinguishes the *Auratum*. All have red-gold anthers that stain the face and hands with saffron—the stigma of the lily fancier. These lilies have high-sounding names like Empress of India, Crimson Glory, Imperial Silver, and for once they are deserved. Massed in a bed, they take the breath away—and as if that weren't enough, they smell like the winds of paradise. There is a school that claims to detest the scent of lilies: 'like a funeral' is the phrase. Personally, I don't associate lilies with funerals, but if I did, what a way to go! No flower perfume is too strong for me. The stupendous lily bouquets that stand on our grand piano during July and August send an essence up the back stairs that finds its way into my bedroom and my dreams at night, and I am sorry for those whose senses don't allow them to enjoy this pleasure.

I have named only the best known of the modern lilies, those found in most catalogues. There are dozens more. Rex Bulb Farms, my sole supplier (see CATALOGUES), listed nearly two hundred cultivars in 1979, fifty of them new or reintroduced. (I would make the trip to Washington state just to see their fields, which must be extraordinary.) Many breeders appear in this catalogue, including Stone & Payne, creators of the Connecticut hybrids I take a special interest in, and all are distinguished names. But the king of modern hybridizers is surely Jan de Graaff, whose lilies (sometimes listed under the trade name Jagra) are the most beautiful of the lot. De Graaff is, of course, of Dutch descent—the great-great-grandson of Cornelius de Graaff, who was breeding lilies in Holland in the late eighteenth century. His lifework, however, has been accomplished in Oregon, and we can fairly claim him for our own. Indeed, I think even the English would acknowledge that we lead the world in modern lily-breeding. Why, then, don't we avail ourselves of this national resource more than we do? One would expect to see American lilies in every garden, but that is far from the case.

One reason may be the unfounded fear that they are difficult to grow. Their princely air does make one think of greenhouses and expert attention. In fact, they are far less demanding than roses, and any novice can raise them. The modern hybrids are free of disease, don't attract pests (mine don't, anyway), and don't need staking. All they require is a hole dug for them in sun or semi-shade, the latter for preference because full sun bleaches out the colors and shortens the life of the blossoms. I plant them a little deeper than is usually suggested, putting into the hole a table-spoon of bone meal or dried cow manure topped with pad of sand for good drainage. Then I forget them—which is why a label with their names must be attached to a stick placed in their vicinity. Lilies don't come up early, or all at the same time, and it is fatally easy to lose track of where they are. At least one bulb a season falls victim to sloppy work with the trowel, and this is a sickening event. Ideally, they would have a bed to themselves where that wouldn't happen, but I haven't the space for such luxury.

A further caution: Never let a seedhead develop on a lily stalk. It will sap the strength of the bulb. On the other hand, the stalks of a spent lily must be allowed to stand until the leaves turn yellow and fall off, because, as with all bulbous plants, it is the leaves that feed the storeroom below ground. For this reason, you shouldn't really cut lilies for the house. It deprives the plant of just that much nourishment. But I am not capable of this self-denial, and therefore I divide my lilies into those on display in the peren-nial beds and those I grow in a less conspicuous place beside the driveway, specifically for cutting; and even with these I go easy, trying not to remove more than half the stalk. Some lilies are more vigorous than others. The June-flowering Asiatics don't care what you do to them. They can be cut quite close to the ground and still return in full force the following year. The others seem to know they are more beautiful and expensive, the trumpets especially, and to cut them severely is to court their oblivion.

Only three lilies have failed me utterly, none a hybrid. The first is, strangely enough, the oldest in cultivation: *L. candidum*, the Madonna lily. I don't know where I go wrong, but others have found them troublesome. Constance Spry's *Garden Notebook* (1940) says to plant them in a trench filled with wood ashes. According to her, that is how cottage gardeners grow them. I'm sure she's right, but it didn't work for me. Nor am I more success-ful with the lovely *L. formosanum*, a species lily that blooms late in September after all the others are gone. Wilson and Bell (*The Fragrant Year*) say it is 'quick and easy to flower from seed' and that 'even tiny bulbs will produce a bloom or two.' They also say it requires a strongly acid soil, and that because it is so virus-prone it should be grown far from other lilies. Perhaps my soil isn't acid enough, but if virus is the problem it must attack the bulb underground because I have never seen so much as an emerging leaf of this 'easy' lily. *L. nepalense*, my third failure, is rather different—a genuine rarity that Rex Farms carries from time to time and always with the warning that it is a problem child. Truth to tell, it sounds rather awful. The colors are parrot-green and purple. I want it because its home is in the high valleys of the Himalayas and I can't resist that kind of provenance. I need only to read that a plant 'was discovered growing among pockets of rocks amid dense thickets of forest in the Ichang Gorge of the Yangtze river,' and I must have it. Partly this is because in the bad old days of American imperialism in China my father commanded a gunboat on the Yangtze river, and at the age of seven I was aboard a Standard Oil boat being hauled upstream over the rapids in that same Ichang Gorge by several thousand human bodies attached to ropes. I wish I could say I minded the experience. But I wasn't a sensitive child (is there such a thing?), at least not to human suffering, and what I chiefly remember is the dazzling beauty of that steeply walled and forested gorge. Naturally, I want the lily that E. H. Wilson (for it was he) found there, and never mind that it is plain old *L. Henryi*, a scentless Turk's-cap not half as handsome as its hybrid descendants. Or is this, in fact, a legitimate reason for coveting a flower? Probably not. Very likely it falls into the same category as enjoying paintings that 'tell a story.' However that may be, I am an eternal sucker for plants with glamorous backgrounds, and species lilies are always that. Their homelands are the world's loveliest landscapes: the Himalayas, Szechuan, the Sea of Japan, the shores of the Aegean, Mount Hood and the Cascade Range.

Connoisseurs have more respectable reasons for valuing them. Species lilies are much subtler flowers than the modern hybrids, more delicately constructed, hence in many ways a more sophisticated taste. Also, of course, they tremble on the brink of extinction, which gives them the terrible poignance of all doomed things. I can imagine becoming an impassioned collector. But I prefer not to. Though not in general an advocate of 'bigger is better,' and as noted elsewhere not at all in favor of indiscriminate hybridizing, I feel that the modern lilies are an exception. Here, in some miraculous way, the hand of man has worked without succumbing to vulgarity. The standard, so far, has been high, and it would seem to me foolish to forgo the pleasure of owning these glorious flowers in favor of the wild forms—nor is there any reason not to grow both.

Christopher Lloyd, who writes a learned gardening column in the English magazine *Country Life*, once put his finger on the single valid objection to growing modern hybrid lilies. They are, he remarked, the world's most expensive annuals. That is a slight exaggeration. Annuals they aren't, but many could be called biennials, which comes as a shock to those who believe what they read in books and catalogues. 'Naturalizes easily' is a well-worn phrase, and if you live where the lilies were grown originally—in the Pacific northwest—it may be true. For the rest of us, it isn't. The June-flowering Asiatics can confidently be expected to multiply. The Aurelian trumpets and August-flowering Oriental hybrids, in my experience, do not—though I believe that under the right conditions they could be made to. What happens is that the bulbs split, and these divisions when left in the ground produce plants that are steadily smaller and feebler. Nurserymen don't leave them in the ground. They dig them up, separate the cloves (which closely resemble those of garlic), and replant each one in rich new soil. In a year or two, these will develop into full-sized bulbs and can be transplanted to the garden beds. But all this is beyond the ordinary gardener. It requires a nursery bed for the baby clones, and several seasons of patience. The rest of us, confronted with a lily that either disappears or isn't worth keeping, often give up altogether—meanwhile swearing at the expense.

That isn't quite fair. The cost of lilies is relative, even that of the short-lived ones. Certainly, it is more economical to pay $2.35 for, say, a Connecticut Lemonglow that will endure and increase than to lay out the same sum for Golden Splendor, a trumpet I have never kept for more than three years—not to mention squandering $4.95 for Empress of India, which in my garden has been a biennial. But look at it this way: A florist sells the Orientals for $5 *per bloom*. That means that the bulb you paid between $3 and $5 for is giving you about $75 worth of flowers. This isn't, in fact, how I calculate the value of lilies. Such a show of beauty can't be measured in dollars and cents. Unless I lose my head completely, I order lilies only every other year and spend, each time, about $100. I waste twice that on cigarettes. As I say, it is all relative, and considering the pleasure they give, lilies are a bargain.

LONGEVITY

The kiss of the wind for lumbago,
The stab of the thorn for mirth,
One is nearer to death in a garden
Than anywhere else on earth.

I like this little quatrain better than the one it parodies but the
facts are otherwise. Before the era of pesticides and atomic fallout
a garden was about the healthiest place on earth and gardeners'
longevity in impressive defiance of the actuarial tables. Theophrastus, Aristotle's heir at the Athens Lyceum, teacher, botanist
and gardener, lived to be eighty-five—something of a feat in the
second century B.C. But then so did Cato the Censor, the harsh old
Sabine farmer (see ASPARAGUS) who was devoted to cabbages and
wrote excellent directions for growing them in his *De re rustica*.
Marcus Terentius Varro, who produced *his* book on horticulture
when he was over eighty, lived another nine years after that but
didn't set a record. Pliny describes for us the Roman botanist
Antonius Castor, spry as a cricket among his specimens and sound
in mind and body: He was over one hundred when Pliny visited
him.

Lives in the Middle Ages were briefer than those of the sturdy
Romans and those of saints apt to be briefer still. Yet Albertus
Magnus, theologian and horticulturist, whose success at forcing
plants under glass attracted charges of witchcraft, went to his
reward at eighty-seven. Petrarch, who among other things was the
first gardener to have what we would call a modern sensibility,
died at the relatively youthful age of seventy—youthful, that is,
for a gardener; he still outlived most of his contemporaries, and
that continued to be the rule rather than the exception. Pirro
Ligorio, creator of the Villa d'Este, survived all his noble patrons
and lived to be eighty-seven. All the Mollets, gardeners to two
generations of French kings (Claude, who worked for Henri IV,
introduced box edging), lived longer than their masters. Le Nôtre
did not, but he had a longer life than Louis XIV did, expiring after
eighty-seven years of perfect health.

A French list could indeed be expanded indefinitely, and must have something to do with the climate of the Ile de France, where plants as well as men seem to live forever. The pear trees planted by La Quintinie at Versailles in the seventeenth century flourished well into the nineteenth, and two of them until 1963, when they were dug up. The cedar of Lebanon planted by Bernard de Jussieu in the Jardin des Plantes in 1734 is still there and in fine shape. Whatever the cause of this longevity—and it produces whole neighborhoods of octogenarians in the older parts of Paris, all apparently hale and hearty—it is reflected in the life spans of French gardeners. One thinks of Bernard Palissy (1508–89), out of favor at court on account of his Protestantism, persecuted, yet living to a ripe old age at his place in Normandy, dreaming of the grottoes and temples of living trees described in his book, *The Delectable Garden*; of Olivier de Serres (1538–1619), author of the fascinating and influential *Le Théâtre d'Agriculture*, absorbed in his experimental farm (the first of which we have a real record) and his silkworms; and one of my favorite minor geniuses, Thomas Blaikie, one of a long line of Scottish gardeners to make a name for themselves in a foreign country. Blaikie was the foremost exponent of the English picturesque style on the Continent. He worked on the fantastical Parc Monceau, and laid out the ravishing Bagatelle for the Comte d'Artois. But he was also an eminent plantsman and his own forty-acre garden at St. Germain, full of rarities, was visited by half Europe. There, crusty and opinionated, a thorough Scot to the last, he died in 1838—two years shy of ninety.

So many English writers have been gardeners and vice versa that one can't always say which occupation came first, or most conduced to a long life. How would one classify Evelyn? Horace Walpole? William Beckford? All at any rate took an active interest in gardens both as practitioners (Beckford once boasted of having put *one million* trees into the ground within a single year) and polemicists, and all three lived into their eighties. The professionals did as well or better. Henry Wise, gardener to Queen Anne, and one of the founders of the first commercial nursery in England, died at eighty-three. George Russell, who gave us the finest of the lupin race, was hard at work at his hybridizing at the age of ninety-four. Gertrude Jekyll and William Robinson survived to eighty-nine and ninety-six respectively.

The record in this country is less salubrious—perhaps because the climate is; perhaps because, for all our tremendous contribution to botany and hybridizing science, we have been rather notably short on great gardeners as such. Only two American presidents have taken a serious interest in gardens (as opposed to innumerable kings and statesmen in other countries, not forgetting Winston Churchill), and Jefferson (Washington was the other) lived to be eighty-three. Our designers of note haven't been many, but let Frederick Olmsted, designer of Central Park and some forty others, go into the longevity book. He lived from 1822 to 1903. Among plantsmen, include Charles S. Sargent (1841–1927), whose leadership made the Arnold Arboretum near Boston the best of its kind in America. But famous amateurs among us have been few, so it is a pleasure to report that Ruth Stout, the doyenne of organic gardening in America, inventor of the permanent hay mulch and contributor to *Organic Gardening*, died only recently, at age ninety-six.

I like to think of these statistics when I am down on my hands and knees grubbing, while my non-gardening friends are out on the tennis court or jogging past the fence. The athletic tend to look down on gardening—until they try it. Then I am amused to hear their moans and groans: 'My *back*, I can't believe it.' I can. I go through it every spring, and the cult of fitness has no part in my psychology. I loathe sport in nearly all its forms except horseback riding. But I figure my chances for a long life are at least as good as the average athlete's, and maybe a lot better.

MAGIC

Do you believe that crops whose yield is above ground should be planted during the waxing of the moon, root crops when the moon is on the wane? That plants should be saluted before picking or digging and told why they are being molested? No? Then what about this? Plants respond to music, preferring Mozart or classical Indian sitar music to rock, which causes them to wilt. Or this: Plants know you are there, and when you approach them knife in hand, they utter tiny shrieks; on the other hand, if you talk to them kindly or pray over them, they reward you with better than average growth. What would you say if told that plants under stress give off a gas that attracts their worst enemies, rather as if they were human beings sweating with fear? Or conversely, that some plants manufacture their own repellents? Could you accept right- and left-handedness in plants?

Cyril Connolly once defined the victory of science over magic this way: Let someone say, 'If I put this pill in your beer it will explode,' and we might believe him; but were he to cry, 'If I pronounce this spell over your beer it will go flat,' we would be incredulous. Connolly's conclusion: 'When I read science I turn magical; when I study magic, scientific.' I feel the same about garden lore. The first two statements above belong to the oldest category of belief. 'Planting by the signs' goes back to Babylonia at least, and probably earlier; and millions of people, including Americans, continue to garden by astrological calendars, which are available by mail order from several southern sources. As for the emotional life of plants, ancient Hindu manuals speak of *dohada*, the practice of singing and dancing to plants, or alternatively kicking them to get results. (Modern man kicks the television set or the car for the same reason.) Are these superstitions or scientific facts? The answer would once have been unequivocally in favor of superstition. Now even some scientists aren't so sure. The effect of sound waves on plants is still under study, and it isn't excluded that they do in fact respond to different kinds of music. I don't myself find this at all unbelievable. Who wouldn't crumple and fade under the onslaught of rock, revive at the first strains of the *Jupiter Symphony*? Less convincing is their reaction to hostile thoughts—and this in recent tests could not be proved. Yet a test I would have thought impossible of success *did* succeed; I saw it with my own eyes, as they say, on television. The man who claimed he could pray plants toward better growth was made to do his stuff under controlled conditions: corn seed was mixed and planted by the laboratory technicians and placed in sealed glass boxes where no tampering was possible. And lo and behold—the plants he prayed over sprouted and grew far more impressively than those he ignored. To speak literally, God knows what this means. The scientists did not. They had no comment to make. Nor have I. I have spoken to plants myself, and if pressed for conclusions would have to say that those I threatened did better than those I—well, I wouldn't say prayed over, but pleaded with, cajoled. A rhododendron that hadn't bloomed for six years was flatly told it would be removed the following year if there were no flowers. Need I say that it has bloomed profusely ever since?

That sort of thing aside, the distinction between magic and science does seem more and more difficult to make. That gas mentioned earlier: Research at a Colorado laboratory has shown that injured trees give off ethylene gas from their decaying tissues and that this alerts bark beetles to begin an attack. But if you pinch the leaves of a tomato plant, you activate a hormone fatal to attacking insects—this according to Dr. Clarence Ryan of Washington State University. As for right- and left-handed plants, pepper seedlings are of both kinds and a plant scientist at MacDonald College in Canada reports a 20 percent higher yield from those that are right-handed, i.e., whose leaves spiral in a counter-clockwise direction—something to look for when buying them.

One of the many reasons I am a lifetime subscriber to *Organic Gardening* is that it is an unfailing source of facts like these—to me endlessly engaging. It isn't that the editors believe in magic, they don't; but neither do they believe that anything to do with plants can be an exact science, or that we have found out all we need to know. The door is open, and it is up to the gardener to walk through, look about him, and perhaps make a finding of his own. Until the advent of modern science, horticultural knowledge was entirely based on observations by those who dealt directly with plants, soil and weather, and the old gardeners weren't fools. That body of knowledge, long dismissed as folklore or old wives' tales, looks better every day. Some of the food systems devised by the ancients were models of efficiency compared to ours. No Indian farmer used up five to six pounds of topsoil to produce a pound of corn, and the Iowa farmer does. No wonder the 'new' ways to farm and garden so often turn out to be several thousand years old. It was, after all, 'primitive' peoples ignorant of chemistry who identified the plants containing basic drugs like quinine, caffeine and digitalis, who without having heard of vitamins located the plants richest in them; who discovered hallucinogens. No findings of comparable importance have been made by modern plant scientists, who are spending more and more of their time trying to understand why so many techniques practiced by the technologically backward have been so successful, i.e., the Chinese method of interplanting crops.

The lesson for the gardener is not to swallow everything he reads in books, especially books whose bias toward establishment thinking is betrayed by their unquestioning acceptance of pesticides, herbicides, etc. (See PESTS AND DISEASES) They aren't in touch with the real world of gardening, which is more than half an as-yet-unsolved mystery. If you have a question, don't write your newspaper either. Better to consult the old lady down the road, the one whose porch is covered with moon vines and who grows the blessed thistle (*Cnicus benedictus*) in her garden.

MAKING NOTES

(*June*) *9th, Monday.* In the morning W. cut down the winter cherry tree. I sowed French Beans and weeded. A coronetted Landau went by, when we were sitting upon the sodded wall. The ladies (evidently Tourists) turned an eye of interest upon our little garden and cottage. We went to R. Newton's for pike floats and went round to Mr. Gell's Boat, and on the Lake to fish. We caught nothing—it was extremely cold. The Reeds and Bullrushes or Bullpipes of a tender soft green, making a plain whose surface moved with the wind. The reeds not yet tall. The lake clear to the Bottom, but saw no fish. In the evening I stuck peas, watered the garden, and planted Brocoli . . .

DORTHY WORDSWORTH
Journals

Along with the urge to make a garden usually comes the urge to keep track of it in writing—to note planting dates and the weather, and the outcome. (Dorothy's peas turned out well; they were eating them all through July and into August. But I can't make out what happened to the broccoli, which on looking it up I find the English don't distinguish from cauliflower.) Once started, the habit is hard to break. It expands to include lists of plants ordered, maps of the vegetable garden (illusory because real vegetables won't conform to them), hints and comments. 'Frank says must cut back all raspberry canes longer than 4 ft., calls these rogues,' 'Try Epsom Salts on roses,' and, furiously underlined, 'Windstorm *laid corn flat*,' are random entries that strike my eye as I turn the pages of various journals kept over the last twenty years.

I notice, too, the changing character of the handwriting. Some of these entries seem to have been written rather late at night, under the influence of Mr. Weston's good wine and a session of bad weather. Others flow as smoothly as a summer breeze. In both, the evidence of a state of mind is just as evident as the state of the garden and makes me wonder if the garden would exist without the journal, much as a life may appear half-lived without a diary to record it. I don't reread my notes as often as I should, and frequently find I would have saved myself considerable grief if I had. One forgets, repeats mistakes. Rereading a real diary won't, unhappily, prevent one from tumbling into the same pitfalls over and over again; a faithfully kept garden record can. And besides, one is in good company.

Though not perhaps the earliest holograph record of the kind, Petrarch's notes in faded ink on the margins of his copy of Palladius's treatise on agriculture must be among the most moving. They are in the Vatican Library and I haven't seen them, but Georgina Masson, who has, describes them in some detail in her *Italian Gardens*. Here the poet, whose classical studies and love of nature mark him as the first of the humanists, noted the day, hour and phase of the moon when he transplanted or sowed seed—and his disappointment when the spinach, fennel, parsley and beets in his Milanese garden didn't come up. He makes a lawn and plants fruit trees and herbs. And he worries at going against Vergil's advice in the *Georgics* on the grafting of vines, is amazed when his own do well anyway.

Petrarch's was an age when everything was to be relearned, not only the arts and sciences but the most elementary techniques of horticulture, as his references to the classics show. The Romans had known all about budding, grafting, seed selection, composting, green manuring. They could build hothouses, do topiary work, shape espaliers, blanch lettuces. Two of Vergil's methods for propagating olives are still in use. Most of what Cato had to say in his *De re rustica* about vegetables holds today. Then the curtain fell. Literate men forgot and the peasant, groping for survival, had no way to transmit such facts as chanced to live on in folk memory —which incidentally is in my experience much shorter than is generally believed. The Sicilian peasant transplanted to America, if not an instant victim of amnesia, is close to it and quickly forgets the old ways of doing things. I have found myself explaining how to prune a peach tree to Portuguese and Sicilian helpers whose fathers would have disowned them for their ignorance, whether real or (as is always possible) feigned. And by the third generation the process is complete: Every trace of hereditary knowledge has disappeared from the genes.

Our time has been compared to the fourteenth century, wrongly I think, because we aren't emerging from a dark age but are perhaps about to enter one if injunctions like 'Bomb them back to the Stone Age' are obeyed, as indeed, on a small scale, they already have been. Moreover the extinction we may face would be global, which wasn't the case after the fall of Rome, when Arab and Chinese civilizations were flourishing and even the overrated Byzantines were holding their own. Where, next time, would be the nucleus of a new start? But like most people I can't really accept doomsday. The slow-motion collapse of the technological structure that supports us is easier to visualize: a world in which the few who knew how would be planting vegetables, chopping wood and raising chickens among the ruins. The ants who had done their homework would no doubt be armed to the teeth against the marauding grasshoppers who had sung all summer while the last drops of oil ran out. The avant-garde already installs solar heating systems and will soon be testing electric cars; but the means of survival may ultimately be far more primitive than that. How different then become the motives of Petrarch and his contemporaries from our own. They read the classics in order to rediscover a civilization infinitely more complex and refined than the one they knew. We study manuals like the best-selling *Foxfire Books*, in which Appalachian old people were pumped for recollections of how to build a log cabin, make soap, plant 'by the signs,' distill white lightning in the woods. These books and others in the same genre (*The Whole Earth Catalog*, etc.) feed, it is true, a nostalgia for lost innocence that is endemically American. For us, the frontier is never farther away than the nearest TV screen. But the success of the *Foxfire Books* with an urban, educated, mostly affluent audience was a little different. Many obviously saw them as a survival kit that might some day come in handy.

And so it might. I'm not laughing. I belong to that audience and share its terrible uneasiness. Some days, I look at my garden and wonder if it will turn out to be the last ditch, if not for me then for the next occupants. I am not thinking of building a bomb shelter—as one of our wealthier citizens did some years ago. I have no desire to survive the holocaust if it comes, and not much chance either, living as I do within a twelve-mile radius of the Groton submarine base, a prime target, and the atomic reactor at Waterford. No, what I have in mind is the long haul of adjusting to simpler, cruder ways, a possible return, in other words, to what the village was in the first place, when this house was built with their own hands by a clergyman and his two sons. Rather a botch they made of it too, hanging some of the doors upside down and patching the upstairs floorboards with Yankee thrift if little aesthetic sense. Nevertheless, the house has stood for two hundred years and could stand for two hundred more unless wiped out by unnatural means. By the same token, I don't think it pompous or self-inflating to conceive of a time when my notes on weather and crops and such tricks of the trade as I have picked up might be valuable to somebody.

The clergyman clearly had a garden of sorts. He must have raised vegetables because everybody did—though what I mostly find is ancient horseshoes and mysterious pressed-metal objects of unknown origin—and I know he had a well. Would he had left some written record of where he dug it. (Our outrageous water rates being what they are, I need to know.) I would like to know, too, about the famous summer that was no summer, when frost hit in July owing to changes in the weather brought on by the explosion of a Javanese volcano. (Was it 1833? Thereabouts, anyway.) Did the village suffer? And was he the one who planted the opium poppies? (See ANNUALS.) Probably not, but I wish whoever did had made a note of it, along with what varieties of beans and corn did well here.

A school of modern historians relies heavily on statistics to disprove long-held theories (i.e., that slavery was uneconomic and therefore doomed without the Civil War) and establish new ones; and in principle I am on their side. I am also deeply skeptical. If by some hazard my records of a southern New England garden circa 1960–80 were fed into a computer a hundred years from now, they would foul the works completely with their implication that berry patches, kitchen gardens, small fruit trees and herbaceous borders were common. They aren't, and I'm not really interested in the possibility that my notes might be used for such a purpose. I keep them primarily for myself, and only after that because I feel—the writer's itch for posterity no doubt—that *we should write down what we know*, not for the computer but for another human being. We are, after all, the ancients of the future.

∞

MAZES

Should you ever find yourself lost in one, choose either the right or
the left wall and follow its every turning. You can't fail to emerge.

∞

MULCHES

After compost itself, mulches in general are the subject most ac-
tively boring to the organic gardener's friends. People will ask me
how it is that my garden does so well even in a drought year like
the one we are enduring at this writing. But they would rather
attribute its condition to some mysterious good fortune ('You're so
lucky') or questionable action ('I suppose you water a lot') than
hear the real story. In fact, I am not a darling of the gods, and I
don't water a lot. Like many communities, ours is at the mercy of a
cozy little monopoly that exploits its stranglehold by regularly
raising its rates to heights locally believed to be the highest in the
East, while supplying us with water so full of chemicals and on
occasion so Ganges-like in aspect that many human beings can't
drink it, and I hesitate to use it on plants. The greenness and
fertility of my garden are due to vast quantities of mulch, everything from compost to salt hay and seaweed, and I would be
happy to explain this, enlarging on the virtues of each, if I couldn't
see my audience melting away on contact. Even the few gardeners
I know who take pride in their flower beds and carefully trimmed
evergreens are satisfied to apply wood chips or pine bark or peat
moss to their ornamentals, mostly in the interest of neatness and
keeping down weeds. They don't want to hear about compost—
their leaves are bagged up and carted away to the dump in the
fall, their grass clippings removed by the man who mows the lawn
—and still less about seaweed, though it is free for the taking on
local rocks. Pausing by my front door, on either side of which

grow two standard lilac trees, one of our respected matrons asked me the other day, voice vibrating with disapproval: 'Surely that is *eelgrass*?' Surely it is, wrapped securely around the feet of these shrubs whose western exposure, unshaded since the elms died, makes them particularly susceptible to the effects of drought. Eager for a convert, I tried to go on: 'It's wonderful stuff, you know, keeps the ground damp, and did you know it has twice the potash content of barnyard manure . . .' Smiling, she went her way, as so many others have before her, leaving me with my lecture undelivered.

So here it is, my undelivered lecture, and readers who want to skip it are welcome. A mulch can be almost any substance laid on the surface of the soil—even newspapers and old carpets. Stones are a form of mulch and, horrible to relate, so are plastic and aluminum foil. To non-organic gardeners, mulch's primary function is to keep down weeds and conserve moisture in summer; in winter they may also use evergreen branches or hay to keep the soil from freezing and heaving around favored perennials. But to gardeners of my persuasion, mulch is much more: It is an organic substance whose benefits extend to the soil itself, improving its structure and enriching its fertility to the point where it needs nothing else. An organically mulched vegetable garden never requires tilling, digging or hoeing, and is scarcely weeded. If it seems to require more fertilizer than it is getting, that too goes on as mulch—in the form of composted animal manure. You can't over-mulch, though you can do it stupidly—applying it to waterlogged land or to very young seedlings. But it doesn't burn or cause sudden spurts of unhealthy growth as artificial fertilizers may—it is long-term in its effects.

Wood chips and peat moss are the most popular mulches today, so it shouldn't come as a surprise that neither is much in favor with organic gardeners. They are expensive commercial products with several disadvantages. Wood chips (like sawdust, pine bark, or any wood by-product) are not only low in nitrogen, they deprive the soil of it as they decay and can be used only in conjunction with a high-nitrogen fertilizer. Most often this is a chemical, and plants thus treated don't thrive. If you must use wood chips, pile them on top of well rotted cow manure or mix them with cottonseed meal. But for my taste, don't use them. They are the staple of every corporate planting, every landscaped factory, gas station, and shopping mall, and I would be against them for that

reason alone. I also notice that in my neighborhood most of the
evergreens so treated are dead within a few years; the flower beds
scarcely survive a summer.

Peat moss isn't as obvious on the public scene, being less conspicuous. Homeowners, however, put their faith in it to a distressing degree. It is true that if you are starting a garden from scratch,
with no source of humus, no compost heap, peat moss is the most
readily available, if most expensive, soil conditioner around.
Otherwise there is nothing it can do that compost won't do a
thousand times better, and at no cost. It has little nutritive value,
is rather acid (though not as acid as was once believed), and as a
surface mulch can do the opposite of what it is supposed to, owing
to its capacity to absorb water: It can form a crust that is more or
less impermeable.

The only commercially sold mulches I indulge in are buckwheat
or cocoa hulls, and salt hay. The first two are extravagances, used
only on the rose beds and, if I am feeling rich, on the perennials.
Though they aren't without value—they keep the weeds down and
the soil moist and cool in hot summers—other and cheaper substances would do that as well, and they make no contribution to
the fertility of the soil. What roses *really* like is great heaps of
rotted manure, but my devotion to organic principles doesn't extend to barnyard effects in flower beds. The hulls are frankly
ornamental, imparting a fine-grained, dark brown, uniform finish
to the formality of the rose plots.

Salt hay meets organic standards better than hulls. It is a good
source of trace minerals and decomposes without depleting the
soil of nitrogen. Straw does, and the two shouldn't be confused,
particularly as they differ, or should, in price. Some dealers make
up bales of salt hay that on examination turn out to be as much as
a third straw, and these ought to be rejected. I don't like the looks
of straw either. The *Encyclopedia of Organic Gardening*, however, strongly recommends it if it is mixed with green or animal
manures, and it was the basis for Ruth Stout's no-work system of
gardening. She maintained a perpetual eight-inch straw mulch,
replenished as necessary, and instead of making a compost heap,
threw all her vegetable wastes on top of that. When she wanted to
plant, she shoved the mulch aside and dropped the seeds. I don't
doubt her success, documented for forty years in the pages of
Organic Gardening, but the method isn't for me. Her vegetable
garden must have been an eyesore, and one certainly can't make a

perennial bed that way. Besides, I want to see the soil, at least part of the year. I like salt hay in the vegetable garden, but not everywhere or all the time.

Salt hay is a delightful mulch, easy to move around once it is unbaled, sweet-scented and dry, making it a favorite with lounging cats. I introduce it between the rows in midsummer when the really hot weather arrives. Any earlier than that and it keeps the soil from warming up and interferes, like any mulch, with the germination of seeds and the development of little plants. Later, it reduces watering by half and all but does away with weeding. By late fall it is much decayed and what is left is raked over the vegetables that will spend the winter in the ground.

The ultimate mulch is, of course, compost (see COMPOST) and if I had enough of it I would need no other. But one never does have enough—wherefore the salt hay and, increasingly of late, seaweed. The difference is that the salt hay can be ordered over the telephone and is delivered nicely baled to the back driveway. The seaweed requires a man with a pickup truck and the willingness to scramble over wet rocks wielding a pitchfork, not a combination I find every day. Which is a pity, because, like compost, it is a fertilizer as well as a soil conditioner, one of the oldest known to man. All marine peoples have used it. In seventeenth-century France, royal regulations established the kinds to be gathered and how they were to be used. You still see it in Mediterranean citrus groves, or you did before the growers turned to chemicals. It has, as I tried to tell my neighbor, twice the potash content of barnyard manure, making it perfect for beets, potatoes and cabbages, the potash lovers. More than that, it has the power to unlock minerals in the soil; it contains growth-inducing hormones that will increase the yields of tomatoes, corn and peppers. Plants given seaweed are better able to endure a light frost, and some are made more resistant to insect and disease attack. With these remarkable properties (some of which, it is true, have only lately been established by research), and given the high cost of commercial fertilizers and pesticides, you might expect to see the gardening citizenry of both coasts swarming over the rocks and beaches. You don't, partly because no high-level interest exists to inform the public of the facts, any more than the same interests care to tell us, and the process is evidently quite simple, how to manufacture fuel from vegetable wastes—for the same reasons. Most commercial fertilizers are petroleum products and for all

the talk about conservation, no effort is likely to be made to educate us on how to do without them.

Thus when I say that my garden is both green and productive
with no other aids than organic mulches, plus a small amount of
cow manure and bone meal, that I spend perhaps $25 or $30 a
year on recognized fertilizers and not a penny on pesticides or
herbicides, I am rarely believed. Most authorities would say it
can't be done. Nor do I myself understand exactly why it works
out the way it does. Two very different sets of standards are obviously being applied. Those for artificial fertilizers are well established. They consist of those figures printed on the bags (5-10-5,
etc.) which refer, in the order given, to the nitrogen, phosphorus
and potash content of the product. The requirements for plants
have been similarly worked out. Take, for example, spinach: It
must have soil containing ten parts of nitrogen, nine of phosphorus
and ten of potash, or so they say. Analysis will reveal whether or
not your soil meets these figures, and if not, there is a fertilizer
with the ingredients to bring it up to scratch. It is all very scientific,
and to me so much mathematical gibberish—to begin with because compost is regularly shown to be low in nutrients, with or
without an admixture of animal manure, which also does poorly in
the ratings by comparison with chemicals. How seaweed and salt
hay might be rated I don't know. I doubt if the U.S. Department
of Agriculture has analyzed them, but if it has I can guess that
they too will fail the test. Natural fertilizers always do, and I don't
care in the least. All these figures leave out of account something
far more important, and that is the life of the soil itself. Mine
teems with it. Chemically fertilized soil doesn't.

I should say here that I have never sent my soil for analysis to
my county extension agent, or my compost either. I don't even
know what the pH may be—this referring to the degree of sour-
ness or sweetness. (Roses, for example, like a pH between 6.0 and
6.8, a little on the sour side.) I have heard from old-timers that
Connecticut soil tends toward acidity, and so I put lime on the
lawn and in the compost; but I will never find out whether this is
right or wrong. I ask myself what I would do with that mass of
figures if I had them. Presumably, something like an acre of garden will show many differences in pH and fertility between one
spot and another. Am I then to rush from place to place with a set
of pails, adding a scoop here of lime, a scoop there of 5-10-5 or
some other formula? It would be madness.

I would rather assume that plants, like animals and people, are hungry most of the time and need a balanced diet. I rely on natural substances to supply that, and leave it to the plants to pick and choose what they want. I haven't a shred of proof that they can do this, but the evidence is that they can, since they seem to be thriving, drought and all. Beyond that, I can only invite doubters to come and judge for themselves.

NATURALIZING

There are several meanings to this word. A plant not native to a region is said to be naturalized when it escapes from a garden and establishes itself in the wilds of a new country. America, settled from distant lands, is extraordinarily rich in these plants, including those so familiar we assume they must always have been here. In fact, the western course of the pioneers can be traced by the trail of immigrant plants they left behind them, all too many of them now considered weeds, though they were brought here originally as medicinal herbs or, like privet, for a variety of other purposes. Privet berries made dyes and ink; the bark was used to tan leather; the wood for shoe pegs; the branches as bindings for grain sheaves and hay; the leaves pounded to powder healed scalds, burns and skin troubles; oil from the flowers was a balm to tired farmers' muscles. But our privet hedges today aren't *that* privet: *Ligustrum vulgare*, brought from Europe. They are mostly *L. ovalifolium*, a Japanese import to California in the nineteenth century, which made the customary trip in reverse, from West to East. If you want to see the original privet still growing you must look for it where it has naturalized itself in the wild.

Two outstanding weeds are also imports: plantain and crab grass. The plantain was long thought to be a beneficent herb, whose leaves growing along roadsides were soothing to the bare feet of pilgrims in the Middle Ages, and because so many of these were on their way to religious shrines, it was a holy herb as well, known as the 'follower-of-the-heel-of-Christ.' This association with footprints was, curiously enough, also made by American Indians.

Noticing that it sprang up wherever the settlers appeared, they called it 'the white man's foot,' and I am not surprised to learn that one of its earliest sites was Connecticut. To the Indians, it presaged the destruction of the wilderness. To me as to all modern gardeners, it presages the destruction of the lawn.

Crab grass has a much older and positively distinguished history, if that is any consolation. According to the author of *Green Immigrants*, crab grass is nothing more or less than millet, the oldest grain cultivated by man, grown from prehistoric times in China, India, Africa, and by the Stone Age lake dwellers in Switzerland. It came to America with the wave of immigrants from Central Europe in the latter half of the nineteenth century. The form most familiar to us is native to Poland, Hungary, and Czechoslovakia, where the peasants knew it for a rapidly growing crop easily raised in many types of soil. They abandoned it eventually because corn and wheat were the staples of the new world they found, and fetched much higher prices. The millet seed was tossed away and in due time escaped to every corner of the country. I am rather amused that crab grass is millet, and I pass the fact along because it may come in handy in some doomsday future when those who have survived the nuclear war some of our politicians think is 'winnable' will be scratching around looking for a crop of edible grain whose 'survivability' is only too well known.

Of course, not all immigrant escapees are a curse. *H. fulva*, the common daylily, denizen of old homesteads and cemeteries, is a pleasure to behold in the wild, and so are foxgloves, which are among our most vigorous coast-to-coast travelers—along with the mulleins, first introduced as a medicinal herb and still used as such in the Appalachians and Ozarks. Still others arrived as a blessing, became a curse and eventually turned into blessings again. The Russian tumbleweed (*Salsola kali tenuifolia*) was one of these. It arrived in this country with a group of Russian immigrants who settled in South Dakota in the 1870's, intending to raise flax. The weed was inadvertently mixed in with their hand-threshed flax seed, which unhappily came to nothing while the weed flourished to become the scourge of the prairies—an invader of other crops that nothing could kill, and a rolling fireball into the bargain: The tiniest spark could ignite it. But in the end it was man and not the tumbleweed who ruined the prairies, and after he had turned them into a dust bowl, it was the tumbleweed that helped restore the grasslands left barren by the plow and the winds. Like those mysterious weeds that appeared in the ruins of bombed European cities, the tumbleweed was one of the first plants to reappear on the devastated prairie, and this time it was beneficent. The roots knitted the ruined soil together, helped to retain moisture and keep down dust, thus allowing other plants to get a foothold. In its shade, small animals and birds found shelter, while larger ones like deer fed on the foliage. In this way it served a purpose not unlike that of the man-made English hedgerows that for a thousand years provided a refuge to flora and fauna that might otherwise have perished—and now *are* perishing. (See *Hedgerow*, a remarkable book by Eric Thomas and John White, 1980, which I can't commend too highly.)

These are examples of naturalization in the most exact meaning of the term. Horticulture supplies others. Daffodils, iris, and primulas, for example, are said to be naturalized when the gardener plants them in the grass, beside a stream or in a woodland in imitation of a natural effect, though it is of course nothing of the sort. Rarely is the plant indigenous to the region, or even to the country, and but for man it wouldn't be there. Which leads to the other, most common form of naturalizing, the deliberate transplanting of species from one part of the world to another for the beautification of a landscape that has been found wanting. The impulse has been universal since ancient times. One of the earliest inscriptions we have bears the boast of an Assyrian king: 'Cedars and box have I carried off from the countries I conquered . . . and planted in my own country, in the parks of Assyria.' Rulers have always had a passion for trees—*amor vegetabile, cara ed amabile* in the comic words Handel gave to Xerxes' ode to the plane tree—and enjoyed moving them from place to place. The Moguls took Xerxes' planes to northern India; Kublai Khan made the first Chinese arboretum from trees brought from every part of his empire. Alien vegetation is one of the signs of advancing culture, and progress can be measured by the acquisition of plants that produce food, medicine and new materials: linen, cotton, silk, rubber. But the ultimate luxury is the plant imported for its beauty alone.

All the more curious, then, that Americans should have such a respect for exotics, because in the give-and-take of plantsmanship, we have given more than we have received. Only Asia has been a richer source of flora. Europe is much poorer, making it logical for Europeans to seek exotics, many of them from right here. More than half the conifers beloved of Victorians are of American ori-

gin: the so-called Wellingtonia (which is the sequoia); Sitka
spruces; Douglas firs, Monterey cypress. Even American weeds
have found their way into English gardens. Many an American
tourist has been bemused to find a plant called *Solidago* occupying
a place of honor in English borders. He tells himself it looks re-
markably like goldenrod, and it *is* goldenrod—one of many American wildings to have been domesticated abroad. But in spite of
our resources, we aren't less avid for foreign species than Europeans are. Dozens of trees and shrubs most of us would swear are
natives are not. The royal poinciana admired by visitors to Florida
comes from Madagascar; the California eucalyptus is Australian;
New York City's ginkgos were imported from China. Also from Asia
are the camellia, the golden-rain tree (*Koelreuteria paniculata*)
which Hoosiers think particularly their own; the tamarisk so apparently indigenous to the Southwest that Willa Cather has a little
hymn to it in *Death Comes for the Archbishop* ('Father Latour
had often remarked that this tree seemed especially designed in
shape and colour for the adobe village . . .'); the large flowered
Azalea indica of southern gardens, and many more.

All these have added much beauty to the landscape, which is
the good side to the mania for exotics. The bad has been the
neglect, sometimes to the point of near extinction, of native species
and the resulting homogenized sameness of suburban plantings.
For most of this century, American houses have been built on land
cleared of local vegetation, which was then replaced with aliens.
In California this has meant the destruction of the chaparral that
anchors the earth to the hillsides and can get along with scanty
rainfall. In the Southwest, millions are poured into lawns and
greenery when cactus gardens like those over the border in Mexico
would be more appropriate; while here in the North we struggle
with marginally hardy trees and shrubs, some number of which
can be counted on to be damaged or killed altogether in a cold
winter. For every plant that takes enthusiastically to a new environment there will be another to pose problems of water supply,
winter protection or some other costly form of maintenance. Add
to these hazards the terminal reliance on machines and chemicals
thought necessary to maintain the conventionally landscaped lot,
and you have the basis for a new movement beginning to be much
written about.

Landscape architects call it 'natural gardening' and some of them
have been doing it for many years. The difference today is that

many ordinary homeowners are taking it up for themselves. What distinguishes it from the old-fashioned idea of a natural garden is that all the plants used are indigenous and local—hence adapted to the climate and needing little or no maintenance, as well as providing shelter for wildlife (important to many people today). Such a natural garden may involve no more than a slight and judicious adjustment of existing conditions (where, that is, land hasn't already been cleared), or it may mean re-creating a woodland or a meadow or a piece of desert from local models. What it does *not* mean is a trip to the nursery or garden center in search of the usual shrubs and evergreens, or the seeding of a lawn. In a sense, the aim is nothing less than to rebuild the American wilderness, re-create the original habitats of birds and animals as well as of plants. In short, it has less to do with gardening in the classical sense than with the environmental crusade. It is a revolt against pollution, the waste of natural resources, the extinction of species, and is only incidentally connected to aesthetics—or to my kind of gardening.

And that is why, though I applaud the principle, I can't myself altogether go along with the practice. God knows I am in favor of saving what we can of this increasingly desecrated country; in favor of the intelligent collecting and study of disappearing botanicals such as is being carried out by—to name only one organization—the Northwest Ornamental Horticultural Society centered in Seattle; and God knows I welcome any alternative to the barrenness of the usual domestic landscape. What I object to is the idea that only a replica of the wilderness can qualify as an ecologically sound environment. By all means, let us save the wilderness. But a wilderness and a garden aren't the same thing and I don't see why they should be. I am not attracted to the dismal pioneer scene of the cabin with the forest primeval at the door—and never mind that the cabin is now a set of boxes placed one over the other at right angles, with protruding decks, the architectural cliché apparently inseparable from the back-to-the-wilderness movement.

All accounts of how people decided to make a wilderness garden have a significant feature in common: the way the family lived before they took the plunge. Invariably it was in a denuded suburb or housing development where they had an 'energy-intensive' lawn and a few shrubs, and inevitably they used power mowers and chemicals. Never are we told that they once had flowers, vegetables, herbs, a berry patch, fruit trees, a grape arbor, vines, roses, a compost heap, and the normal complement of bees, birds, raccoons that such an arrangement attracts—and that they abandoned *that*. In other words they aren't and never were gardeners, and they have simply gone from one non-gardening extreme to the other, which is certainly preferable but hardly deserves to be described in such overblown terms as 'the creation of ecological communities,' 'stewardship [that] will establish a bond between the homeowner and his land,' 'add significantly to the growing resurgence of the natural world.' (I quote from a recent article in *The New York Times*.)

This is heavy stuff when all that is being suggested is that the homeowner stick to indigenous trees and shrubs and underplant them with local ground covers and wild flowers. Nothing wrong with that, certainly, but is it really the only way to get in touch with the land and make one's contribution to the natural world? It seems to me that my version of a cottage garden, organically grown, does these things at least as effectively and maybe more so. I eat my own uncontaminated vegetables, fruits and berries for three-quarters of the year. I fill my house with flowers. I may not have created an ecological community—the woods and pastures are full of those already—but I have perhaps struck a blow for civilization as it once was, and I don't think that a less worthy aim. But of course my garden is 'energy-intensive' in a way that has nothing to do with lawn mowers and chemicals; the energy it consumes is mostly mine. And so I can't help wondering whether, in spite of high-minded talk about the environment, these so-called natural gardens aren't just another manifestation of the well-known American distaste for old-world horticulture, for mastering the art of growing things by hand, and for the manual labor involved. Am I hearing the ghost of Thoreau? I rather think I am, and if he couldn't convince me of the moral superiority of the wilderness, those who are translating his message into modern jargon never will.

--- ◇ ---

NIGHT

A garden, however familiar, is another place on a summer night, and I don't mean those changes wrought by stage designers with 'moonlight' and veils—nothing operatic. There are, to begin with, peculiar noises, faint rustlings whose source may be revealed by a flashlight picking up a pair of frozen green eyes. Or the drumming of katydids. Or a sound that occurs in August in a corner of my garden and is answered in the one across the street. In both places, someone seems to be hard at work on a typewriter, clackety-clackety-clack. Answer: clackety-clack. What on earth are they? Not locusts or cicadas, which have a different sound. The most bizarre and least likely explanation yet offered me is that they are raccoons. *Raccoons?* 'Well,' said the man who told me this, 'that's what my cousin who owns the garage out on Route 1 says, and they're all over the back of his place.' Why not, when you come to think of it? Perhaps, in lieu of the chimpanzees who one day will write *Hamlet* if the laws of probability are allowed to operate long enough, raccoons are hammering away at *The Theory of the Leisure Class* somewhere in my shrubbery.

Scents are stronger at night. Everybody knows that but not that they are also different. Faint whiffs of sweetness in nicotiana and clethra acquire a dose of pepper after midnight—when, on the other hand, the carnations, at their most powerful at dusk, seem to go to sleep and stop smelling. But the biggest change is that of proportion and texture produced by seeing things in black and white. My first experience of this phenomenon wasn't in a garden, or at night, but in Rome in broad daylight, in the company of a friend who is color-blind. I had always known this about him and never grasped the significance until the day I stupidly said something about the apricot glow of Roman palaces. 'You forget,' he said gently, 'I don't see that. I don't know what you mean.' The words were more than an embarrassment, they were a revelation, for he was the subtlest of observers, who had often pointed out to me details and refinements in paintings and architecture, and even plants, which—blinded in my own way by color—I had missed.

Thereafter, I observed things with different and in some ways better-informed eyes, and I haven't forgotten the lesson.

To see things in black and white is to see the basics, and I would now recommend to any designer of gardens that he go out and look at his work by the light of the moon. He may well see that a certain bush is too large for the space it occupies, another too small, that the placement of a flower bed needs adjusting. Above all, he will be more conscious of the importance of form. Strolling among the ruins on the Palatine, my color-blind friend had again and again identified the wild flowers growing there by their shapes, pointing out to me especially the beauty of the acanthus, so loved by the Greeks they made it the capital of the Corinthian order, and reminding me that Pliny made beds of acanthus alone, not for the flowers but for the leaves.

The Impressionists saw nature as color swimming in light, but in most of the world's great gardens color has counted for very little. Masses of brilliant shrubs and flowers are a modern idea and not necessarily a good one. Subtract the color from a garden and it can prove to be an ill-planned scramble. One way to find out is to walk around it on a summer night. But not, please, with the aid of floodlights. No matter how skillfully carried out, I abhor the introduction of electricity into a garden. Lighted pools, false dawns among the shrubs are to me both ugly and vulgar. (No, I don't like *son et lumière* either: The Parthenon bathed in lavender is a horrid sight.) A path or driveway may need to be discreetly lighted to keep people from breaking their necks, and hurricane lamps on a terrace where one is dining are more than permissible. I love an old-fashioned Japanese paper lantern stuck with a candle and hung in a tree like a moon. A spotlight trained on a fountain, no. A garden at night should be itself—a place at rest, a haven for creatures, and for me too when I want to lie in the hammock in the dark.

ONIONS

Cooking onions aren't among the vegetables I find it worthwhile to grow. They take too long from seed. Growing them from sets is faster, but old hands say the mature onions so raised will have thick necks and won't store well, and I have found this to be the case. Seedling plants (differing from sets in that they have roots already growing) are satisfactory but can't be picked up anywhere as sets can. They must be ordered, aren't cheap, and the varieties offered are the same as those in the store. So as I don't find the quality of home-grown onions appreciably better than that of those bought at a good grocer's, I have eliminated them.

Some gardeners say they find Egyptian or multiplier onions (*Allium cepa aggregatum*) a good substitute. Yes and no. The Egyptian onion is a curiosity. From a single bulb it sends up half a dozen stout, hollow stalks each of which sprouts a bulb cluster rather like shallots. When the weight of these brings them to the ground, they root in their turn, and in no time you have a hydra-headed monster ready to take over the whole garden. (The original bulb also forms clumps underground, from which other shoots will appear.) The monster does, it is true, supply you with some form of onion most of the year. The bottom shoots can be dug as early as March. They look like a giant scallion and can be used in any recipe calling for chopped onion, though not, of course, in one where you want the onions to keep a recognizable shape. The bulblets meanwhile can, if you catch them before they have sprouted, be separated and used like shallots, except that they aren't half so good. I puzzled over Egyptian onions for several years, thinking there must be some way to put such a prolific and sturdy plant to good use. A lazy gardener who was also an indifferent cook might find one. I never did. It is a poor compromise between shallots and scallions, either of which is perfectly easy to grow separately.

Why we allow shallots to be palmed off on us as a 'gourmet' vegetable, outrageously priced, is more than I can understand. Nothing could be easier to grow, and they cost no more than the initial investment of buying a small bag of them. Separate the cloves, plant them very shallowly in a rich bit of ground and for-get all about them while they multiply. Some five months later, after the green stalks have yellowed off, brush the soil aside and there are the golden-brown or purplish clusters waiting to be lifted —not pulled or dug, just lifted. Spread them out to cure for a few days, then wash off the dirt and bring them into the house to be stored in a net bag. (You can either break up the clusters into individual cloves at this time, or leave them in a clump as you do garlic, to be snapped off when you need them.) Set some aside for next year's planting, and you will never buy a shallot again. They keep almost indefinitely.

The old rule, based probably on their Middle Eastern origin, was to plant them on the shortest day of the year and harvest them on the longest. Obviously, you can't do that in New England. Mine go in the first week in April and are ready in late August or early September. I read that they can develop powdery mildew and a disease called blast. Neither has happened to mine, which is for-tunate since the recommended cure is the usual dousing with poison. If I saw signs of disease, I would simply pull them up and throw them away. But in my experience they are singularly healthy. That, and the ease of raising them, makes it the more unconscionable that they are classed as an expensive delicacy. But because they are, a little bag of them makes a welcome present to a city-bound cook.

Scallions, for which I have an ungovernable appetite, can be cultivated in two ways. I associate them with those icy days in early spring when the seagulls, alighting on the tower of the Con-gregational church, howl with laughter to see me venturing into the kitchen garden once again. To this derisive accompaniment, I scrape a little ditch, kneel, and from a paper bag extract a couple of dozen onion sets which, business-end down, go into the ditch and are covered lightly with soil. They are the first things to be planted; the peas come next, then the lettuces. But the onion sets will sprout before anything else, and when they are five or six inches high, I pull them. The rotted remains of the set slip off like a dirty glove, and there is a silky scallion, needing only to have its white roots nipped off with a thumbnail then and there to make what is to me a heavenly treat. Freshly pulled scallions taste so unlike the specimens found in even the best markets as to qualify as a different vegetable, so delicate is their perfume, so mild their flavor.

But onion sets won't give a constant supply of scallions after early June. By then they are sprouting in their paper bags faster than you can plant them and there will be no more for sale. For a long season of scallions, put in successive sowings of bunching onions—eternally immature in that they never develop bulbs. They are, in fact, the scallions sold in markets, and they haven't the sweetness of those grown from sets; but a few pulled from the garden will always be better than any you can buy.

Leeks, like shallots, have an unearned reputation for being a fussy, foreign-born vegetable. Foreign they are (I can remember when you couldn't buy them outside of big cities), but in other countries the leek is a poor man's vegetable, common in soups and stews. An old recipe I have for the Scotch soup cock-a-leekie, calling for a rooster, a bunch of leeks and a handful of barley, directs that one cook them together 'until the bird is in ribbons and the soup divine.' It is, too, but hardly a refined dish. No more is the pot-au-feu in which leeks play a part. The only really classy leeks are those fat white columns served in France with a vinaigrette sauce as an hors d'oeuvre or winter salad. These are superleeks, raised in the richest soil, a couple of inches across yet tender as the youngest scallions, and any resemblance between them and the tough, tasteless vegetable sold in American grocery stores is in the name alone.

Anything up to the standard of the French leek is, I think, beyond the resources of the average home gardener to produce, even with French seed. Though this is much better than ours (order from Vilmorin if you can get hold of a catalogue), something in our climate or soil must be wanting. But at a lower level it is still possible to raise leeks without undue fuss. A good garden leek is of moderate size, not the colossus you might hope for but not requiring to have all its outer leaves stripped off in order to reach an edible center. There are various ways of growing leeks. I plant the seed outdoors first thing in spring and let the plants grow to the size of a slim pencil. I then dig them up, separate them, snip off the reedy green tops, and replant them in a trench up to their tips, about four inches apart. This gives a head start on blanching. They will sulk for a bit, then start growing again at a brisk pace. Blanch them by hilling up the earth around them, and when they have outgrown that, throw extra compost or soil against them. The idea is to keep the stalks buried up to the point where the leaves begin to unfurl, and it may sound like a lot of trouble, but really

it's a matter of a shovelful every now and then. Leeks are otherwise a sturdy crop, with no enemies I know of, and can be harvested for the best part of six months if you blanket them with hay
over winter.

Onions are so indelibly associated with the table that we sometimes forget the ornamental types bearing the generic name of
the family: the alliums. The most familiar is *A. giganteum*, which
bears a lilac-colored globe of florets on a naked stalk. I don't like it,
possibly because it is carried by so many sleazy catalogues. But
there is a host of smaller, more delicately proportioned alliums in
pretty colors that fit charmingly into odd corners. They dry well,
too, I am told, without recourse to messy boxes of borax or gel.
Like herbs, which in a sense they are, they need only to be hung
upside down in a dry place out of the light and they will keep
their color. I haven't tried this. I am not good at drying flowers in
general and anyway am in two minds as to whether I really like
them. There is a starry little white *A. neapolitanum* that florists
desecrate by dipping it into red or blue dye, and even without the
dye I would be afraid of producing something similar. On the
whole, the ornamental onions don't interest me half as much as
their edible relatives—which as a matter of fact are ornamental
too. Let a leek go to seed and you will have a flower handsome
enough for anybody.

ORIGINS

It is reasonable to ask how much has been accomplished in the
introduction or creation of new economic species in the last five
thousand years, that is, since 3,000 B.C. In spite of advances in
cytogenetical technique made since the beginning of the present
century, and notwithstanding the admittedly greater intelligence
through which our crops have been made more adaptable to the
demands of modern agriculture, it has to be admitted that not a
single species comparable to bread wheat, Indian corn, rice or the
soybean, or in fact to any of our important food annuals has been
added by modern man to the economic flora of the world.

It is also reasonable to ask how long before 3,000 B.C. it was that early man began his colossal task of plant amelioration. If a standard for measuring undated time could be created, based on the relative accomplishments of man in antiquity compared to his accomplishments in recent years, it is obvious that five thousand years is too brief a period. It must be multiplied many times, otherwise the period is not long enough for what took place in the evolution of agriculture in the Old World previous to 3,000 B.C.

Far be it from the botanist to dispute the theories based on sound anthropological evidence of man's origin or arrival in America. No doubt the migrations and discoveries surmised by anthropologists all took place, as did the recorded discoveries of Magellan, De Soto, Hudson and others. Nevertheless, the hypothesis based on the evidence presented by the enumeration of economic annuals shows that it would have been impossible for wandering tribes, starting from Bering Strait, to travel more than five thousand miles to tropical South America, and discover there the ancestors of a number of useful American plants, and within a period of two or even ten thousand years develop them to the state of perfection they had attained as proved by the prehistoric remains of 1,000 B.C. When observed by the first European explorers in 1492, all of these economic species had been diversified and greatly ameliorated, and some of them had been adapted to every climate from south of the equator to Canada. They had been spread over vast areas of North and South America; they had been rendered dependent on man; they had been so deeply rooted in tribal history that their origin was attributed to the gods. This is too great a task to assign to primitive people in the time allotted. . . .

Biological evidence indicates that man, evolving with his food plants, developed horticulture and agriculture in both hemispheres at a time which may well have reached far back into the Pleistocene.

OAKES AMES
"Economic Annuals and Human Culture."
Quoted in *Plants, Man and Life* by Edgar Anderson

PARTLY CLOUDY

The drought is serious, the corn crop threatened, lawns are burning up and water restrictions forbid us to water them. Turn to the evening weather forecast and there is a grinning young man surrounded with weather maps and radarscopes to assure us we haven't a worry in the world: 'The threat of shower activity has passed and it looks like a gorgeous weekend.' Or it is winter and a snowfall in prospect. Panic: 'It could be as much as four inches and travelers' warnings are out for the metropolitan area and eastern Long Island.' Nightly, some variation on these themes is enacted in the grotesque ritual called a weather forecast but more accurately described as pandering to infantilism. It is a frightening revelation of how insulated we have become from the natural world.

I assume that in those parts of the country where sufficient rain is still a life-and-death matter the forecasters show a little more sensitivity, though I wouldn't bet on it; and surely the states whose economy depends on snow to activate the ski resorts don't allow an imminent storm to be forecast as though it were a plague of locusts. Elsewhere, the weather is treated as something between a threat and a joke. The 'meteorologist,' having read out the figures we can see for ourselves on the screen and relayed predictions that come to him from computers at the National Weather Service as though they were his own, then engages in heavy banter with the fellow who broadcasts the news: 'Don't give us any more of the white stuff, Bill.' 'I'll do my best, Jim.' Thus is the power once attributed to Jove and his thunderbolts transferred to a man in a sports jacket—a quaint conceit indeed in a scientific age, and one with disturbing implications that the viewer is a child on perpetual holiday, his only interest in going out to play.

Unfortunately, that assumption seems to be correct. Americans resent the vagaries of weather to a degree unknown to other peoples. England's generally abominable climate is forecast in positively poetic terms—'Intervals of sun and cloud over East Anglia' —and in Italy a light chop on the Mediterranean sounds Vergilian. The majority of Americans crave a sunlit perfection, as if hell itself weren't a warm, well-lighted place, and have accordingly migrated by the millions to the Sun Belt, where the real prediction, not often uttered, is that they and their crops, planted in areas never intended by nature to support such exploitation, will die of thirst within twenty years unless a miracle occurs. Not only that: Bulldozed and overbuilt southern California is regularly burnt over by man-kindled fires and bids fair to be destroyed by mudslides well before the long-predicted earthquake comes along. Californians are only continuing the well-worn practice of building where floods and washouts are regular events—all our alluvial plains are examples of the same recklessness. We aren't, of course, the only people who have chosen to live on the brink. Ancient history testifies to that. From the flood plains of Mesopotamia to volcanic regions around the world, always heavily populated, the record is of one catastrophe after another, beginning with the Flood. But we are surely, in modern times, the least realistic and least equipped to deal with quite ordinary and predictable happenings. Our cars are so constructed (they didn't used to be) that an inch or two of snow is enough to swamp the roads with accidents. I don't know how they do it, but in northern and Alpine Europe (and Japan's northernmost island, Hokkaido), trains race through blizzards and arrive on the minute. In the United States, a commuter railroad like the Long Island, with no mountain passes to cross, no elaborate connections to be made with other international trains, can and has collapsed for more than a week after a snowstorm. No wonder the prospect of a little bad weather makes us nervous. We aren't equipped to handle it physically or—what is more important in the long run—psychologically either.

Weather is a force we have lost touch with. We feel entitled to dominate it, like everything else in the environment, and when we can't are more panic-stricken than primitives who know that when nature is out of control they can only pray to the gods. We pray, too—to the electric company on whose vulnerable wires our lives depend. When we first moved here, the local company was called the Mystic Light & Power, a name that made me laugh whenever I made out a check. Now it is Northeast Utilities, which doesn't inspire the same confidence. Nor has Northeast moved to change the scary system of wires, strung overhead where they can be smitten by lightning and tree limbs, that was installed about the turn of the century. In Europe, these tangles are underground and not allowed to disfigure the streets and endanger the citizenry.

Why are they here? Nobody can tell me. There they hang, one more reason to fear the winds that can't be stopped from blowing. Only last week, lightning struck the maple across the street, bringing down the wires interlaced in its branches and leaving us powerless for a night and half a day. Powerless is the word. It was almost comic that I couldn't even brew a cup of coffee.

It probably goes without saying that that particular storm didn't figure in the evening forecast—neither its violence nor where it would strike. 'Possible late afternoon or late evening thundershowers' is a prediction we hear day after day all summer and have learned to ignore until we see the thunderheads. It is the forecasters' way of not getting caught, just as ever since the unannounced 1938 hurricane of terrible memory they have been careful to inform us of the least tropical depression developing in the Caribbean. But having lived through many later hurricanes, I have noticed that the nearer the storm, the less accurate the plotting of its probable strike. We are told the 'eye' will pass over Montauk (which on the usual north by east course means, in short order, us), or no—it will pass over Bridgeport (which doesn't), or it has already gone out to sea. The same with snow, which will accumulate to two inches, four inches or, suddenly, amount to little or nothing. Not the least of the sins of the forecasters is their unreliability. Many years ago, my father believed there would be a revolution in forecasting as soon as Arctic weather stations and an efficient system of radio communication were established at various points across the globe. A Navy man, he had a particular interest in the subject, especially as it applied to military operations like the Normandy landings, which it will be recalled nearly foundered on account of an unforeseen storm. He died before the invention of weather satellites and other advanced technology like computers, which would have given him even higher hopes. What would have been his feelings to learn, thirty years later, that our military weathermen in the Arabian Sea were unaware of a vast sandstorm hovering over the Iranian plateau at a critical moment —a locality where such storms are common at that time of year? Is it reasonable to expect the little chap on the TV screen, who gets his information from a less vitally concerned source, to do better? I would rather trust the farmer who holds his finger to the wind, anyone, indeed, who lives outside the technological cocoon. I remember that when my father was in charge of a naval station on a West Indian island in the 1920's, he had received no official word of an approaching hurricane. It was the inhabitants who gave him warning of the need to take precautions. Reading the motion of the sea, the clouds, feeling in the barometer of their bones a sudden drop a thousand miles away, they muttered for days, 'Hurricane coming, hurricane coming.' They were right. A couple of hours after the official warning arrived, the storm struck the island like a sand-blasting machine and nearly blew us off the map.

Such skills have largely been lost. Hence, in part, the inordinate fear of weather and the dependence on the idiot box to feed the dream of eternal sunshine, or the nightmare of a couple of inches of snow. In our civilization, if that is what it is, only farmers and gardeners are free of these fantasies. We don't care if your weekend *is* ruined by the rain we need. We curse the wind the Sunday sailor wants for his outing (it dries up our peas, just coming to perfection), and bless the snow that blocks your roads but keeps our plants and the winter wheat safe. We must collaborate with nature whether we like it or not and perhaps need a special weather service of our own.

Something of the sort exists, and I don't mean the old black magic, not but what I don't rely on it on occasion, and in the short run. Rain really is imminent when the leaves turn their backs to the wind, smoke goes to ground and the earthworms rise to the surface. It may not be true that if St. Martin's Day is fair and cold the winter will be short, but I would give it a try. A Mexican-Indian gardener once told me at the beginning of the dry season in October that it would rain heavily for three days in February—I forgot which saint's fiesta was involved and anyway the saint was undoubtedly a thinly disguised Aztec god—and not thereafter for three months. The prediction was correct and amazed me at the time. It doesn't amaze me now. It never pays to underestimate folk wisdom. Neither does it pay to overestimate it. The 'natives' don't know everything or they wouldn't be 'natives.' But neither do we, or we wouldn't be in the awful pickle we are. What I seek is a scientific approach that takes into account information gathered down the ages by observant human beings—and goes on from there.

Such a minor discipline is at hand in a development called phenology: the study of the growth stages of plants, which can be used to predict the approach of spring and all that implies about planting dates, the emergence of insects and other data vital to farmers and gardeners. The name is modern, the practice as old as

the hills. The Chinese and the ancient Romans were using phenological calendars a couple of thousand years ago, and real farmers,
as opposed to those engaged in mass agriculture, have always been
aware of the principle—which simply consists in noting the dates
when one or more plants known as 'indicators' burst into leaf or
bloom. Given this information, it is then possible to predict other
events like the warming of the soil, the likelihood of one area
remaining persistently colder than another, and so on. It has long
been understood that plants are sensitive weather instruments,
registering temperature and humidity. Indicator plants are simply
more reliable than others. The common lilac, for instance, won't
open its buds until it is safe to do so (which is why the flowering
can vary by as much as three weeks from one season to another),
and the farmer or gardener who takes phenology for his guide will
watch for this flowering rather than go by the books and perform
certain tasks at a fixed date. In Montana, the blooming of the lilacs
tells farmers they have ten days to cut the alfalfa and eliminate
the first brood of alfalfa weevils. Truck farmers on Long Island
count on the flowering forsythia to signal the arrival of the cab-
bage-root maggot. In New England we used to plant our corn
when the elm leaves were the size of a squirrel's ear, knowing the
ground would then be warm enough for the seed to germinate.
The elms are nearly gone but oak or maple will do as well. Using
the lilac, or the dogwood—another indicator plant—it should also
be possible to locate the best place on a property to plant a tender
fruit tree like an apricot. Where either of these flowered consistently earlier than others of their kind would be a warm spot that
could save the fruit buds from late freezes.

A number of countries in Europe maintain networks to gather
phenological information as part of their national weather services. We don't. Such a network was established here in 1904 by
the Weather Bureau but abandoned for lack of funds. Now,
however, there seems to be a revival of interest. A few states are
developing programs and the Department of Agriculture is col-
laborating with some of them. Phenological maps have been compiled. But it will be a long time before the nightly forecast
includes the latest word on lilac time. Meanwhile, there is nothing
to stop the amateur from making his own observations. I scored a
minor success, though not with phenology, in long-range forecasting in the fall of 1979, when we had an exceptionally early snow-

fall, one that took place while the roses were still in bloom and the leaves green on the trees. That, I announced grandly, meant we would have no more snow until February and an exceptionally dry winter. This was based on nothing more than notes in my garden log which recorded two similarly premature snowfalls in the early 1970's, both followed by dry winters. It may well have been coincidence, but I turned out to be right. On the number of times I have been wrong, misled by the behavior of squirrels with nuts and the amount of moss on the north sides of trees, time-honored omens, I naturally don't enlarge. But then I notice that those who predict weather never do mention, or apologize for, their failures.

PATHS

Russell Page says a path must always lead somewhere, and when you come to think of it, that is a very English conception. The formal French and Mediterranean gardens weren't for walking. The open parterres were to be looked at from above, not strolled about in; and people were carried across the vaster open spaces or driven in little carriages down the broad *allées*. (I often think of those as I trudge the last weary mile of some royal park.) Grassy paths, seats to rest upon, objectives to make for during a walk, these were the inventions of a race mad about taking exercise in the open air. But even in England it hasn't always been demanded that a walk have an object. The winding paths of the early nineteenth-century style called the gardenesque led nowhere in particular. J. C. Loudon, the great promoter of this style, even suggested that 'an author, if he can afford any other garden than a plot of mint, should surround this plot with an oval path, that he may walk on without end, without any sensible change in the position of his body' while he unravels the complications of his thought. Different again was the function of the Chinese garden path. Here, to quote Sirén, the stroller is 'led on by ever new impressions, farther and farther into the composition that is never completely revealed, and which for this reason retains something of the secret charm and allurement of the unknown.' In that most exquisite of garden manuals, the *Yüan Yeh*, such paths are said to 'meander like playing cats.'

A path, then, may be winding or straight, lead somewhere or nowhere, but whatever its purpose garden designers East and West and in all periods agree on one thing: It must be well made of materials as carefully chosen as any others in the garden, and not be an afterthought. This doesn't, of course, mean laying a walkway arbitrarily, least of all in the small modern garden where one is well advised to take note of those routes already established by human traffic—for if these are ignored in favor of some alternate way, be it ever so attractive it won't be used. Beyond that, I am on Page's side. I do think a path must lead somewhere, and I can't see myself taking turn after turn around my circular rose bed, or even, following a much older tradition, pacing a philosopher's walk like those of ancient Greece and Rome. In some Roman gardens the length of these promenades was inscribed on a marble tablet so that the walker could calculate the amount of ground covered—rather as in the dear dead days of ocean liners it used to be posted how many times around the deck made a mile. Pliny had walks like these, one under a pergola 'where the soil is soft and yielding even to the bare foot.' But I am not a pacer and have never acquired the habit of cogitating in the open air. My only path is utilitarian. It leads to the garden shed, is made of ancient stepping stones and lined with gray-foliaged herbs and pinks. This doesn't exactly make me an expert on paths, which are nevertheless an aspect of garden design I have strong feelings about.

Take cement block, or rather don't take it. I see a lot of it nowadays, either laid like stepping stones or butted together, and I don't think it's any improvement over the poured concrete of an earlier day. Asphalt is ugly too and can't be disguised as anything but what it is. Gravel is handsome, and beastly to walk on if like Pliny (and me) you go barefoot, and those who have it tell me it needs constant grooming. I assume the same would apply to stone chips or ground oyster shells or any similar material—which I couldn't walk on either. Wood chips or tanbark are fine for a woodland path. I feel they give a garden an unbecoming resemblance to a riding ring. Some people make stepping stones from sections of tree trunks or barrel tops. The effect is too self-consciously rustic for my taste, and I have skidded on these in wet weather.

This leaves stone, brick or plain grass. What I would like best would be European cobblestones, which make lovely, simple paths, countrified without being quaint, and very durable. These being out of the question, my next choice would be a mosaic of tiny pebbles, with or without a pattern and in several natural colors, set as closely as possible and pounded hard into the ground. You see these in Mediterranean countries, though they may have been a Chinese invention. The *Yüan Yeh* has directions for making them, sometimes combining them with brick. It also points out that 'even small bits of waste brick may be used for paving. The small square bricks should be collected; they can be used around the plum trees, where they are laid out in a pattern of cracked ice.' Trust the Chinese to find the right image. Say 'crazy paving,' which is what the English call irregularly laid stone, and one's reaction is an instant negative. These little bricks in a pattern of cracked ice immediately sound like a charming idea, and one that might be well worth trying.

Brick, anyway, is a lot easier to handle than stone and owing to its association with colonial America is, I think, particularly appropriate to gardens attached to old houses like mine. It is true that New Englanders didn't use it much—brick really means Philadelphia and points South—but I let that pass. I have bricked in our dooryard rather than try to cope with ground covers or grass; also the space between back door and back gate. Both are entirely satisfactory, and were I to embark on another path, I would have that of brick as well. Page says that bricks should always be set on edge, and he is right. Not only do they look better and allow for a greater range of patterns, they go that much further into the ground, lessening the need for a deep base of sand and ashes. Unfortunately, setting them on edge uses up three to four times as many and multiplies the expense accordingly. Perhaps it's worth it. Mine, however, have been laid flat except at the border line, and I am not unhappy with the result. (A word of caution to would-be bricklayers: Don't set them in cement, and don't just lay them end to end as for a wall. Bricks can have almost as many 'stitches' as embroidery—herringbone, basket weave, etc., many of them to be found in old books, and to me at least great fun to work out.)

Finally, there is grass—plain or mixed with those matty herbs like pennyroyal and shepherd's thyme—hemmed in with herb or flower beds, which should be called walkways, perhaps, rather than paths. These are the joy of the English garden. Here, they pose the same problems as those of lawns in general, and if all you can produce in the way of a lawn is weeds and crab grass, your grassy walk will do no better. Otherwise, the great thing to keep in mind is that they *are* walkways, not spaces between the beds. When our perennial borders were set out, this salient fact wasn't appreciated. We were thinking of the massed effect of the flowers, presided over by our resident goddess, a copper weather vane in the form of Columbia-the-gem-of-the-ocean designed by Benjamin Franklin. Columbia, mounted on a bit of rough wood, stands at the confluence of four island beds, arching her arm toward the phloxes in the left-hand ones. Nothing could be prettier—and anyone who has to mow the lawn has complained ever since. The grass strips just barely accommodate a mower, which can't turn the corners at the center of the cross but must approach it from the four cardinal points of the compass. This nuisance also applies to strollers who can't walk two abreast while admiring (one hopes) my handiwork. These grass strips, or walks, should be two or three times as wide as they are, a defect that could be rectified now only at the sacrifice of valuable plants in the beds. The moral is the same as that for making any sort of path: Have it broad enough to fit yourself and a friend, as attractive as possible to the eye and kind to the foot.

———— ∽ ————

PEONIES

A fashion photographer I once knew, famous in her day, was in due course obliged to retire to a farm, thereby causing much anxiety to her friends. What, they wondered, would this dynamic woman, whose perfectionism had terrorized the studio, do with her old age? She took to raising tree peonies, and these beautiful, temperamental plants clearly came to replace the models she had alternately bullied and coaxed to do their best for so many years. I last saw her in her potting shed, surrounded by notebooks in which she recorded the genealogies of her favorites, absorbed in questions of drainage and soil, happy as only the obsessed can be;

I have no doubt that her peonies, not in bloom at the time, were faultless. They are, as everyone familiar with their images in Oriental paintings, silks and porcelains knows, among the world's loveliest flowers, at once sumptuous and subtle in their golds and moonlight-pinks and snowy whites; their finely cut foliage makes that of the common, herbaceous peonies look coarse. They are in short the royalties of the peony world; and perhaps for that very reason I have come to feel they belong to those gardeners with a streak of fanaticism, to whom the shortcomings of the race are a challenge rather than an annoyance, the kind of person who will cherish a plant for twenty years for the sake of a few, jewel-like flowers—someone like my friend.

I am not of that order. I have a few tree peonies but am in no sense a connoisseur, and I have several objections to them. To begin with, and on all but one of my plants, those dazzling flowers are nearly invisible, hidden beneath the foliage. To admire them I must cut them and they don't make good cut flowers. The heads are too heavy for the short, flimsy stems, and so they end up in shallow bowls or in a bud vase, not my preferred ways of arranging flowers. (The exception is Renkaku, meaning 'flight of cranes,' a Japanese variety, white and the size of a dinner plate—which, however, and contrary to its reputation, flowers so sparsely that in a decade it has never produced more than three blossoms in a season, and its upright, solid stalks can't quite make up for such a parsimonious habit.) Nor do any of them have much scent—that of the white, faint as it is, is distinctly rank, rather like a mushroom going bad.

It has, of course, occurred to me that something is wrong with the way I grow them—though I can't think what. The plants are large and healthy, if scarcely to be described as trees. That is a misnomer. Tree peonies are small shrubs with a woody skeleton that doesn't die down in winter as the stalks of the herbaceous peonies do. I have been told that the two shouldn't be grown in the same bed, though no such warning is given in books and their requirements (rich soil, good drainage, shelter from wind, etc.) are as far as I know identical. Mine, however, *are* planted together, and if that is a mistake, the purveyors ought to say so.

But I am beginning to think that the small group of people involved in the breeding, propagating and selling of tree peonies in this country must constitute a tight little island of specialists catering to other specialists, without much interest in communicating with the rest of us. The same names appear and reappear: The late Professor Saunders of Clinton, N.Y.; Lyman Glasscock of Ellwood, Illinois; William Gratwick; Nassos Daphnis; Toichi Domoto of Hayward, California; David Reath of Vulcan, Michigan—all are breeders and some are (or have been) sellers as well. My first tree peony came from William Gratwick, who then operated a nursery in upstate New York—now, I gather, out of business. Or is it? Wayside's 1980 catalogue offered 'Daphnis-Gratwick' hybrids, implying a partnership—somewhere. Wayside further stated that these men were the 'successors' of Professor Saunders. But if that is the case, what is one to make of the following in David Reath's catalogue: 'In 1966 Silvia Saunders [daughter of Professor Saunders], was searching for someone to continue the propagation of her peonies as she was preparing to retire. We were very pleased to have been asked to do this.' Who, then, are the successors of Professor Saunders? (To complete the confusion, Reath also sells 'Daphnis hybrids'—minus Gratwick.)

None of this is very important and could perhaps be cleared up by the American Peony Society (250 Interlachen Road, Hopkins, Minn. 55343). My point is simply the inbred nature of the tree-peony business, which together with the understandably sky-high prices of the plants (tree peonies are propagated by grafting and a minimum of five years is needed to judge success or failure) makes for a kind of exclusivity that doesn't feel the need to explain itself. The onus is on the outsider who tries to get into the club, usually by the back door.

A back door exists. Tree peony plants are often sold at garden centers—packed in cardboard cartons and unlabeled as to variety; also by mass-production nurseries who classify them by color only. These cost a fraction of the cultivars offered by nurseries specializing in tree peonies ($7.00 or $8.00 versus $20 or $30, and I am not speaking of the rarities, which can go as high as $75)—and by rights should be correspondingly inferior. With plants as with everything else you usually get what you pay for. Not with tree peonies. Not only do the prices vary wildly within the precincts of the club (the *lutea* hybrid Age of Gold costs, for a two- or three-year-old graft, $15 at Reath's, $29 at Wayside), but there is no assurance that a plant, picked up at a garden center or ordered from a third-class source, will be a whit less beautiful or prolific than a pedigreed cultivar. All it may lack is a guaranteed lineage, a name.

I don't approve of the situation. I only say it exists, and in proof

I offer the distressing fact that the most beautiful tree peony I own came from just such a dubious source some years ago, at a cost of $7.95. At the time, I didn't know what it was, and didn't care. I now realize that it is a *lutea* hybrid and a rare one at that, on account of its green-gold color. The *luteas* are the only truly yellow peonies, but none I have seen is this extraordinary shade or has this form: globular and heavy in the hand as a ball of silk. It lasts longer, too, than one of its pedigreed relatives I own, Souvenir de Maxime Cornu, a rumpled yellow edged with crimson— which is to say that it may survive as long as five days in water before it shatters, as all peonies do, overnight, casting its petals all over the ebony surface of the piano and revealing, like a peach, a bloodstained heart. And while I am on the subject, I should also mention an anonymous white, apparently a duplicate of the 'flight of cranes,' purchased I don't remember where, which covers itself with bloom and for which I can't have paid more than $10.

I am not doubting the integrity of those who dedicate their lives and fortunes to the breeding and propagation of tree peonies. I am suggesting that something is wrong with the way the business is regulated, and the plants themselves defined. When I pay a steep price for a named cultivar I ought to be getting more than a fancy title: the plant itself should perform better than the anonymous specimen costing less than half as much; and mine just don't. In the last analysis I'm not even prepared to say they are more beautiful than the common herbaceous peonies that everybody grows and nobody makes a fuss about. They are less varied in form and color, and if a display of great big gorgeous flowers is what you are after, the herbaceous peonies are my choice.

The herbaceous peonies stand straight and tall, don't hide their heads and are magnificent for cutting. They aren't temperamental, deciding, for inscrutable reasons, to withhold their bloom for a year. They are almost immortal, even when hopelessly neglected in the backyards of old farms. They can stand temperatures below zero. Tree peonies are sturdy too, but because they don't die to the ground as herbaceous peonies do, their superstructure is liable to winter damage. Often, in fact, they will look quite dead at the end of a bad winter, tempting you to cut back the wood. Don't. Concealed in a scaly brown casing is a pink bud that if no permanent damage has been done will burst forth when the proper time comes. All peonies suffer when a heavy rain hits them, and by the law of averages a deluge will occur at least once in the blooming season. Heavy rain will ruin the more delicate blossoms of the tree peonies, which don't like hot, bright sun either—and I hear of gardeners who place open umbrellas over their plants to protect them, a quaint effect, perhaps, if the umbrellas were Japanese parasols, but can you imagine doing it? To such lengths I will not go, and with herbaceous peonies need not. They love sun, and after a rain need only be given a good shake to revive.

Colette says, 'The peony smells of peonies, that is to say of cockchafers,' and only she would know what cockchafers smell like. Lilacs, she further says, have the 'discreet smell of scarab beetles,' whatever that may be. I am not good at such comparisons. Peony scents vary greatly, from one so like a rose I couldn't in the dark, tell the difference, to an acrid sweetness not unlike the lilac's. The doubles smell better than the singles and the herbaceous better than the tree peonies—to me. As with roses, one is confronted with stark divergences of opinion. The authors of *The Fragrant Year* say all the Japanese tree peonies have scent, the more perfumed of them 'a yeasty sweetness that shades from narcotic and repelling to something quite delightful.' Never having visited a great tree-peony collection (for example, that at Swarthmore College in Pennsylvania, which is said to have over two hundred named varieties), I can only retort that mine don't—and that includes Souvenir de Maxime Cornu, which they think outstandingly sweet. They also find the odor of the old-fashioned Memorial Day peony, *Paeonia officinalis*, 'unbearable,' and I don't agree about that either. (Is this perhaps Colette's cockchafer-scented flower?) Further, I notice that today's catalogues haven't a word to say about scent, from which I conclude, perhaps wrongly, that the modern hybrids have little or no perfume. But as I never buy them, I can't say.

That may or may not be one of the drawbacks to peonies. Once you have them, you have them for a lifetime and can pass them along to your grandchildren, which makes for an unadventurous spirit. Unless you have occasion to start a fresh collection, there is no incentive other than curiosity to buy new plants. Most of my herbaceous peonies have been in place for the better part of forty years, quite long enough for me to have forgotten what they are— or what is more reprehensible, to try to find out. Trying to identify them would be rather like suddenly asking your oldest friend his mother's maiden name. To me, they are just peonies: double pinks, whites dribbled with crimson, shell-colored singles with golden hearts, ruby-reds. Having had them so long, I can predict almost to the hour when they will come into bloom—beginning with the tremendous pink ball at the fence corner—and nearly as accurately when they will come to an end, six weeks later. (The tree peonies, blooming earlier, are less predictable. Sometimes they overlap their herbaceous cousins, sometimes not.)

Yet this predictability is not a bore. One looks forward to the peony season as to the yearly visit of friends one loves, and the impulse to go whoring after novelties is, in me, quickly stilled. I could no more dig up these old friends and replace them with new ones than I could tell a human being that after thirty or forty years I was tired of his company. Moreover, peonies (of either type) need time to settle down and do justice to their capacities. Properly cared for, which is a simple matter of enough water and plenty of fertilizer/mulch, they improve with age, like wine, and if you have a clump you like, my advice is to leave it be. Given the unavoidable hazards of gardening, the droughts and killing winters, the attacks of insects, a perennial that is immune to all of them is a godsend.

———— ❧ ————

PERENNIALS

In its heyday, forty or fifty years ago, what the English call an herbaceous border and we call a perennial bed could be hundreds of feet long and wide as a stream. With its infinite variety of flowers planted in great billows of color, those at the back rising to six-foot spires, those in front lapping like wavelets at the shore, it was a far cry from the cottage beds that had inspired it, and required many highly trained gardeners to keep it up. For a start, it was double-dug to a depth of several feet, then filled with well-rotted manure, ashes, sand, etc., and as if that weren't enough for a lifetime, it was taken apart every third year, dug over, replenished with huge amounts of fertilizer and fresh soil. At that point, new plants were put in, old ones in need of dividing were broken up and reset, and the whole elaborate complex reassembled.

So much for the basics. The color scheme also had to be carefully thought out. Gertrude Jekyll, who invented the herbaceous border, sent her clients the originals (many of which survive in her own hand) of those scale drawings still used in gardening books, which indicate the exact placement of iris, delphiniums, etc., according to color—and, of course, height. In her own Surrey garden, the spectrum moved from blue, white and yellow at each end of the border, through pink and purple to a bonfire of vibrant reds and oranges at the center. The plants used weren't, in fact, always herbaceous or native: Yuccas, cannas, half-hardy annuals and some roses were included, but the backbone of the border was hardy perennials.

At the time, Jekyll's schemes were revolutionary, and a much needed departure from the rigidities of carpet-bedding with annuals. But eventually they, too, came to seem old-fashioned and lacking in that quality of improvisation desired by gardeners in the 1920's and 1930's. 'An air of rapture and spontaneity' is how Russell Page describes Norah Lindsay's 'subtly controlled sea of flowers' in her famous walled garden at Sutton Courtenay. Lindsay was an amateur consultant who flourished between the wars, and her *modus operandi* was very much of the period. She would arrive at a great house, trace out a whole garden with the tip of her umbrella, make a long and brilliant list of suggested plants on sheets of flimsy paper, and be on her way—'leaving the rest to nature and the astonished gardener.' She liked big drifts of opalescent flowers interplanted with old roses and smoky-leaved artemesias, lavenders and senecios, effects that were widely copied. At V. Sackville-West's Sissinghurst, the beds might be all white, or all red, as well as mixed colors, but they, too, had a studied air of untidiness. For as Page points out, herbaceous perennials are basically meadow flowers, and the border should recall something of their native habitat.

Page, however, isn't an aficionado of herbaceous borders. Few designers are, and most gardeners, too, have lost interest in them, partly because of the shortage of skilled labor, and partly because flowers per se are out of fashion. It is also true that they don't fit into a starkly abstract design. But unless one is dealing with the ultimate in modernism, the owner of a small park by Le Nôtre, or a garden on the shores of the Mediterranean, I continue to feel that a flowerless garden is a sad place; and I would add that if you do want flowers, this is much the easiest way to grow them.

The chief drawback to the English model was size. Some borders appeared to extend a good quarter of a mile. Obviously, nobody is going to attempt *that*, and it isn't necessary. A perennial bed should be generous enough to accommodate, say, a dozen varieties in good, big clumps without crowding—dinkiness is to be avoided—but no larger than that. Nor is it necessary to double-dig. Ordinary digging in of natural fertilizer at the start, and liberal additions of enriched compost after that, are perfectly adequate. As for those planting diagrams, copied from Jekyll's, that one is advised to make before putting a spade to the ground, I don't believe they serve any useful purpose today. They are based on improbable premises—the first that you know enough about plants and their habits to be certain in advance of what you want; and the second that you will be able to find it.

It doesn't often work out that way. Plants ordered by mail, even from the best nurseries, may be out of stock, delivered too late to make a good start, or turn out to be the wrong varieties. At the very least, they will be discouragingly small. Instead, locate if you can the kind of family-owned establishment where the people on the premises have either raised the plants themselves or know where they came from. We were fortunate to have such a nursery close at hand when our perennial beds were started years ago, and it saddens me now to pass the Ramada Inn standing squarely on top of the spot where once I could choose peonies and hand-pollinated lilies, and consult the owner about which phloxes I would be happy with. Mr. Lamb, who was as gentle as his name, spent hours with his clients, and I learned more about perennials from him than from any book. (I still have his plants, too, thirty years later.) Alas, the nearest such place is now fifty miles away. Never mind. If one is serious about growing good perennials, and particularly if one is starting from scratch, there is no substitute for choosing them in person and on the spot. Catalogue orders, and the occasional mass-produced specimen at the garden center, are only for those with established beds, where a disappointment won't leave a hole. It is true that the perennial border made this way won't bear much resemblance to the one you saw in your mind's eye. But given the eccentricities and inevitable failures of plants, it probably wouldn't anyway; and I prefer to apply my paint, as it were, straight to the canvas, scraping away the mistakes as they occur.

Much more important than choosing plants ahead of time is deciding on the location, size and shape of the beds themselves. You can't keep digging up the lawn as you change your mind, or make the belated discovery that the spot you have picked is in deep shade all afternoon. A bed can be any length, but no wider than can be reached for weeding by someone on hands and knees. Island beds can be broader than a border beneath a wall, because there is access from both sides. But on no account should any bed be so wide that it must be waded into bodily to get at the plants. As to shape, I prefer the rectangle. For reasons I can no more analyze than defend, I can't abide flower beds with sinuous, irregular outlines. Something in my brain demands a Euclidean geometry—which doesn't exclude the circle but does rule out the meandering shapes that many, perhaps the majority of gardeners, seem to like. I also want them securely bricked in, the bricks laid at a 45-degree angle so that only the top third is to be seen.

After planning, the aspect of perennial borders most worrying to beginners is 'succession'—the idea that there must be at all times and in every quarter a mass of bloom. This is nonsense. Some professionals do produce that effect, and they cheat. Look closely at those photographs purporting to show the same border in spring, summer and fall, and you will see how. Notice the wall of snapdragons (which aren't perennials) that has sneaked in where the faded iris would be, and mark the spot where the sweet Williams of early summer have been replaced by chrysanthemums that weren't visible in the first photograph. A gardener with a greenhouse has made those changes, introducing new plants as they were required during the season; and the amateur shouldn't feel inferior because he can't do the same thing. Gaps *will* open up when the foliage of the bleeding heart and the Oriental poppies ripens and disappears. Clumps of late bloomers like Michaelmas daisies are flowerless for months while they wait their turn. I can't see that it matters. Indeed, I don't want a solid mass of flowers. It would exhaust the eye. Rather, I try to see that each of my four island beds has in it something for three seasons of the year, and let it go at that. With the enormous variety of plants there is to choose from, it isn't difficult.

I began by saying that perennials are the easiest flowers to care for, and I stick to that. Two thirds of them, once established, and with a good supply of compost dumped on them every fall, simply come up, year after year, with no further effort. I never take the beds apart in the English manner; and I don't divide the clumps more often than every seven or eight years, if that. As noted (see BLUES), the itch to divide perennials, abetted by garden books, is to be resisted unless the signs that they need it are unmistakable.

Weeding a perennial bed is also a less demanding business than it is among annuals. Weeds don't find it easy to get a foothold in the solidly rooted clumps, and the spaces between them are easier to deal with. Deadheading and cutting down are other chores that must be done, but less frequently than with annuals. The thing to be learned is when. Some perennials, which include coral bells, columbines and astilbes, bloom once, and when that is over the stalks should be removed, leaving the foliage at the base. It is very pretty and will last into winter and beyond. However, there will be no more flowers. Other perennials (delphiniums, lupins, Italian bugloss, centaureas, etc.) will be making new growth even while they bloom. When the flowers have faded, cut down the stalks to a point just above the fresh foliage, and if you are lucky, you may get a second flush of smaller flowers later on. Yet another class of perennial, notably the phloxes, have a long season of bloom which can be prolonged still further if you snip off the faded flower trusses a little above the place where they join the stalk. In due course, smaller side shoots will appear. In the fall, the whole plant is cut to within a few inches of the ground. None of this is as complicated as it sounds. The categories are clearly recognizable after a season or two, and the plants almost tell you what to do with them. Obviously, you don't cut away fresh growth; neither do you leave spent stalks and dead flowers, which not only look awful but are bad for the plant, and an invitation to disease.

These jobs cannot be called onerous. If regularly performed, a few minutes a day suffices. But, as usual, I have left the bad news to the last. Many perennials can't stand on their own. They need support, which means enclosing them in wire hoops or tying them to stakes, and both are hateful procedures. Wire hoops have legs fiendishly designed to slide around uncontrollably and stab the ground at crazy angles, while the hoop itself pops open. The double hoops for peonies are beyond description maddening to unfold and set in place. Two people are needed, one of them with better control of his temper than I have. And one's fury is all the greater for knowing that the struggle is quite gratuitous. Simpler and better versions of the hoop can be seen in medieval paintings; the Victorians had a model with a single stout leg that looks admirable —as does a modern one with a grid across the top, advertised in English magazines.

The alternative is to tie the plants to stakes, and it isn't much better. String doesn't look attractive (and the stain in green string washes out); plastic-covered wire is dispensed from a container guaranteed to fall apart, while the wire coils and recoils like a boa constrictor. Tie the plants too early and the string is too tight. Tie them too late and the stalks, belatedly confined at the waist, look like a witch's broom or a pot-bellied vase. So it goes. Bamboo stakes are handsome but the largest isn't strong enough to hold a clump of dahlias. Wooden pales, which are, have to be driven in with a sledge hammer and aren't a pretty sight. Green-painted metal stakes are nice, and much too short to be used with many perennials. With these devices to assist him, no gardener is going to enjoy this aspect of growing perennials. But as used to be said to me when I was a child who hated having tangles combed out of her hair: '*Il faut souffrir pour être belle.*' It would be unreasonable to demand that anything as lovely as an herbaceous border in full bloom be achieved without a little suffering.

◇

PESTS AND DISEASES

Central to organic gardening is the belief that plants so grown are healthier to begin with, hence more able to cope with attacks from whatever quarter; that preventive measures are better than drastic attempts at cure; and that natural remedies must be substituted for those man-made ones that are 90 percent toxic in one way or another. As a corollary, nature left alone will strike a tolerable balance among the predators. And we organic gardeners had better be right, because time is running out on the indiscriminate users of chemicals. A point of no return has already been reached in several parts of the world where more and more deadly pesticides are deployed against insects more and more able to resist them, natural controls are destroyed, and the ecology is in ruins. Diseases aren't being cured either. On the contrary, as more land is devoted to single, high-yield, high-profit crops like wheat and soybeans planted in the same soil year after year, blights are both more frequent and more devastating. Finally (and this may save us where missionary work has failed), the whole appalling array of chemicals (pesticides, herbicides, fungicides, etc.) is now so expensive that the cost may soon be prohibitive to farmers and home gardeners alike.

You would expect the agricultural establishment, dominated as it is in large part by the petrochemical industry, to set its face against change and to loose a barrage of defensive propaganda—and it has. What you ought *not* to expect is for the gardening press, with so much less to lose, to follow suit—as *it* has. Gardening books, newspaper columns, radio programs devoted to answering gardeners' questions, continue to give the impression that sprays (and chemical fertilizers) are the answer to everything, with no hint that alternatives exist, let alone that there is a school of thought totally opposed to both. Even the U.S.D.A., until recent years the faithful servant of the commercial interests, knows better than that and is in fact examining and testing alternatives to chemical extermination, while gardening editors as a whole seem blissfully unaware of what is happening or what can be done about it. I sometimes wonder if they read the news in their own papers.

Take the recent banning of the pesticide aldicarb or Temix, a favorite with Long Island potato farmers. It was banned because it was belatedly found to be contaminating wells and streams—and, one would infer, the potatoes themselves. Yes or no? The question was asked and the official reply was that while it may have, most people don't eat potatoes every day and that therefore the level of the poison consumed could be considered safe. A leading newspaper, and the one I judge by, ran this story on the front page, then let it drop. The gardening editor never referred to it—though it was surely of concern to home vegetable gardeners who have also been using aldicarb on their potatoes for many years. (My own reaction was to conduct a small poll on who *does* eat potatoes every day, and anyone could have predicted the result: People living on limited incomes eat potatoes once and often twice a day—they are a staple food. Only the diet-conscious with money to spend on meat do not. So much for that—except that it didn't occur to the newspaper to pursue the obvious point.)

Even so, it didn't surprise me that this story was ignored, not only, be it said, by newspaper gardening columns but by most of the gardening press. Worse things have happened, most notoriously with the herbicide 2,4,5-T, which the Environmental Protection Agency only got around to outlawing some eight years after the Vietnam war, in which it did horrendous damage not only to the wretched Vietnamese peasants and their land but, it now develops, to the American soldiers who handled the stuff: 2,4,5-T is an ingredient of the infamous Agent Orange. But it was also an ingredient of the herbicides American gardeners were spreading on their lawns, and how many knew that? How many know it now? The casualness with which the whole affair has been handled is staggering, and the gardening editor of the newspaper referred to above is, once again, typical. She is as high on herbicides as ever and only the other day listed no fewer than five to be applied to lawn weeds, beginning with 2,4-D and something called Banvel. Then apparently a warning light flickered, and she added a footnote for the benefit of those who might be frightened by that sequence of numbers. Noting that the E.P.A. has suspended the sale of 2,4,5-T, she wrote: 'The herbicide 2,4,5-T was an ingredient of the Agent Orange and is not to be confused with 2,4-D.' No comment on her own past recommendation of 2,4,5-T, and no reason given for why we should now unquestioningly accept 2,4-D. Are we not entitled to know what the significant difference between them is?

She might reply that the responsibility for guaranteeing the safety of these products rests with the United States government, not with a newspaper, and up to a point she would be right. But as a reporter and adviser to the public she surely has a responsibility of her own to go beyond a supine acceptance of whatever the government may be saying at the moment. She can't be unaware of how often and how disastrously we have been misled on everything from atomic fallout to chemical dumping. 2,4,5-T isn't an isolated case. For decades the government ignored the evidence against the commonly used pesticides in the group called chlorinated hydrocarbons, which includes DDT, dieldrin, aldrin, heptachlor, endrin, lindane and chlordane. These have been denounced for years by independent scientists as indiscriminate killers of a broad range of life forms. They don't break down into nontoxic materials soon after application and are suspected carcinogens. The first four have now been taken off the market. The others haven't, though they may be at any moment. Meanwhile they are still being recommended in the gardening press without a caveat to innocent readers. The general attitude seems to be that it's our funeral—as indeed it will be—and when it is you can be sure there will be no expressions of regret. It is one of the nastier features of the chemical world that repentance is never forthcoming for past errors, however lethal they may have proved.

The organic gardener can't be detached about the situation, which will enrage or depress him according to his temperament. But it doesn't affect him directly. (I have had to check the spelling of all those sinister names and have some trouble keeping them straight since none has ever entered my gates.) He is under no obligation to produce blemish-free crops of fruit and can put up with a mild case of powdery mildew on the lilacs, knowing that neither is fatal. He can do himself nothing but good when he banishes chemicals from the premises, and I guarantee that if he then takes certain measures he needn't look forward to insect invasions or epidemics of disease. (I have no experience of either—Japanese beetles excepted, and I will get to those in a moment.) All he has to do is to follow the simple rules of good husbandry, and instead of trying to keep up with the latest in chemical extermination, educate himself a little on how to run a garden without an array of bags, bottles and aerosol cans in his shed.

Compost of course is basic. Aside from its fertilizing and soil-conditioning properties, it teems with antibiotics and is thus the best insurance against disease. Keep the garden clean: Get rid of anything that looks really sick and compost the rest. Old stalks and litter lying around aren't organic so much as a sign of laziness. Bugs and blights can multiply in trash as opposed to the compost heap. Then, if you are growing vegetables, rotate the crops—no matter how small the kitchen garden may be. This is important protection against root rots and nematodes, which are tiny, eel-like worms that attack root systems. Compost is a help here too because it is a breeding-ground for certain fungi that devour nematodes. Rotation discourages the pests from building up a population in the spot where their favorite vegetables grow year after year. Give them something they don't like and they starve. What they like best are the midsummer vegetables such as tomatoes, peppers, eggplant, okra, melons, etc., so be careful never to grow these more than once every three years on the same land. (I make a note in my garden book of what went where—I can remember for one year but not for two.) Stay away from all plants after a heavy rain—moving around among wet leaves spreads any diseases that may be about—and don't embark on wet-weather weeding for the same reason. Some vegetable diseases breed on weeds and are conveyed from plant to plant by moisture.

Plants imported to the garden may, of course, be infected too, and this is one of the best arguments for raising your own if you can. If not, do at least stay away from those emporia whose stock comes from a distant source they can't vouch for, and try to find a local nurseryman you can trust. Seed catalogues make a point of noting which varieties are disease-resistant, and these would be the ones to order if you were having troubles. On the other hand, catalogues dealing in perennials, bulbs, shrubs or trees are apt to be reticent on this subject—though some of the species they are selling are notoriously susceptible to disease and to insect attack as well. You must do your own homework. Ask a neighbor who has a tree you are interested in, or look it up. Had I had the sense to do this some years ago, I would have spared myself the expense of a row of Lombardy poplars, installed under the influence of romantic European memories, only to be removed a few years later in disgrace. Had I inquired, I would have learned of the poplar's propensity to canker and scale, which attacked mine more or less simultaneously. Thus bitten, I am now shy of ordering, say, English hawthorns, though I long for a dense pink hedge of them. But I now know that in this part of the country they, too, have a bad name and must be regularly sprayed if they are to do well.

There are other secrets to a healthy garden, and one of them (though we had no idea of this when our original layout was made) is to have it full of a number of things: vegetables, flowers, herbs, small fruits and berries, rather than the sparsely planted modern plot. The kitchen garden in particular oughtn't to consist of a limited number of vegetables in segregated rows. This may satisfy a sense of order but is an invitation to predators and diseases to demolish a crop overnight. Short rows of different vegetables interspersed with herbs and flowers have a contrary effect. Not only do they limit the spread of a blight, they discourage methodical attack by insects whose appetite for one kind of plant can be deflected by the near presence of another they dislike. In other words, the cottage garden, which in one form or another has flourished the world over since the beginning of time, is now seen to be scientifically sound. It remains to sanctify its procedures with a name and to find an explanation of how it works that will be acceptable to the agricultural establishment.

The name is companion planting (or interplanting), and the practice is based on the observable fact that plants in cultivation, as in nature, seem to reinforce one another when grown in mixtures.

Partly, this is because some plants are naturally repellent to certain insects and can therefore protect their neighbors, though what the repellent properties may consist of is only now being seriously investigated. But there can be no doubt that they exist. Marigolds and garlic are perhaps the most famous all-purpose deterrents to a variety of pests from root nematodes to borers, and it at once occurs to the rationalist that it was on just such simple foundations that the whole Gothic edifice of plant mythology was built. (What more natural than to deduce from the effect of garlic on sucking insects that it would also work on vampires?) But however off-putting that edifice may be to some of us, the original thesis does prove out in practice. Beside marigolds and garlic, geraniums, nasturtiums, petunias, and many herbs—notably tansy, the mints, rosemary, and summer savory—actually do behave as claimed and repel a wide variety of pests. Still other plants are useful in specific situations. Snap beans and horseradish are distasteful to potato bugs; and the wormwoods to cabbage butterflies. (Hemp, i.e., marijuana, is said to be the most powerful deterrent of all to these pests. Dutch cabbage beds were surrounded with it throughout the nineteenth century, but I haven't been willing to risk a police raid to prove the point.) A comprehensive list of insect-repelling plants would be too long to give here. Those inclined to join the faithful can consult *The Encyclopedia of Organic Gardening* or the excellent *Companion Planting* by Louise Riotte, available from Garden Way Publishing, Charlotte, Vermont 15445.

There is more to companion planting than putting in marigolds to ward off the Mexican bean beetle. Subtle patterns of interaction between the plants themselves are manifested in curious friendships and antipathies, and in this area I am bound to say I think the organic press has done a terrible job of explication. It is all very well to say that such relationships exist—to assert that potatoes don't do well in proximity to tomatoes, squash, or cucumber but get along beautifully with beans, corn, and cabbage, while cabbage doesn't want to be near beans or tomatoes, which in turn are compatible with onions but inimical to potatoes and cabbage, and so on, ad infinitum. Such assertions seem on the face of it to countermand the premise that mixtures of plants are a good idea. Furthermore, the gardener who tried to accommodate so many likes and dislikes would be in the position of a hostess making out a guest list and trying to remember out of half a hundred people who is or isn't on good terms with whom—and going out of her mind. And the more so in this case because the 'rules' of compatibility are often in conflict with those of crop rotation, and those at odds with others applying to insect control. (Example: Flea beetles are repelled by tomatoes interplanted with cole crops, but tomatoes, we are elsewhere told, don't *like* cole crops.) Lastly, I question whether all this juggling accomplishes anything. My experience doesn't verify the quaint vision of vegetables turning from one another or alternatively falling into each other's arms. It seems to me they rub along pretty well together, and if they don't I haven't noticed. There are, to be sure, variations from year to year, but I can't determine that they have any connection with my having introduced a tomato, say, to a fennel—which according to *Companion Planting* is so unpopular with so many other vegetables it shouldn't be asked to the party at all but planted outside the kitchen garden.

I have other objections to what is called trap-cropping. This consists in growing a bug's favorite meal next to something you want to protect from its depredations, and it has a prominent place in organic literature. I don't see the sense of it, not because it doesn't work but because it does. It is quite true that eggplants next to potatoes will be more attractive to the potato beetle than the potatoes are; that zinnias (especially in white or pale colors), white roses and white geraniums will lure Japanese beetles away from other plants; and that dill charms the tomato hornworm into deserting the tomatoes. What of it? What of the eggplants, zinnias, white roses, dill, I have lost in the process? Even more to the point, what if I also prefer the beetle's first choice to its second, would rather have the eggplants than the potatoes, the white roses than the beans? Trap-cropping may serve a practical purpose for the farmer or the orchardist. To me, it is an exercise in futility.

In any case, and whatever you do, insects of some sort are going to visit you sooner or later. Deciding what constitutes an infestation is then the beginning of wisdom. It also helps to know what the insect is. So distant are most Americans from the natural world, so thoroughly have they been brainwashed on this topic, that the majority fear anything that flies or crawls. Should you encounter an object some five inches long that seems to be constructed of wire and toothpicks, which turns a tiny triangular face in your direction, you may be slightly unnerved even when you know perfectly well what it is: a praying mantis, of course, so greatly valued for its consumption of aphids, tent caterpillars, leaf hoppers, locusts, chinch bugs and half a dozen other menaces that organic gardeners order its egg cases by mail and carefully attach them to the branches of shrubs and trees in hopes that a population of mantises will emerge. Or perhaps you notice a congregation of ladybugs on a rose stalk. Don't invoke the old nursery saying and ask them to fly away home. Their house is not on fire. Your roses are, with aphids, which the ladybugs are feeding on— and you can bless yourself that they have come to your rescue. Ladybugs are a boon, and another insect the organic gardener takes pains to import if he hasn't got them already.

These are examples of the famous 'balance of nature' we're always talking about, and the principle is the same as that of the old balance-of-power politics. Every harmful insect has a mortal enemy. Cultivate that enemy and he will do your work for you. Observe the tomato hornworm. Bright green and stuck all over with white pins as often as not, this decorative creature is on its last legs when you see it: those pins are the larvae of a wasp and they are eating the worm alive. Wasps are, in fact, one of our more valuable allies owing to their parasitic habits. The trichogramma wasp lays eggs inside the eggs of other insects such as the corn borer, the cabbage looper, the codling moth, and once hatched the baby wasps consume their hosts. Organic apple growers rely on them for help in producing worm-free harvests, and like mantises and ladybugs, the trichogramma is sold commercially. But try telling that to those who panic at the sight of any flying object. Strong men in my employ have been incapacitated by a single sighting. I recall one idiotic youth who arrived panting at the back door. 'Have you,' he demanded, 'ever seen a *white-faced wasp*?' 'I have now,' was my reply—which attempt at humor didn't stop him from buying a gas bomb to destroy these imaginary enemies. He had, of course, to go. Had he chanced to lay eyes on one of those insects that go by the names of ambush, assassin and damsel bug (fierce devourers of caterpillars and grubs) he would probably have fainted away. Even the lovely lacewing (a predator of aphids, mites, mealybugs, etc.) might have been too much for him.

I make fun of him, but really there is nothing funny about the prevailing fear of insects and the indiscriminate use of sprays it leads to. It can't be said too often that spraying is like using a bomb instead of a bullet, killing the good along with the bad; and

the psychology of those who defend it is perilously close to that of
the general who wanted to destroy the village in order to save it.
In the end it isn't even effective. The history of the Japanese beetle
in this country is instructive. Accidentally introduced in 1916, it
quickly became one of the worst of garden pests. Yet it hadn't
been in Japan. Why? As early as 1933, government entomologists
isolated a bacterial organism that produces a fatal disease in Japanese beetle grubs. They called it milky spore disease after the
whitish look of infected insects, and it then turned out that it is
naturally present in the soils of Japan. Here, it wasn't, and the
beetles were soon out of control. In the 1950's and early 1960's, we
were engulfed in beetles, but nobody told us about milky spore
disease. Spray and spray some more was the advice handed out,
and it was worse than useless. The beetles quickly developed immunity. Nor, I have to admit, did I succeed in knocking them off
with garlic planted in the rose beds. Praying mantises couldn't
seem to get a grip on the situation either. Not until milky spore
disease became available in powder form sold commercially were
the beetles finally routed. (Several laboratories produce it under
license from the U.S.D.A. and market it under the names Doom or
Japonex.) It is applied mostly to lawns, where the beetle grubs are
hatched, is harmless to everything but the beetles, and once established is said to last indefinitely. Why, then, did it take so long to
appear on the market? Why isn't it sold, even now, at every garden
center? One may well ask.

Milky spore disease (*Bacillus popilliae*) is called a biological
control. Another such is *Bacillus thuringiensis,* or simply BT
(trade names are Thuricide, Biotrol and Dipel), which is fatal to
the larvae of many serious pests, particularly tent caterpillars,
peach tree borers, cabbage worms, codling moth worm and the
gypsy moth caterpillar. The last is of special interest at the moment because, and not for the first time, it is infesting large
sections of the northeast. But in spite of the availability, safety and
known effectiveness of BT, and still more to the point, past experience with chemical spraying of this caterpillar that killed birds,
bees, small animals and deer in large numbers without having much
effect on the gypsy moths, the battle is still being fought between
those who insist on chemicals and the environmentalists begging
that BT be used instead. The lesson is never learned.

There are other forms of biological control but they are too
sophisticated for the ordinary gardener, who anyway doesn't need

them. For us, the simplest measures usually suffice: a blast of water from the hose to dislodge the aphids, a saucer of beer for the thirsty slugs to drown in, a small tin can or a paper collar around young plants to foil the cutworm. The squeamish brush visible pests into a can of kerosene carried about for the purpose. I crush beetles and aphids between thumb and forefinger and leave the victims on the battlefield as a caution. Coming across the mangled remains of one's kin is evidently as unpleasant to bugs as it would be to human beings, and they usually leave the scene. (On the same principle, some organic gardeners grind them to a pulp in a blender, dilute the strained juice with water and use it as a spray.)

Organic gardeners are enthusiastic concocters of homemade sprays—infusions of hot peppers, wormwood, a medicinal bark called quassia, garlic, horseradish and other nippy substances, but although these are probably harmless, *The Encyclopedia of Organic Gardening* takes rather a dim view of them since they, too, might upset the balance of nature in some unforeseen way. Ideally, one should use no sprays at all unless in extremis, but one or two organic products are considered acceptable: rotenone (but not if adulterated with synthetic toxins—read the label); dormant oil spray (without additives); pyrethrum, the least toxic of any.

Most gardeners, I think, come to organic gardening through the kitchen door. Their first concern is fresh, uncontaminated vegetables, and it may seem less important to apply the same principles to trees, shrubs, lawns and flowers. But it doesn't make much sense to keep the kitchen garden free of poisons if you apply herbicides to the lawn and something that smells like boiled rubber to the flowers. A garden is a world, and its parts are not separable.

POISON

It astonishes me that so many plants we see all around us, some of them common as weeds, are or are believed to be poisonous. Who would have thought that larkspur can be lethal to cattle—as are buttercups? That the laburnum is considered the second most

poisonous tree in Great Britain, the first being English yew?
Deadly nightshade carries its warning in the name—provided you
recognize the plant—but one should also know that the potato,
which belongs to the same family, may secrete a poison in the
areas that turn green on exposure to light. Castor beans are
deadly, and the velvety wisteria pod carries seeds that have made
children ill. Jimsonweed (*Datura Stramonium*) is a menace in all
its parts, including the white trumpet flowers that give it such
distinction. Everybody knows about the toxicity of poison ivy but
not many are aware that English ivy (*Hedera helix*) has been
considered poisonous since Pliny's day. The lovely *Daphne
Mezereum*, whose rosy blossoms signal an early spring, is a dangerous little shrub which should be kept clear of. Rhubarb *leaves*
are extremely poisonous. Those of foxgloves (*Digitalis purpurea*)
might benefit a heart patient if he knew the right dose; otherwise
they, too, can be fatal. As for house plants, so many are on the
danger list one wonders how anyone dares keep them about. The
latex exuded by poinsettias is a skin irritant; the leaves are said to
be poisonous. Take a bite out of a *Dieffenbachia Seguine* stalk
(though who would?) and your tongue and throat may swell so
you can't speak for days. Cats have died from nibbling at philo-
dendrons. Jerusalem cherries (*Solanum Pseudocapsicum*) are to
be regarded with suspicion (no recent cases of poisoning proved),
but oleanders, which many people grow indoors in winter, were
well known to the ancients to be toxic, and so were the pearly
berries of the mistletoe. Lantana is poisonous.

There are many others, but lists and documentation aren't easy
to come by, evident though it is that we are surrounded by natural
poisons. Americans aren't given to harvesting in the wild as Europeans are. The English go after nettles for soup, the French and
Italians root up a number of greens that go by the name of field
salad, and are insatiable hunters of truffles and wild mushrooms.
So are Hungarians, Russians and Poles. In Hungary I ate a number
of sinister-looking fungi gathered by the cook in field and forest,
and as none of us died I assume she knew what she was doing. I
have no such confidence in myself. Perhaps because I use so much
compost, my garden produces a fair number of mushrooms—some
under trees and hedges, others on the open lawn. They are, I'm sure,
common types but although I have several scholarly books on the
subject, the descriptions in them never quite tally with the speci-

men lying on the kitchen table. There are too many variables except in the most obvious cases: morels; the all-too-appropriately named *Phallus ravenelii* or stinkhorn; the *Clavariaceae*, like clumps of coral; the unmistakable *Amanita muscaria* (scarlet with white warts), and so on. My fungi tend to be pinkish-greyish-beige with gills, which applies to dozens of varieties; or they are boletes with spongy yellow flesh that may or may not be poisonous depending on certain characteristics I can't quite pin down, even with the aid of photographs. Not that it matters. Neither I nor any member of my family has sufficient faith in my diagnoses to touch a wild mushroom cooked by me. So there they sit, one more potential witches' brew in a garden that already contains deadly night-shade, digitalis, monkshood, laburnum, English ivy, wisteria, and yew. Yet I would never think of calling my little paradise a dangerous place.

<hr />

POPPIES

Somebody asked the other day if I had ever seen a flower open, to which I replied carelessly that of course I had. Only later did it come to me that I haven't; nor I think has anyone, not that act of unfolding one sees in slow-motion films. A bud may be swollen to bursting, ready to open at any minute; but however long you stare at it, like the watched pot it won't boil until you turn your back. In particular I found myself thinking of Oriental poppies, of which I grow quite a number because I think them among the most ravishing of flowers: the blotched silky petals, the seedcase marked with a design in flocked velvet, the quivering stamens like those of the sea anemone are amazing, and all this beauty is packed into a hairy calyx that swells and swells until you can plainly see the crushed petals inside and long to release them. That would be a mistake—however teasing the suspense. Poppies, like all flowers, open according to their own internal clocks, and if you mess with them you ruin the blossom. But I have also heard that the act is triggered by the first rays of the rising sun, and since many of

them open at the same time it must be an extraordinary spectacle
—like watching those Japanese paper blossoms that magically ex-
pand in water, only on a grand scale. I say 'must be' because I
have never witnessed it. It is true I am not an early riser, but in the
years when I worked in the city I did have to be up with the sun in
order to catch the first train on Monday mornings; and many a
dawn did I carry my cup of coffee into the dewy garden hoping to
catch the poppies at their performance. As I never did, I conclude
that the report is false, or that they saw me coming and altered the
schedule.

But although you may never see a poppy burst into bloom, few
flowers can give greater pleasure, whether the great big *Papaver
orientale* or the annual Shirley and Iceland poppies. Hybrid Orientals come in wonderful colors beside the basic red and orange—
and a ghostly white is perhaps the loveliest, though when you see
the raspberry pinks you want those too. Neither type demands any
particular know-how. My soil is too rich for the annuals, which are
really wild flowers and prefer a poorer, dryer mixture than I can
give them, and anyway don't belong in perennial beds. But the
Orientale, which reaches to about three feet and grows in permanent clumps, is a superb perennial plant whose only drawback is
its disappearance from view for about three months after it has
bloomed. The considerable hole it leaves can be disguised by a
nearby cloud of baby's-breath or simply left until the new crown
of leaves appears in early September or thereabouts. Never try to
move a poppy. The annuals should be sown where they are to
grow and not bought in flats as seedlings; they don't transplant
well. The perennial has a taproot of immense length. Nurseries
send it in deep pots from which it should be extracted intact—and
planted with care. That much it will stand. Begin moving or dividing in a year or two and it may well decide to disappear forever. In
fact, the less attention paid to poppies the better they like it.
Cage them in a metal hoop to keep them from flopping over in
rainstorms (I leave these hoops in place from year to year), and
that is all you need to do for them.

POTATOES

Lacking proper space, I didn't grow potatoes until a few years ago, when a holiday in France reminded me of a European variety I had forgotten: the little potato about the size and shape of a small sausage, with a thin skin and firm, yellow, waxen flesh that is the only kind the French use for potato salads, and that can also be sautéed in clarified butter as an accompaniment to meat or fish. Since it is common in Central Europe as well as France, I was fairly sure it must be grown by German-Americans in this country, but I had never seen it in an American market or catalogue. I determined to have some, and nothing, it turned out, can be easier than to find seed potatoes in the heart of Paris. Along the quays opposite the Ile de la Cité they sell every plant and seed known to horticulture. (And if you happen to be in the market for a badger, Madagascar finch, racing pigeon, long-tailed Japanese rooster, mink, or goat, they have those, too.)

Locating a two-kilo netted bag of *jaune d'hollande*, the name of my potato, was child's play. Getting it home was another matter. Seed can be imported legally—I think: I smuggle it anyway, just in case. Potatoes, I know, aren't on the legal list. So I mailed myself one kilo in a shoe box marked—what else?—'used shoes.' The rest I carried around in a suitcase for the three weeks that had to elapse before I flew home, and by that time they were sprouting nicely. Customs inspectors luckily aren't on the watch for potatoes, only dope, and I got them safely home—where I found the shoe box had also arrived undetected. This minor crime was rewarded with a handsome crop I fondly imagined to be an exclusive on this side of the Atlantic. Experienced travelers will guess what happened next. Even as the rug woven by Kurdish tribesmen in darkest Turkey and shipped home with the utmost difficulty will be found the following week on Bloomingdale's fifth floor, so it was with my potatoes. A rival gardener promptly discovered them in Gurney's catalogue, where they are called German Fingerlings and where I suppose they had been all along; and a little later an article about them appeared in the press. So they aren't an

exclusive at all, and you needn't break the law to get hold of
them.

Having no experience with other potatoes, I can't say if their
culture differs. I doubt it, except that they must be planted as
early as the soil will stand disturbance, and even that is a bit late.
By that time, mine have sprouted alarmingly into a tangle of white
growth, though I keep them (in net bags) in the coldest, darkest
part of the cellar. This, I suspect, is due to their European ancestry. In the milder French winters they would obviously be planted
much earlier than can be done in New England; and my race
hasn't recycled itself to our seasons. But though I worry every year
that they are too far gone, they never are and begin to grow as
soon as they are in the ground. Even so, it has occurred to me that
I may be mismanaging them, because a certain number of them
that were missed in the final digging-up invariably live over in the
ground. It may therefore be that they could be planted late in the
fall, and do even better, but I haven't dared risk it.

Their culture is otherwise very easy. I set them, whole, in a
trench about six inches deep and hill them up as they grow. By
the Fourth of July I have my first harvest, which I get by clawing
around under the plants, disturbing them as little as possible. (A full-
grown *jaune d'hollande* is about five inches long and the diameter
of a quarter, but many never attain that size. Take the big ones
first, the opposite of what you do with ordinary potatoes.) Right
after that, I mulch them heavily with salt hay. They don't like
heat, and as all potatoes do, turn poisonously green if exposed to
light while they are growing.

I have to confess they aren't as easy as ordinary potatoes to
prepare, and that may account for their rarity in this country. The
skin is a mere film and so delicate that a peeler strips them to the
bone. To cook them for a salad, wash them before dropping them
into boiling water. They cook quickly and must be skinned while
they are hot, a messy business best done by rubbing them between
towels while gingerly plucking away the ribbons of thin skin.
Then follow Julia Child's recipe in *Mastering the Art of French
Cooking*, Vol. I, for *pommes de terre à l'huile*, slicing and plunging
them into a hot bouillon to steep while you beat up a mustardy
dressing and prepare whatever herbs you have—parsley, chives, dill,
tarragon (one or the other of the latter but not both)—to sprinkle
over them. Drain, immerse them in the dressing, sprinkle with the
herbs and you have a potato salad that, warm or cold, so far out-

classes any other that there is no comparison. Their firm, waxy flesh doesn't crumble but absorbs the dressing; and the rich, nutty flavor is quite different from that of any white potato. Since the preparation is so fussy and time-consuming, I make big batches of this salad, which keeps well, and even improves, but must always be brought back to room temperature before serving.

Sautéeing these exquisite little potatoes is much simpler. Scrub them as before, this time not worrying whether the skin is completely removed, drop them into bubbling clarified butter and roll them around until they develop the ghost of a crust. Salt them, then turn the heat down and let them cook for another fifteen minutes. They are done when they turn a deep gold, and like pasta should be served *al dente*, not left to steam. As I have explained elsewhere (VEGETABLES), limited space forces me to grow only those vegetables that are either unobtainable in the market, or so inferior to the home-raised as to make the effort worthwhile. *Jaune d'hollande*, or German Fingerlings as the case may be, qualify on both counts. I can't buy them, and for the purposes described, they are better than any I can. I imagine, too, for those who worry about such things, that they are lower in calories than the floury white potatoes. I care nothing about that. For me, they are simply a delicacy and as such I commend them.

---------- ∽ ----------

PRUNING

Never before or afterward did a gardening style evoke so much attention, generate so much literary heat, as the one that overthrew the formal garden with its geometrically determined spaces and sculptured evergreens, and replaced it with an imitation of wild nature. Writers, painters, philosophers on both sides of the Channel were involved, but the landscape movement originated in England and the landscape park is a *jardin anglais* on the Continent to this day. The leaders were Pope, Addison, Horace Walpole, and their friends among the Whig aristocracy, aesthetes like the third earl of Burlington.

Each of the writers had his opinion and produced his manifesto

—surely a unique instance of literary men leaning over the shoulders of garden architects, who for their part probably drew more inspiration from Arcadian visions of Italy as interpreted by Poussin and Claude Lorrain, not to speak of the natural beauties of the English landscape itself, than from the philosophically oriented advice heaped upon them. The most famous of them, Charles Bridgeman, William Kent, and Lancelot ('Capability') Brown, don't seem to have been intellectuals in any sense of the word. Yet the movement itself, allied to romanticism and the rise of libertarian ideas, certainly was.

The opening gun may be said to have been fired by Pope in his *Epistle to Lord Burlington* (1731), which contains the famous phrase, 'Consult the genius of the place,' and denounces the garden where 'the suffering eye inverted nature sees, Trees cut to Statues, Statues thick as trees.' Topiary was Pope's *bête noire* and his satire, *The Essay on Verdant Sculpture*, was the hatchet job that finished off this art form for all but a few conservatives, virtually forever. His catalogue of topiary subjects offered by an imaginary nurseryman has been quoted to death, but a few examples bear repetition: 'A Queen Elizabeth in phylyraea, a little inclining to green sickness, but of full growth. An old maid of honor in wormwood. A topping Ben Jonson in laurel. Diverse eminent poets in bays, somewhat blighted, to be disposed of, a pennyworth. A quick hog, shot up into a porcupine, by its being forgot a week in rainy weather. Noah's ark in holly standing on a mount, the ribs a little damaged for want of water.'

From this it can be seen that Pope's real target was something more than topiary, or even the kind of garden it adorned. The formal garden had come to be the symbol of a social hierarchy with an absolute monarch at the top, the open 'natural' landscape to stand for liberty if not yet for equality, since the only men in a position to commission these private Arcadias for themselves were landowners whose liberalism was bolstered by large private fortunes and thousands of acres of land. The philosophical implications of the landscape movement were enormous, and too complex to go into here; but the political aspect wasn't less significant, and must account for the otherwise inexplicable interest the subject aroused. If garden design hadn't been a metaphor for larger issues, who would have cared if paths were straight or crooked, trees trimmed or untrimmed, brooks left to babble or confined to canals? It was odd enough that poets and intellectuals should occupy themselves with such questions, odder still that a reading public followed them with fascination in the press. To get an idea of what the situation would be like today, try to imagine, say, Gore Vidal, James Merrill, and Susan Sontag arguing the merits of garden design in *The New York Review of Books*. You would then have an approximation of what readers found in the pages of Addison's *Spectator*. Go a step further and imagine that one of the century's seminal thinkers (here, analogies fail me) takes some of his theories from theirs, and that these lead him to become one of the fathers of an earth-shaking revolution. Preposterous, of course —and exactly what happened. Rousseau was indebted to Addison's essays for some part of his obsession with the sanctity of nature; and at least one scholar (A. W. Adams: *The French Garden—1500–1800*) has noticed that not coincidental resemblance between Addison's own wild garden with its winding walks, untrained vines and native flowers and the famous wilderness in *La Nouvelle Héloïse*—in its turn Rousseau's paradigm of a free society.

In England, these ideas weren't that new. They were only less concealed in metaphor than in the previous century, when the Stuarts forced the issue between king and commoner. That was the point when the question of what gardens should look like—or, more accurately, represent—became more than one of aesthetics. The Stuarts had foreign tastes. Charles II was half Bourbon and a quarter Medici (has anyone remarked on his startling facial resemblance to his garden-loving ancestor, Lorenzo the Magnificent?), and neither inheritance disposed him to the unfettered style, in politics or in gardens. One of his first and least popular acts after the Restoration was to Gallicize the gardens at Hampton Court à la Versailles, with radiating avenues and formal canals—a fashion that was followed by royalist aristocrats. The succeeding Dutch dynasty brought more box parterres, more tortured evergreens. Both Hampton Court and Kensington Palace were so choked with box that there was no room to walk. (Queen Anne, who hated box and her brother-in-law King William about equally, had all this torn out.) Or so the critics said, and it is obvious that the English in general weren't captivated by these symbols of foreign-minded kings, whose instincts couldn't be trusted to respect English nature, English liberties. Unless this is understood, many of the Puritan poets appear to be raving when they write about gardens. Listen to Marvell: 'Luscious earth' stupefies the plants, and fertilizer is bad—'The pink grew then as double as his mind,/The nutriment did change the kind.' Grafting is dangerous: 'No plant now knew the stock from which it came;/ He grafts upon the wild the tame,/That the uncertain and adult'-rate fruit/Might put the palate in dispute./His green seraglio has its eunucks too,/Lest any tyrant him outdo.' There is much more, and all splendid poetry, but you might think him deranged unless you caught a deeper drift.

Milton in *Paradise Lost* makes the same points with his 'Eden's waters flowing free' (a pox on your French or Italian fountain-makers with their knowledge of hydraulics), his flowers 'which not nice art/In beds and curious knots, but nature boon/Pour'd forth . . .' (which were to become Addison's in the next generation). His 'Insuperable heights of loftiest shade,/Cedar and pine, and fir, and branching palm,/A sylvan scene, and as the ranks ascend/Shade upon shade, a woody theatre/Of stateliest view' might, but for the palms, be a description of the landscape park as eventually realized a century later, and directly anticipates Pope's 'genius of the place,' which 'helps the ambitious hill the heav'n to scale,/Or scoops in circling Theatres the Vale, Calls in the Country,/Joins willing woods, and varies shades with shades.' The pictorial imagery, in both cases, undoubtedly derives from Italianate sources, but the spirit itself is new, iconoclastic, and was one day to sweep a mob to the gates of Versailles.

None of this might be important to Americans, if it weren't that the English mistrust of formality and artifice, with all its religious and political implications, had been transferred to Puritan New England, whence it spread from sea to shining sea. Beginning with the grim little band who descended on Plymouth Rock, as blissfully innocent of horticultural skills as even Marvell could have desired, a deep vein of contempt for order imposed on nature has been part of the American ethos. It is all there in Thoreau, the Yankee Rousseau, with his seven miles of untended beans, his dream house, 'omitting other flower plots and borders, transplanted spruce and trim box,' fronting a quaking bog: 'If it were proposed to me to dwell in the neighborhood of the most beautiful garden that ever human art contrived, or else of a Dismal Swamp, I should certainly decide for the swamp.' Thoreau has always struck me as an exhibitionist, a thoroughly unsympathetic character who thought he was more original than he was. The fact is that most of his fellow-countrymen agreed with him, which is one of the reasons for the slovenliness of the American backyard. 'From the time I entered America,' wrote Mrs. Trollope, 'I had never seen the slightest approach to what we call pleasure-grounds; a few very worthless and scentless flowers were all the specimens of gardening I had seen in Ohio; no attempt at garden scenery was ever dreamed of . . .'

For the most part, it still isn't. We have our great historical gardens, and all of them are in the South, built with slave labor—a fact that wouldn't have escaped Thoreau. Allowing for differences of climate and flora, they were mostly provincial copies of the cavalier style, the social values of the southern slave-holder having differed in no important respect from those of the Tory Englishman, whose income not infrequently derived from a similar source in the West Indies. (It should be noted that the Tory rich tend to have the same tastes in every age: today's millionaires, basking in the Sun Belt, commission gardens in which 'abstract' is the substitute for 'formal,' but whose intent is the same.) It is at the lower, more democratic level that Thoreau has prevailed, substituting for artifice a kind of featureless and disheveled conformity. That something in the national character which doesn't love a wall (and loves Robert Frost, Thoreau's successor, for saying so), doesn't love an espalier either. Like Addison, it would rather 'look upon a tree in all its abundance and diffusions' than one 'cut and trimmed into a mathematical perfection.'

The landscape movement came late to America, about a hundred years late. It was introduced by A. J. Downing, and carried on by Frederick Olmsted, whose masterpiece, now atrociously vandalized, was New York's Central Park. (Fortunately, the great garden he designed for Cornelius Vanderbilt at Biltmore, North Carolina, is in good shape.) A certain gloom hovers over Downing's achievements, which were too late to be original, and have left a dreary legacy. Like all garden architects, he worked for the rich, who happened, in his era, to be a particularly tasteless lot—in that sense, the self-made Sun Belt entrepreneur with his willingness to try anything, and to employ truly experimental architects, is an improvement, whether we old-hat easterners like it or not. In Downing's day, the aim was a conservative imitation of a style already dead in Europe, and we haven't got rid of it yet. In debased form, it is what we see in the better-heeled but declining sections of old suburbia, such as Scarsdale. With even those references almost obliterated, it can be traced to unpruned bushes in unfenced yards, the urge for the asymmetrical even in the crude terms of tract building, the universal reluctance to take hold of a plant and train it even if we knew how—which hardly anybody does.

I have accordingly been amazed to read in Anthony Huxley's *Illustrated History of Gardening* (1978) that Americans excel at stylizing plants. 'Apart from trained fruit trees in espalier and many other forms,' he writes, 'examples can be found of forsythia, pyracantha, and even magnolias trained either as espaliers or in more complex patterns.' That is what comes of being a distinguished botanist and horticulturist whose hosts in a foreign country take pains to show him only what they want him to see. Where can Mr. Huxley have derived such an impression? At Longwood Gardens in Pennsylvania, perhaps; at Mount Vernon or the Mellon estate in Virginia; or in the plutocratic purlieus of Texas and California? In the country as a whole, nothing, alas, could be farther from the truth. I myself never return from abroad without being struck by the disheveled air of our domestic landscape, the scragginess of gardens and parks, the low condition of street trees. The latter provide an especially dismal example of how and why pruning is done here, when it is done at all. Yearly, the utility companies send out cherry-pickers to hack out the center limbs, the disfigurement being inflicted so that wires not be interfered with; and no one protests this barbarous practice. Yet if it were to be suggested that these same trees be pruned in the European manner, cries of horror would go up.

In *Wyman* there is a photograph of pollarded sycamores on a French street. The caption reads, in its entirety: 'This is not a good way to grow trees in America.' That is arguable, but it is certain that if it *were* a good way, there would be no one to perform the operation. I doubt if there are more than a few hundred men in the whole country who are trained to such work. Most of them would be of foreign extraction and 90 percent of them in the employ of the very rich. It follows that the average amateur wanting a little formality must either buy his espaliers and standards already trained, or be prepared to master the techniques himself; and both are extremely difficult to do.

What price those espaliered magnolias? No firm that I know of sells flowering trees or shrubs in even the preliminary stages of training. Henry Leuthardt's nursery on Long Island is the only specialist in espaliers in the East to my knowledge, and it deals only in fruit trees, mainly apples and pears. Wayside Gardens offers a small selection of standards—lilacs, pyracantha, etc.,—and there may be one or two others (I know nothing of suppliers on the West Coast). Standard rose trees can be had, and the scions are mostly the wrong kind of rose, long-stemmed and needing to be constantly pruned, rather than the bushier bedding types. And that's about it. The aspiring gardener is thus faced with coping for himself, and up till now the literature on the subject has been far from satisfactory. Most gardening books are too general even in describing ordinary pruning—failing to note exactly when a given variety of shrub should be cut back, on old wood or new, and approximately how far. Espaliering is sketchily handled, on the (correct) assumption that not one gardener in a thousand will put his hand to it. Topiary work, making standards, are also defined but not described in detail. Now at last a first-class textbook has appeared: The volume called *Pruning and Grafting* in the *Time-Life Encyclopedia* series, and it may be a harbinger of sorts. Just as people forced to do their own cooking turned ultimately to sophisticated foreign sources and became experts at techniques undreamed of by their mothers, so may American gardeners come to hanker after the horticultural arts unknown to earlier generations.

I certainly hope so. (Why else would *Time-Life*, which must have its ear to the ground, have published this particular volume?) Guided by its excellent directions, I myself am thinking of reproducing diverse modern poets in bays. Why not? My prejudices having placed me, by my own definition, on the side of the divine right of kings and slave labor, in favor of order and against liberty, I can't do less than atone by trying to produce at least one well-managed piece of topiary—instead of, as I have done, letting the hemlock hedge go to hell in its own way.

———— ✎ ————

REWARD

Finally I reach a garden where I am to uproot
the last parsnips for my sisters' dinner
Not parsnips mastodons   But this year's greens

> already frill them and they pull easily
> from the soft ground   Two of the finest
> are tightly interlocked have grown that way   They lie
> united in the grave of sunny air
> as in their breathing living dark
> I look at them a long while
> mealy and soiled in one another's arms
> and blind full to the ivory marrow
> with tender blindness   Then I bury them
> once more in memory of us

>   JAMES MERRILL
>   'From the Cupola,' in *Nights and Days*

Others might not be as moved as I am by that particular passage in the poet's glittering *oeuvre*, but they wouldn't have my reasons. Those parsnips, you see, were mine. I planted them, then went away that winter, commending the vegetables to his care. Gardening can be a discouraging business. We all have our days when we moan that it isn't worth it, nobody appreciates our efforts, etc., etc. Then comes a Christmas package like this one. The parsnips have made it into literature. Onward!

---------------- ∽ ----------------

ROCK GARDENS

Any garden employing rocks as a prominent feature can properly be called a rock garden, whether it is full-scale replica of a landscape or a miniature, and either way it has a long history. Miniature landscapes were constructed in the peristyles of Roman houses, and Pliny mentions a portion of his Tuscan garden laid out 'in imitation of the negligent beauties of rural nature.' Both had dwarf trees, though whether rocks were included to imitate mountains isn't clear. Very likely they were, because such toy landscapes existed and were called *topia*—a word that also applied to a type of trompe l'oeil fresco or bas-relief depicting rugged shorelines and hills that was used to bring the illusion of a view in to courtyards and colonnades. (Confusingly, *topia* was a Greek word —the frescoes having been a Hellenistic invention—later Latinized to apply to the gardener who did topiary work: the *topiarius*. Research hasn't revealed to me what the connection was.) The Romans, at any rate, employed rocks for landscaping in various ways. Aside from grottoes and nymphaeums, it is believed that they designed whole gardens in imitation of wild scenery—forerunners of the style not seen again until the eighteenth century. These have vanished, but the rocky little valley called the Vale of Tempe at Hadrian's villa near Tivoli is known to have been laid out in the manner of the *ars topiaria*, the artificial landscape.

All these, however, pale beside what must have been antiquity's rock garden to end rock gardens. This was at the villa of one Faustinius near Monte Circeo on the Tyrrhenian coast, and it is wonderfully described by Georgina Masson in *Italian Gardens*. From the remains that have been found—fragments of monsters, men in terror-struck attitudes, the prow of a ship—it is deduced that Faustinius's idea was nothing less than to carve a scene or scenes from the Ulysses legend (a frequent subject of the *topia* frescoes) out of the living rock of the coastline where they were believed to have occurred. The site is incompletely excavated but appears to have been a natural grotto, which with the surrounding pools and outcroppings was transformed into a mythical seascape that was either pure magic or pure nightmare—like the monster-filled glen at Bomarzo, it was probably a bit of both. A certain freakishness and horror are hallmarks of rockwork, an art full of pitfalls.

Grottoes and boulder-strewn cascades came to France and England as part of the cult for the picturesque modeled after Vergilian landscapes, like Hubert Robert's view of the gorge at Tivoli. Some of these, as we would say, 'worked.' Many more didn't. The grotto at the entrance of the famous Désert de Retz near Paris—an ominous cave guarded by satyrs carrying torches—must have been hideous; and the Doric temple set under a crown of jagged teeth at the Folie de Saint James almost as bad. Worse was to come. In England the idea of copying an Alpine setting was introduced about 1830. Gibbon, remember, had studiously ignored the Alps near Geneva during his residence there: no classical associations. But by 1830 English travelers were converging on that centerpiece of the picturesque, the Mèr de Glace at Chamonix, and soon after we find a rockpile to represent it at Hoole House, near Cheshire. The type throve, waxing in vulgarity, until the end of the century, the climax being reached at Friar Park in the Thames valley.

Seven thousand tons of stone were hauled in to make a 'Matterhorn,' complete with models of chamois, and beehives in the form of Swiss chalets.

Such conceits began to lose their attraction with the advent of a serious interest in alpine plants, first promulgated by William Robinson, and later by Reginald Farrer, whose book *The English Rock-Garden* became a classic on both sides of the Atlantic and is still worth reading. Farrer, whose prose is high Edwardian, couldn't abide what he called 'dog's graves,' and 'devil's lapfuls.' He was a botanist of genius, and his care was for the plants—tiny, jewel-like rarities that are the only excuse for this type of garden. Your true alpinist has nothing to do with banalities like alyssum. He seeks the two-inch primrose, *P. Bilekii*, found only in the Brenner Alps, and would make the voyage to the Himalayas for a really fine specimen of *Spathoglottis ixiodes*, a high-altitude orchid. I respect all this scholarship, and the little plants are exquisite. I only wish I had ever seen an artificial setting worthy of them, one that didn't have something of a devil's lapful about it. Arrange it how you will (and I understand the trend is now toward fewer and smaller rocks, raised beds rather than a moraine), the world of miniatures is at odds with the garden as a whole. One's sense of proportion is disturbed without being charmed into credulity—the contrary of what happens with Japanese miniature landscapes, where the eye is fooled into judging size and distance to be greater than they are. The focus of the rock garden is on teeniness, and the effect is the more disconcerting when, as I often see it, the arrangement is backed against the wall of a building.

It may be that Europeans simply don't understand the principles of the rock garden, as Orientals undoubtedly do. Ostensibly, the objective is the same—to reproduce a wild landscape within a small space. But the analogies are superficial. European rockeries, especially those of earlier centuries, were representations of the *somewhere else* of romantic fancy—the Alps, Italy, even the Orient—and therefore at odds with their surroundings in a way that the Chinese and Japanese rock garden is not. These match their backgrounds to a degree not easily grasped by someone who hasn't been there. Those carved peaks wreathed in cloud, rising from inland seas, actually exist, and in the garden are merely repeated or suggested on a smaller scale. The Western version is thus an escape from the world as it is; the Eastern accepts and celebrates it.

In the Taoist philosophy that underlies the Chinese garden (and here I quote Osvald Sirén, the great authority on the subject), the earth is a living organism built up of the same elements of which man is made. The artist's task, whether he works with ink and brush or with living materials, is to employ these in such a way as to invest his creation with an expression of life, whether symbolically or literally. It follows that stones and water should have a significance we don't begin to attach to them. Stones especially. As Sirén points out, water is common in the pleasure gardens of many civilizations. Hollowed and furrowed blocks of stone (the most prized being limestone modeled by water) assembled in the form of mountains occur only in China, or in gardens under Chinese influence: 'The garden rocks are the expression of a very old cultural tradition, a deeply ingrained interest in the beauty and significance of the mineral kingdom which has been directed not only toward the "mountains" of the gardens, but also towards smaller picturesquely formed stones that are used as ornaments in dwelling-rooms or on desks—not to speak of the popular inkstones, or the most costly specimens of jade, rock crystal, or other semi-precious minerals that the Chinese have collected as eagerly as works of art.'

Given these profound differences in outlook, it isn't surprising that perhaps the least successful form of rock garden in the Western world should be our imitations of the Chinese and Japanese. These have been in vogue at intervals ever since the Jesuit reports of Chinese gardens first reached Europe, nearly always in garbled form. Sir William Chambers, who made the famous Chinese garden at Kew and may or may not have actually visited China, conceived of the Chinese landscape as a litter of pagodas, 'impending rocks in gloomy valleys,' raging torrents and heaven knows what other absurdities. Better acquaintance with the real thing produced better results, but the correct use of the Oriental idiom continued to elude European gardeners. (At one time, between 1880 and about 1907, Japanese water gardens were all the rage in England. A well-known one in Scotland, jammed with Japanese features, was made by a Miss Ella Christie, who with true Victorian grit had traveled all over the East, even into Tibet, but returned more enamored of the Japanese style than any other.) There is the story of the Japanese diplomat who on being shown an allegedly perfect copy of a Japanese garden hissed politely, 'Wonderful! Wonderful! We have nothing like it in my country.'

With the advent of modern architecture, times have changed a little. 'Oriental' gardens no longer contain lanterns, bridges and heaps of boulders. In keeping with a severer attitude toward architecture as a whole, the Japanese sand garden is now the thing to have. The inspiration for these is, of course, the celebrated stretch of raked sand punctuated by fifteen stones and enclosed by a low wall that belongs to the Ryōanji temple near Kyoto. No garden can have had the same impact within living memory, and it isn't hard to see why. In the words of Arthur Wexler, whose book, *The Architecture of Japan* (1955), was the first to call attention to it, the Ryōanji's 'field of empty space remains a tangible sign of Zen Buddhist speculation; austere, deliberate, and perhaps bitter,' which puts it perfectly in tune with modern sensibilities—and probably accounts for the failure of earlier generations to notice it. It wouldn't have appealed to the nineteenth-century fans of *japonaiserie*, who opted for Japanese prettiness. Every age makes its own borrowings from Oriental culture, which isn't to say that it always profits from them.

The Ryōanji has been exactly copied at least once—by the Brooklyn Botanic Garden, who built a replica in 1964. How many times it has been inexactly replicated or alluded to would be impossible to say, but surely it would run into the dozens. I disapprove of all of them. Even with a Japanese artisan to construct it, with sand and stones brought from Japan, the Japanese sand garden (and there are many others beside the Ryōanji which have also been copied) remains alien in every respect. You can't, for instance, set foot in it. It is a picture to be looked at, and a very beautiful one, but still outside our experience. What do those stones mean to us? Why are there fifteen and not nine? There are answers to all these questions but they aren't our answers. Buddhist myth can no more be re-created in twentieth-century America than in eighteenth-century England. Still less does American gravel set with a few boulders constitute a meditation on the meaning of Zen.

It will be seen that I have nothing useful to propose to the rock gardener, whose art I do not care for except in the Oriental context I don't think belongs here. If I were to have a rock garden, nature would have to give it to me—as well it might if I lived a mile or so inland where the characteristic New England landscape of heaved-up ledges, abrupt little cliffs and a multitude of bouldery hillsides begins. But a curious thought occurs to me: Nowhere in this neighborhood have I seen such a natural rock garden put to use by its owner. Why is this? Probably it means that rock gardens, too, are falling victims to the labor shortage, and if so, I won't be sorry.

⎯⎯⎯⎯⎯ ⬦ ⎯⎯⎯⎯⎯

ROSES

Dreadful confession for a gardener to make, my favorite rose bush is an artificial one. Made of pure gold, crumpled and pleated and adorned with a single cabochon sapphire, this masterpiece of fifteenth-century jewelwork was the gift of Aeneas Pius Piccolomini, that most sympathetic of Renaissance popes and memoirists, to his native Siena. It is just under life size, about two feet high, and realistic enough to identify as an alba, yet it is an altogether poetic conception no real rose tree could match. Or so I feel after some thirty years of looking after countless specimens of the real thing. There are times when I long for a Midas touch to transform them into artifacts and relieve me of their care.

Four rectangular rose beds were in place when we bought the property, stocked with relics of many years' neglect. I haven't much recollection of them. I knew nothing about roses in those days, but I do remember that they gave us little trouble, and so I guess that most of them were what we call old-fashioned, a vague term that generally refers to roses bred before 1900. The lone survivor, whose age I can't guess, is a cabbage or Provence type, and it is still going strong. The others may have been of the same vintage. In any case, they wintered without protection, and were free alike from aphids and black spot. We rather despised them. They didn't look half as glamorous as those we saw in the catalogues—modern hybrids elegant in form and exciting in color—and most of them bloomed intermittently, if at all, after the June outburst. So we got rid of what may have been an interesting collection, and thereby embarked on the slavery of watering, mulching, pruning, spraying for pests and diseases, that is the price of growing the modern hybrids. We hadn't anticipated that. My father managed the roses, and it was for him to learn the hard way how to cope with Japanese beetle traps, canvas hoses supposed to soak the soil without dampening the leaves, and defective sprayers. To him, it was worth it. He loved roses (many men do, for some reason), and cosseted his favorites: red-and-gold Condesa de Sastago, white Frau Druschki, above all that favorite of retired warriors, Peace—introduced in 1945.

Peace has a romantic story. It was bred by the distinguished French house of Meilland. In 1939, when Francis Meilland discovered in his nursery a ravishing rose growing from a single seed he had planted, he knew he had something extraordinary. The beginning of the war kept him from finding out exactly what. All he could do was to ship unnamed and largely untested cuttings in all directions, hoping that one or another of them would arrive safely and survive. Those consigned to the American grower Robert Pyle, in Pennsylvania, were aboard the last plane to leave France in November 1940, a step ahead of the Nazi armies. The Meillands waited for four years to learn its fate, until August 1944, when a letter arrived from Pyle. 'Whilst dictating this letter,' he wrote, 'my eyes are fixed in fascinated admiration on a glorious rose, its pale gold, cream and ivory petals blended to a lightly ruffled edge of delicate carmine. There it is before me, full of promise, and I am convinced it will be the greatest rose of the century.'

He was right. Peace was skillfully promoted. On the day Berlin fell, it was given its name at a ceremony in California, attended by rose-lovers from all over the country, at which doves were set free. When the delegates to the San Francisco Conference arrived in their hotel rooms, each found a vase containing a single specimen, and a message from the American Rose Society conveying wishes for peace and good will. But in spite of the rather crass exploitation of the name (in Germany it was called Gloria Dei, in Italy Gioia, in France simply Mme. A. Meilland), Peace deserved its acclaim as the archetypal modern rose. The pity is that it should also have the archetypal modern faults. Beautiful though it is, it has no scent; and while it is fairly hardy, it is susceptible to every rose plague in the book. It was bred for looks alone and that, by and large, has been the aim of all modern breeders.

Peace is a hybrid tea, a class introduced about a century ago, and the most widely grown rose today. The others are the floribundas, developed in the 1920's, and the grandifloras, which date from 1954. Neither is an improvement in my opinion. The floribundas (crosses of the hybrid tea and the polyantha) bloom in multiple clusters and are slightly hardier than the hybrid tea. They are nice for picking because one cut procures a whole bouquet; but they, too, have been steadily deprived of scent, and they lack the elegance of the hybrid tea. The grandifloras I haven't a good word to say for. To me, they personify every wrong tendency in rose breeding, beginning with the pointless pursuit of novelty for its own sake. They are a recross of floribundas with hybrid teas, which causes them to produce flowers that bloom in clusters like the floribunda's, only slightly larger. There are no singles (a loss), and they have a narrower color range than either parent. Few have any perfume worth speaking of; and of all the unwelcome attributes in an age of smaller gardens, the bushes can be enormous.

At the other end of the scale from these monsters are the miniatures. These have their uses as pot plants (which is what they really are), but to promote them for beds and borders, as I constantly see done, is scandalous. The tallest is less than a foot high; yet because they are roses like any others, they, too, must be deadheaded, sprayed and fertilized—presumably from a prone position. To pretend that they are suitable for gardens in the last quarter of the twentieth century, when the luckiest of us is dependent on the part-time services of a slouching adolescent or a senior citizen dying on his feet, when many gardeners are senior citizens themselves, is a pathetic example of how a business can lose touch with its logical clientele. Why not admit that they aren't for gardens, where few people plant them anyway? They are most often sold as single specimens, 'conversation pieces,' or as florist's offerings for Mother's Day. (One baby polyantha is *called* Mother's Day. Another is Happy, after one of the Seven Dwarfs—need one say more?)

The search for new colors isn't of the same order of folly. It is, or was, a pursuit that added many beautiful shades to the repertory, particularly among the golds and yellows. The first true yellow garden rose was Soleil d'Or, a hybrid tea introduced about 1910 by the French breeder Pernet-Duchet. Rose lovers owe so much to the French, whose preëminence goes back to the late Middle Ages, and who have been responsible for every major development up to and including the hybrid tea, that I often want to remind them of that old Gallic adage, *Le mieux est l'ennemi du bien*, which roughly translates as, Let well enough alone. I am thinking

just now of Ambassador, a Meilland grandiflora proudly introduced by Wayside in the 1980 catalogue. Ambassador is a glistening apricot and could be considered gorgeous if experience hadn't
made me wary of its 'fashionable orangy color.' This range, a
clamoring chorus of Sunkist oranges and corals, has increased by
leaps and bounds since the 1960's. Katharine S. White (*Onward
and Upward in the Garden*) was, I think, the first to object to
them, pointing out that they look hideous planted with other, traditionally colored roses, and alongside a lot of other flowers as
well. They need a bed apart, near marigolds or tiger lilies, and
even then their autumnal colors are a jarring note in a summer
garden. But worse is to come. We are promised a brown (or tan)
rose someday. That sounds to me like something Chanel would
have wanted to go with her Coromandel screens, not a garden
flower. The rose world, like Detroit, seems to have put its faith in
perpetually new 'styling' to attract a fickle public, and I predict
that the results will be the same.

To a great extent, they already are. Statistics show that rose-
growing is in decline in this country and has been for a long while.
Wayside's catalogue for 1960 had thirty pages devoted to roses;
in 1981, there were ten. Jackson & Perkins, once synonymous with
roses, has drastically reduced its catalogue and has diversified into
other plants. Still other companies have gone out of business.
Books talk of some 5,000 varieties being available. I would like to
know where. The average gardener who orders from catalogues, or
shops at garden centers and nurseries, has access to a couple of
dozen at most, and I sense that the supply more than meets the
demand. People have lost interest in roses. Partly this is due to the
difficulties of growing them, which breeders have done little to
alleviate. They don't seem to realize that most gardeners haven't
time to embark on elaborate programs of spraying and fertilizing,
and that environmentally sensitive gardeners refuse to spray,
whether they have time or not. All that is out of date. And so, in a
curious way, are the roses themselves with their neon colors and
disappointing fragrance.

Again, the resemblance to the American car is striking. Not for
nothing was a well-known modern rose called Chrysler Imperial.
It was christened in 1952, the heyday of the overgrown gas guzzler
with fins. Perhaps a plant ought not to be made to bear the burden
of a breeder's bad taste in nomenclature. On the other hand, there
is more than a casual relationship between the two. A flower

whose grower thinks of it in terms of advertising and brand names ceases to be a flower and becomes a product to be marketed like any other. So it proved. Until recently, dozens of new models were introduced every year, heavily promoted and allowed to lapse from sight. It often happened that a rose one liked couldn't be replaced after a year or two. Rejection by the public may have been one factor, but there were disturbing analogies with a policy of planned obsolescence. Modern hybrid roses, like modern appliances, seem made not to last. Either they succumb to cold—and I find it ridiculous that living as I do on a coastal area of the moderate Zone 6, I should have to smother bushes in salt hay and wrap the standards like mummies or bury them alive—or they suffer from premature senility.

There are signs that the rose industry may be seeing the error of its ways. Although there is still talk of finding a better spray for black spot, a rose with inbred resistance to the disease is also being worked on. Bowing to the howls of rose lovers, some breeders are also trying to recapture lost perfume. For two decades, 'moderate' or 'slight' fragrance have been code words for 'little' or 'none.' 'Strong' is now beginning to appear in catalogues. Usually, it is an exaggeration, but it does signify a change of heart.

It may be too late to bring the disaffected back into the fold. Many gardeners who still love roses have been turning back to the species, and to those old and now rare types bred before 1900 which some call 'heritage roses.' I haven't the statistics but I would venture that they are the only roses whose cultivation is increasing. Certainly the catalogues that carry them are as fat as ever. The best known, *Roses of Yesterday and Today*, put out by the late Will Tillotson's firm in California, had more than two hundred entries in 1980, the majority of them roses of yesterday. (See CATALOGUES.)

Old roses are a subject that either fascinates or bores, depending on whether you are in the mood to trace genealogies as complicated as those of the English royal family, or of a mind not to give a damn whether Henriette d'Angleterre was the mother or the sister of Charles II. It would help if one, just one, absolutely authoritative and clearly written book existed. I can testify that it doesn't. Those that do exist contradict one another on virtually every point, and are calculated to drive the researcher mad. To straighten it all out would be a life's work. I know because I've tried. Still, there are some things one ought to understand before trying to grow old roses, and I will try, in a general way, to make them clear.

Before the end of the eighteenth century, there were two distinct kinds of cultivated rose: the European and the Oriental. The European include the antique French roses (the Gallicas and centifolias); the damasks (notable for their perfume); the albas, and the musks. (In addition, there are the species roses like the dog rose, the eglantines, the rugosas, and others.) All these have certain traits in common. Their flowers are what professionals call 'unimproved,' meaning that even when the petals are multiplied a hundredfold they have a recognizable kinship with wild roses. Nearly all of them are distinguished for their powerful perfumes, derived from rose attar, a floral essence the experts have some trouble defining. The authors of *The Fragrant Year* have this to say: 'Of course, it can be claimed that all sweet-scented roses have an attar, an inexpressible oil of some sort. However, only certain roses produce true Attar of Rose. *R.* × *bifera* and closely related damasks, *R. centifolia* and its sports, and the Hybrid Provence roses have it in greatest abundance. The type Rugosas are particularly rich. . . . Then with a scent out of all proportion to their mere five petals, most American species are generously gifted with the fragrance of Mediterranean Damask.' (Elsewhere they add, confusingly, that 'Alba perfume is Damask.')

This matter of perfume is important to anyone interested in making potpourris. *The Fragrant Year* is emphatic that the roses mentioned are indispensable for the authentic rotten pot. No others will do no matter how sweetly they may smell in the garden. I have found this to be true, if one is going to use the moist method, which doesn't resort to fakery with oils and additives. The moist potpourri isn't attractive to look at. It's a brown mess to be cured and stored in a closed jar, and it lasts indefinitely. But don't try to make it with modern hybrids, which go sour or lose their odor altogether. They can be used in the so-called dry method, where the emphasis is on prettily colored petals left uncovered in a bowl, and most of the scent is supplied by additives. The two have very different results, and the dry is rather despised by connoisseurs. (But see *The Fragrant Year* for a detailed essay on both methods, and a list of twenty-five old roses most productive of attar.)

The unforgettable perfume of old roses, which comes as a surprise to noses accustomed to modern hybrids, is a delight. Whether it is sufficient reason for growing them is another question. They have drawbacks. Many of them, for example, are large bushes with long arching canes, and they take up a lot of space. More serious is their annual blooming habit. The exception is the repeating damask, *R.* × *bifera*, known to Vergil as the rose of Paestum, and in the Middle Ages as Rose des Quatre Saisons. The others rarely if ever repeat, making them poor subjects for a small rose garden. As against that, they are hardy as rocks, immune to disease, and last practically forever.

Very different are the Oriental types, those called China and tea roses, in Latin, *R. chinensis* and *R. odorata.* When they began to arrive in Europe toward the end of the eighteenth century they were a revelation to gardeners. The form was unfamiliar—high centered and finely modeled, even after the buds unfurled—and so was the scent. *R. odorata* was called tea rose because the aroma was thought to be like that of a newly opened tea chest. I rather guess the name to have come about through association, the roses and the tea having traveled from the Orient aboard the same ships. Personally, I can't detect the odor of pekoe others claim to identify in tea roses. To me they have fruity bouquets—or so I remember them. I don't get much chance to smell them any more. The tea roses I grew up with in the South aren't hardy in this climate, and that is their principal weakness. They are tropicals who possess no early warning system in their genes to alert them to approaching cold and direct them to go dormant—which is how the roses of the temperate zone save themselves from death by frost. The Chinas and the teas bloom and go on blooming until death strikes.

This trait of continuous bloom was another revelation to European gardeners, who naturally thought of cross-breeding the native races with the Orientals to produce offspring with the best qualities of both: the hardiness and strong perfumes of the European types, the refined form and everblooming characteristic of the Oriental. The history of the modern rose may be said to begin the moment that union occurred, and oddly enough, though the hybridizers were already at work, it happened by accident and far from Europe. French settlers had planted the repeating damask, *R.* × *biferia*, and the China rose we call Old Blush together in the hedgerows on the Ile de Bourbon (Réunion) in the Indian Ocean. Seedlings produced from this idyllic mating reached Paris about 1822, and the Bourbon rose was born.

To me, the Bourbons and their close relatives, the Noisettes, are the most exquisite of all the nineteenth-century roses—at once voluptuous and delicate. Their form is globular, as if they had been pressed into a teacup, and their perfumes are heavenly. They can have tremendous canes (pink Zephirine Drouhin, with copper foliage, can reach twelve feet by summer's end), and they are hardier than their China parent, though not reliably so in the North. I have grown Reine Victoria, a lovely pink Bourbon; I can't manage Maréchal Niel, a climber of vast dimensions with heavy heads of pure lemon-gold and intense tea-fragrance. So there is evidently a good deal of variation. (Confusion, too: Reine des Violettes, a deep violet, pepper-scented rose I adore is a Bourbon in *The Fragrant Year*, a hybrid perpetual in most other sources.)

These mix-ups are normal, as you discover in a jog through the literature. What, for instance, is a hybrid perpetual? This rose is a descendant of damask, China and Bourbon dynasties, but nobody seems to know what proportions of each went into it. Or how exactly to define it. It is either the last of the historical roses or the first of the modern hybrids, depending on what book you choose to follow. It is historical in the sense that it isn't being bred any more, and perhaps also because it isn't truly perpetual. It blooms inter- mittently, like the roses of an earlier day. But its size and showi- ness are modern (a hybrid perpetual could be mistaken for a Peace), and so is the frequent absence of scent. Hybrid perpetuals may have been the first garden roses to be without it. (However, they are variable in this respect: Snowy Frau Druschki, one of the finest of white roses, has no smell; Général Jacqueminot, General Jack in American gardens, is a red-velvet rose that can knock you down with its blast of perfume.) Hybrid perpetuals are essentially Victorian flowers. That is their charm. They suggest conserva- tories (though they are perfectly hardy) and sentimental courtships—American Beauty, really a French rose called Mme. Ferdinand Jamin if that makes you feel better about it, is a hybrid perpetual—and that may have accounted for their fall from grace. They dominated the rose scene for fifty years before they were more or less dropped from catalogues. Suddenly they looked old- fashioned and that, except to a few faithful fanciers, was the end of them.

Their place was taken by the hybrid teas, and I often wonder how much better than hybrid perpetuals they really are. It is true that they are everblooming. Aside from that, they are less hardy, less disease-resistant. And just as variable when it comes to scent.

In appearance they aren't dissimilar. The first hybrid tea was, in fact, mistaken for a hybrid perpetual, and the class not recognized as a separate one for some years. By most accounts, the first seedling turned up just where you would expect it—in a French nursery near Lyon. The year was 1867 and the grower was J. B. Guillot, who named his new, sweetly scented, silvery pink rose La France. It is thought to have been a cross between the pink hybrid perpetual Mme. Victor Verdier and the creamy white tea Mme. Bravy. La France became world famous, migrating even to the shores of the Black Sea, where the parents of Prince Youssoupoff, the murderer of Rasputin, had literally thousands of them growing on their terraces. The aroma drifting through the palace was one of their son's poignant memories, and is recorded in his otherwise macabre autobiography.

But La France wasn't the perfect rose, nor were its descendants. No rose ever has been that. In each succeeding step of their development, a loss has been registered along with a gain. The ancients who grew roses in the West valued them chiefly for scent, and for medicinal purposes long forgotten except by health addicts who grow rugosas for the vitamin C in the hips. Orientals grew roses for beauty, and theirs was the view that prevailed. Modern roses are much closer to their Oriental ancestors than to their European ones, more like them in appearance, in vulnerability to climate and disease, and in scent. It is strange that rose attar, so much more powerful an essence than whatever it is that imparts fragrance to the Chinas and teas, should in the end have lost out. But so it was. The odor of damask was diluted and eventually overwhelmed by the subtler aromas of the East, to the point where it vanished altogether. No modern hybrid has a trace of it.

It seems to me that no clear choice is possible. Growing the European roses bred before 1800 is inevitably tempting to romantics, who get a thrill from their very names: White Rose of York, Rosa Mundi (believed to have been named for Rosamund, mistress of Henry II), Rose of Castile. Having gone through this phase, I know the satisfactions. I also know that rose beds filled with very large bushes that won't bloom more than once a summer quickly become a bore. A shrub or two of these is sufficient, and not in beds. The same goes for the species. My Blanc Double de Coubert, a double rugosa originally planted in a bed, now occupies a space some four by eight feet near the garden shed, and is still sending up canes. It smells like the distillation of a million apple blossoms and can be detected a good fifty feet away. But it blooms in June, and hardly at all thereafter.

The nineteenth-century hybrids, which must be carefully selected according to one's climate zone, are much more rewarding and I always try to have a few in the beds. They are to the garden what fine antique furniture is to the house. They give it distinction. But the truth is I can't bring myself to turn my back entirely on modern roses. Standard bushes, which I persist in growing (see STANDARDS), are always grafts either of hybrid teas or the polyantha called the Fairy (which I reject). Then every so often a catalogue will turn up a rose that isn't to be resisted at any price. Last year, it was a hybrid tea called Paradise, a deep lavender suffused with ruby, and something close to an authentic tea scent. I don't suppose it will last. I don't, at this writing, even know if it is alive or dead under the snow of this exceptionally cold winter. But I had to have it. When it comes to roses, some of us are incurable.

───────────── ◇ ─────────────

SEEDS

Sooner or later, the northern gardener will try to get a jump on the season by planting seed of tender annuals and vegetables indoors, probably—to start with—in the kitchen window. It's a thrilling business the first time you do it, especially if you are a woman, for then you can tell yourself you are re-enacting one of the oldest of human rituals: making an Adonis garden. Adonis, you may remember, was the beautiful young nature god who fled to the underworld in winter and was resurrected each spring by Aphrodite. Women mourned his departure ('Delicate Adonis is dying'), and women celebrated his return with Adonis gardens: baskets or pots planted with quick-sprouting wheat, fennel, lettuce, barley. In ancient Mesopotamia where Aphrodite was Astarte, these charms to promote the growth of vegetation were ranged in pots along rooftops, a custom that was continued in Greece—and was the origin of pot gardening.

The Adonis cult is with us still in Christianized form. In Sicily just such pots are (or were as late as the 1930's) planted a week or two before Easter and set on the altars of churches, where they sprout on Easter morning. There, as in Greece, Aphrodite has become the Virgin Mary and pursues her Adonis/Christ in candlelit processions through the streets all the night before the Easter dawn. But though I have witnessed these ceremonies I have never been sure how the miracle of the sprouting seeds, exactly timed, was accomplished. Perhaps the women cheat a little. Why not? It is one of the few surviving rituals to acknowledge our fundamental role not only in creating life but as the inventors of agriculture. Men hunted and stole the secret of fire from the gods in order to cook meat. Women stayed home and gathered seed, planted and tended it, and Adam to the contrary, made the earliest gardens.

I was thinking of Adonis gardens when I planted my own first pot of seed one long-ago spring with Easter a couple of weeks away. I am an agnostic. I don't believe a word of any organized religion and go to church only to look at the architecture, listen to music I could hear nowhere else, or be moved in the modern manner by demonstrations of faith I don't share. And yet, that isn't quite right either. When it comes down to it, I am as superstitious as any savage about the origins of life and as disposed to propitiate the powers that govern nature. True gardeners will know what I mean. You can't work among plants for long and remain altogether an unbeliever: it is too obvious that *something is going on.* So I don't think I was guilty of anything more serious than a fit of pretentiousness when I made rather a thing of my first Adonis pot, sown with lettuce seed I hoped would sprout on Easter morning.

How unlucky, then, that the experiment proved to be a triumph for rationalism. The pot sprouted all right, on schedule too, and I was thrilled—until it became plain even to my inexperienced eyes that the little green shoots weren't lettuce but weeds in embryo, and the lettuces when they did appear soon toppled and died. The miracle would have been if they hadn't, because I had done everything wrong. The pot was much too large and deep and you don't plant seed in unsterilized garden soil without inviting damping-off, a fungus disease that destroys young seedlings. You don't learn how to sow seed by studying ancient religious practices either. You buy a book and read the directions.

I don't know how many hundreds, perhaps thousands of plants I have grown from seed since then. I grow most of my own perennials, all the biennials and a few annuals—outdoors. I raise all my

vegetables except tomatoes and eggplants, and I used to grow them
from seed too until I got tired of the fuss of indoor planting. I
don't try anything fancy, nothing that requires greenhouse conditions, but I can claim some thirty-odd years of practical experience. Why, then, should it be getting harder and not easier to
grow my own? I am prepared to say that something is going badly
wrong with American seed. I am not speaking of mislabeling,
though that is more and more common, and infuriating it is to
waste a season on an incorrectly labeled variety. I am not even
complaining about the steep increase in prices (150 percent for
farmers between 1972 and 1977—I haven't seen figures for home
gardeners), or the miserly amounts in the packets: $1.50 for *ten*
Paisley pink seeds last year. I am talking about germination, or
rather the lack of it. I was raising Canterbury bells and Siberian
wallflowers, to give but two examples, before I knew the first thing
about gardening, and never had the slightest trouble. Now I sometimes have to make two or three sowings to get a dozen plants, and
the same is true of many annuals and vegetables.

I can't fault my methods. If anything, I am more careful than I
used to be, and my soil is better. So it has to be the seed itself, and
I am all the more certain of this since I ran a couple of informal
tests by way of comparing American with foreign seed. Twice I
made simultaneous and adjacent sowings of the following with
their American counterparts: sweet William, Shirley poppies, leeks
and celeriac from France; wallflowers and laced pinks from England; *Bellis perennis* from Italy. The results were startling and
depressing, because I don't like knocking an American product.
Our seedsmen enjoy a world-wide reputation, and many European
firms carry American varieties in their catalogues. But there it is.
Not only did the European seed germinate far more rapidly and
vigorously than the American, it made sturdier plants. (Italian
seed, I should note, seems to be the most viable of all, and it comes
in big, generous packets too.)

I have no idea why this should be but I can make some guesses.
For many years now, American seedmen have been striving to
develop seeds that will do well anywhere in the country (Burpee
marks these with a bull's-eye symbol) under a wide variety of
conditions, and it would seem to me that these hybrids might be
less vigorous than the old open-pollinated varieties that evolved in
response to particular conditions of climate and soil. For it is known
that although they have higher yields, hybrids are more vulner-

able to pests and diseases than older strains (see HYBRIDS), and I see no reason why this shouldn't be true of the seed itself. Today's hybrids are bred on an ever-narrowing genetic base, which deprives them of many of their hereditary strengths, and 90 percent of our commercial seed trade is now in hybrids.

As it happens, there is a tremendous row going on about this very subject right now, and there is no foreseeable end to it. It centers on the Plant Variety Protection Act passed by Congress in 1970, and some proposed amendments before the House at the moment of writing. The amendments, which are minor, aren't important. What they have done is to call attention to the effects of the original legislation in the ten years since it was passed, and to many people these are cause for alarm. On the face of it, the law looked like a good idea. It simply authorized the U.S.D.A. to grant patents to the breeders of new varieties of open-pollinated plants—the point being that open-pollinated plants, unlike hybrids, set seeds that anyone, including the home gardener, can harvest and replant, and in theory market under his own name if he wants to go into business. (Hybrids, on the other hand, are self-protecting because they don't breed 'true,' and the seed is valueless.) Patenting clearly prevents this by granting exclusive ownership and marketing rights to the original breeder for a period of seventeen years (eighteen under the proposed amendments), and given the expense of research and development of new varieties, that seems reasonable enough, for unless it could count on the royalties accruing from exclusive ownership for a period long enough to allow it to recoup its investment, a company, or for that matter an individual, might think twice before undertaking such a search. Proponents of patenting point to the example of the Sugar Snap Pea, the smash success of the vegetable world in this decade, which was developed by a small breeder in Idaho who might never have gone to work without the protection (and prospect of future profit) offered by the Act.

Now for the other side: Since the passing of the 1970 legislation, research spending by seed companies has almost tripled, while the U.S.D.A. has reduced its funding for research to the point where public universities and agricultural experimental stations received only 9 percent of the new variety certificates issued by March 1979. Patenting has suddenly meant big money and the emergence of seed companies, once largely in private, family-owned hands, as worthwhile victims of conglomerate takeover, often by petrochem-

ical giants. Most gardeners don't know this. They see the friendly
face of David Burpee and read his message ('Dear Friends and
Fellow Gardeners') on the second page of the catalogue as of old.
But Burpee no longer belongs to the Burpee family who founded
the business in 1876. It is the property of ITT. Purex owns Ferry-
Morse, and Sandoz, Inc., a Swiss conglomerate, owns Northrup-
King. Funk Seeds International, Stewart Seeds and the Louisiana
Seed Company have been swallowed by Ciba-Geigy, while Union
Carbide has taken over the Keystone Seed Company. Shell, Mon-
santo, Pfizer, Celanese and Upjohn all have made inroads into the
seed business in recent years.

Only the most blissfully ignorant will have to be told that this is
sinister news, that the interests of these companies aren't ours. In
theory, of course, the patenting of plants safeguards the small
breeder as well as the large, but it isn't difficult to predict that
given the expense of the enterprise the big fish will devour the
small, and not impossible to imagine that if they gain exclusive
control over enough varieties of plant, they could dictate what is
grown in this country. At the very least, they could, as they already have, concentrate on varieties (often coated with fungicide),
whose survival depends on their own chemical fertilizers and
pesticides. It goes without saying that they haven't been interested
in developing pest- and disease-resistant varieties. Why should
they be when these would put them out of business? Nor does it
need pointing out that they are in a position to fix prices, which is
to say raise them to exorbitant heights, any time they choose, and
this has been a trend already felt in third-world countries.

In case all this doesn't give you fits or seem very convincing,
consider these statistics: Of the patents issued in the last ten years,
30 percent went to five companies or their subsidiaries. Three hold
81 percent of the patents for beans, two hold 41 percent of those
on peas, and four have 58 percent of the patents on lettuce. I ask
myself whether I am to believe that there is no connection between these facts and my dissatisfaction with the seeds I buy.
Manifestly there is, even though I can't define it exactly and even
though the vegetables seem to have been more affected than the
flowers. But there, too, I can speculate on if not prove the possible
consequences of monopoly. Flowers aren't big business today, and
the few exceptions are precisely those—marigolds, petunias, zinnias—that are subjected to intensive breeding by the bigger
companies. Those that aren't best sellers are falling by the wayside

or soon will—exactly what is happening with food crops, which are more and more confined to a few commercial blockbusters: wheat, corn and soybeans. And for this reason I further suspect, but can't prove, that those few companies that still offer a wide variety of flower seed may not monitor the seed of the less popular flowers as carefully as they should. It could be that in spite of germination percentages and dates printed by law on the packets, the seed isn't as fresh as it is supposed to be and may have been stored from unsold surpluses in previous years.

I hasten to add that I don't *know* that any of this is true (I don't, after all, want to be sued for libel). I only say it could be, and if it isn't there has to be some other explanation, and I wish somebody would tell me what it is.

SEED TAPES

Many catalogues, notably Burpee's, offer these ridiculous devices designed for the gardener too stupid to sow seed by himself—and of course charge extra for them; and to put it plainly, they are a swindle. Anyone who can't scrape a shallow trench with a hoe, then walk down it scattering seed from a packet, had better abandon gardening forthwith. Seed tapes are clumsy affairs that have to be unwound and maneuvered into position, then covered with soil exactly as naked seed is. But they don't germinate any better than seed does—rather worse, the difference being that when seed is sown by hand, the inevitable blank spots can be filled with seeds kept in reserve in the packet. When four out of ten seeds imbedded in a tape fail to come up, there is nothing to do about it.

SEEING EYE

The gentian has rather unattractive branches. Yet there is something to be said for it: when all the other flowers have been withered by frost, its colours stand out brilliantly.

Though the amaranth can hardly rank among the more impressive flowers, it is pretty enough as a shrub. Its name is disagreeable, but, written in Chinese characters, it reminds one that the amaranth blooms when the wild geese arrive . . .

The round-leaved violet has little to distinguish it from the common violet; when they have faded, one cannot possibly tell them apart, which I find rather a pity.

The moonflower resembles the althea, and their names are closely related. The flower itself is attractive, and it is really a shame that the gourds on which it blossoms are so ugly. I wonder why this pretty plant should produce such graceless fruit. Instead of gourds, it should have winter cherries or something of the sort. Yet, as soon as I recall the name, 'evening face,' I find the moonflower charming . . .

The bush-clover blossoms prettily with deep purple flowers; and, as it bends down, dampened by the morning mist, it is a most delicate sight. I have heard that this is the stag's favorite plant and that he frequently stands near it; this gives me a very special feeling . . .

When one examines a rose closely, one finds the branches unpleasing; but its flowers are no less beautiful for that. After it has been raining and the sky clears, what can be prettier than a great cluster of roses, growing by the water's edge or near steps of unpeeled log, when the evening glow shines down on them?

> *The Pillow Book of Sei Shōnagon*
> Translated by Ivan Morris

It is hard to believe that Shōnagon wasn't a gardener but a lady-in-waiting to the Empress Sadako during the last decade of the tenth century A.D. Her celebrated diary is full of such exact observations on plants, which remind us that sensibility alone isn't enough. She had plenty of that. She also noticed how many things grew, and when, and where. Nature lovers, take note.

STANDARDS

A rose-tree stood near the entrance of the garden: the roses on it were white, but there were three gardeners at it, busily painting them red. Alice thought this a very curious thing, and she went nearer to watch them, and just as she came up to them she heard one of them say, 'Look out now, Five! Don't go splashing paint over me like that!'

'I couldn't help it,' said Five, in a sulky tone. 'Seven jogged my elbow.'

On which Seven looked up and said 'That's right, Five. Always lay the blame on others!'

'*You*'d better not talk!' said Five. 'I heard the Queen say only yesterday you deserved to be beheaded!'

LEWIS CARROLL
Alice's Adventures in Wonderland

I date my affection for rose trees—and all standards—to that passage, read aloud to me when I was about five, and to Tenniel's illustration, which it will be remembered has the rose tree looming large over the playing cards who are painting it. These seemed about my size, and the rose tree therefore immense; but that didn't surprise me. There were no rose trees on the tropical island where we then lived (and *Alice* was read to me in West Indian accents by my black nurse), but plants just as curious grew in our garden: banana trees, crotons marked like serpents. It wasn't the least of Carroll's genius to detect the underlying menace that all densely planted gardens hold for children. Our West Indian one, in addition to the curious plants, was populated by 'obeahs,' a kind of ghost, and a version of the Tar Baby vividly described by the servants. I had no trouble believing in Carroll's talking flowers and creatures saved from quaintness by their hateful personalities. (I kept a pet tarantula myself.) I still haven't. I recall the insolence of tiger lilies whenever I look at them. And I go on pining for a giant rose tree.

Unfortunately, I can't grow even a small one with any security in this climate, for rose trees are at the perilous edge of hardiness in New England. Like other hybrid roses, they are grafted, but whereas on a rose bush this vulnerable point occurs almost at ground level where it can be covered with earth or straw, on a stand-ard it is several feet above the ground and almost impossible to protect. The method most often recommended is to ease them over on their sides so that they lie flat, and then to heap them with earth. I don't find this feasible. A prone rose tree covered with earth makes an impressive looking grave, and there is no way I can see to keep it from flattening everything in the vicinity for a dis-tance of several feet. I have accordingly tried other ways, once going so far as to construct wooden towers bound in burlap and stuffed with straw. The towers were rather like those used in northern Europe to protect valuable marble statues. In a village garden they looked ridiculous, and in the end were a failure. When the rose trees didn't actually die, they were so severely killed back that they never recovered their pristine symmetry. The only form of rose tree guaranteed to survive this far north is the polyantha called the Fairy, covered with clusters of baby-pink blossoms, a far cry from Tenniel's voluptuous blooms, which I guess to have been that Victorian favorite, the hybrid perpetual. As I have said, I don't like the Fairy at all. (Or, for other reasons, many of the modern hybrids used for rose trees today. The flower stems are too long but that is another story—see PRUNING.)

Other standards present fewer problems as far as hardiness is concerned. Dwarf fruits, hydrangeas, evergreen euonymous, cotoneasters, wisteria, hollies, flowering almond, lilacs, all are perfectly hardy and can in theory be turned into standards. The question is: Who will do it? I can count on the fingers of one hand the nurseries that supply standard shrubs by mail order. Either there isn't enough demand or the labor isn't there to do the job. The cost is clearly prohibitive, and is reflected in the prices such standards fetch if you can find them. The alternative that suggests itself to the enterprising is therefore to have a crack at it, and I wish I could say that I have done this successfully. I can't count my potted kitchen plants—rosemary, scented geraniums, bay—all of which I standardize. They are child's play. Nor would it be fair to include my ten-year struggle to standardize a wisteria on the lawn: I started too late and it was well on its way to becoming a hopeless tangle before I set my mind to it. I did manage to stand-ardize a couple of yews but that was largely unintentional. In the deep shade where they had been planted they fought so hard to reach the light that their trunks were already bare and all I had to do was shape their rather spindly tops.

They do, however, suggest one of the first principles of standardizing: finding a plant with an inclination toward a single trunk, which by pruning and patience can be trained to grow upward and make a ball at the top. The process can take years, yet it is well within the capabilities of the average gardener. A much faster way to produce standards, and one that increases their chances of survival, is by grafting, as is done with roses; and that is another matter. It isn't that grafting by itself is hard to master. Having assisted with the grafting of young fruit trees in my time, I know it isn't, and books give full directions. The stumbling block is what is called compatibility between scion (the crown) and rootstock (the stem), for if there is no affinity between them the graft will fail. Since grafting is one of the oldest practices in horticulture, you might think that the facts about compatibility would long since have been established, and lists of what goes with what would be easily obtainable. You would be wrong. The facts are still very much up in the air, and no book that I know of is prepared to give more than a few examples of grafted standards and the materials they are made of.

Grafting to the ancients was something of an outdoor sport. They would try anything. Columella gives directions for grafting olives to figs. Other writers speculated that oranges grafted to pomegranates might produce blood-oranges, and roses to holly, evergreen roses. These theories are derided today. But although a union between plants belonging to different genera is in some books called next to impossible, there are notable exceptions. Pears can be grafted to hawthorns, lilacs to privet. The *R.H.S.* even has examples of bizarre grafts said to have succeeded between members of widely different families: sunflowers on melons, cabbage on tomato, aster on phlox. On the other hand, while it is by and large to be expected that grafts between members of the same species will take, they don't always. A scion of *Magnolia Soulangiana* won't necessarily grow on rootstock of other magnolias randomly chosen: It prefers *M. Kobus* or *M. tripetala*. Furthermore, grafts within a species may work in one direction—plum on peach—and not the other. One begins to think the ancients weren't so crazy after all. Experiment is still possible, and in *Time-Life's Pruning and Grafting*, it is strongly suggested that this is an enticement to would-be amateur grafters.

I don't agree. Just as amateur cooks don't want to be told to 'use your imagination' in concocting a dish, neither do amateur gardeners want less than precise ingredients and measurements. Experiment is for those who already know the rules—and therefore don't need books. What I require in this case isn't the incentive to experiment but to know the names of hardy shrubs that can be successfully standardized by grafting, and what materials to use for both scions and rootstock. *Pruning and Grafting* tells how to make a rose tree (which I already know, as most gardeners who grow them do); a standard false cypress; a weeping cherry standard (*Prunus subhirtella* on *P. Mahaleb*); little ivy trees that, if one tried to produce them without grafting, with mature ivy, would take twenty-five to thirty years—these, a graft of *Hedera helix* Manda's Crested on a fatshedera trunk, can be had in three or four. Appetite whetted, one looks for more. There isn't any. The other standards shown are of the type made by pruning and training. All are tender plants—geraniums, fuchsias, azalea, lantana, ficus—grown in pots, and in fact not hard to find at greenhouses and garden centers, though their popularity is a mystery to me in light of the problems of carrying them over to another season in this climate. A greenhouse is needed if one isn't to lay out $35 or $40 for what amounts to an annual (don't imagine they can spend the winter in the living room)—and the same objection applies to starting them from scratch oneself. No: I am looking for hardy outdoor specimens: little holly trees; the weeping *Cotoneaster apiculata* standards I see in Wayside's catalogue; Korean lilacs such as I already own, whose rootstock looks to me exactly like privet, though the *R.H.S.* informs me that the use of privet for this purpose is 'universally condemned.' I would also like to try *Kerria japonica* (could that be done?), *Deutzia gracilis* (could that?) and half a dozen more. But I don't know where to begin with any of them. I don't even know what is surely an essential distinction: which should be produced by pruning and training, which by grafting? The first would be well within my reach, the second probably far beyond it. And I am not putting the blame on *Pruning and Grafting*. Other textbooks I am aware of aren't nearly so informative. Anyone can see what the trouble is. I am trying to enter a rich man's world, where one hires a landscape architect or expert gardener who might or might not be able to produce the specimens I want.

STRAWBERRIES

The work in the vegetables—Gertrude Stein was undertaking for the moment the care of the flowers and box hedges—was a full-time job and more. Later it became a joke Gertrude Stein asking me what I saw when I closed my eyes, and I answered, Weeds. That, she said, was not the answer, and so the weeds were changed to strawberries. The small strawberries, called by the French wood strawberries, are not wild but cultivated. It took me an hour to gather a small basket for Gertrude Stein's breakfast, and later when there was a plantation of them in the upper garden our young guests were told that if they cared to eat them they should do the picking themselves.

ALICE B. TOKLAS
The Alice B. Toklas Cookbook

Large-fruited strawberries are among the many plants to have been discovered in the Americas, taken to Europe to be hybridized, and returned to us in improved forms that American growers then proceeded to develop still further. There are now varieties adapted to every climate zone in the country, and American strawberries, unless shipped out of season from long distances, are second to none. It would therefore seem the height of folly to turn to the smaller, less productive European species often called *fraises des bois* or wild strawberries—which they are not. The commonest, *Fragaria vesca*, was transplanted to the kitchen gardens of the Louvre in the 1600's; the Alpine strawberry, virtually indistinguishable from *F. vesca*, has been in cultivation since the eighteenth century. These and other European strawberries resemble the wild not because they have been plucked from some woodland habitat but because they don't hybridize well—as one source puts it, 'Long cultivation neither improved the flavour of the fruits nor greatly increased their size.'

So why grow them in preference to the big, luscious natives? Snobbery pure and simple, and I speak with authority because I must have been among the first to respond to those classy ads for *fraises* the White Flower Farm ran, and still runs, in *The New Yorker*. I grew them for years around my rose beds, and charming they were to look at, like an old engraving with their starry flowers and tiny fruit. But they weren't perfect, even as an edging. They grow unevenly, some into big clumps, some into scraggy little ones, and while they don't produce runners, they do seed themselves all over the place; and the clumps must be regularly divided. And what of the taste? A dish of *fraises*, rustling like taffeta and with a squeeze of orange over it, brings coos of delight from those who have eaten them, preferably under a pergola, in some foreign restaurant: pleasure by association. Their flavor isn't a patch on that of a fat, home-grown strawberry of American ancestry. And the gardener who serves them, whether he mentions it or not, has gone through hell to harvest them. Eternities pass on hands and knees before enough are assembled to make a dessert for six. It isn't an occupation for the middle-aged, and like Alice Toklas I have given it up.

Had I the space I would grow large-fruited strawberries for eating. I haven't, but I no longer consider *fraises* a substitute. Such as survive in my garden, and many do in odd spots, are solely for decorative purposes.

———— ∿ ————

SWEET PEAS
(*Lathyrus odoratus*)

————

Gardeners of a certain age complain so systematically that flowers don't smell the way they used to that the young must be tired of hearing us. Sceptical, too, for isn't this just another variation on the everything-was-better-before-you-were-born theme? I have wondered about this myself. Maybe violets, pansies, roses, the old blue iris we called flag lilies, hawthorn, syringa, really weren't the perfume factories we think we remember. Above all, what about sweet peas, which are so far from smelling as one is positive they did? Well, about the others there may be argument. Though it is unquestionably true that many qualities are deemed more important than scent in modern flowers—size, color, ease of cultivation —we may exaggerate the proportionate loss of perfume. About sweet peas we are right. Any catalogue confirms it: 'heat-resistant,' 'early,' 'larger flowers,' 'don't need staking'—these are the come-ons mentioned, with nary a word about their *raison d'être*, that exquisitely light and delicate yet penetratingly sweet odor which gives them their name. It isn't mentioned because it has all but disappeared.

The old scented grandiflora sweet peas—Miss Willmott, Queen Alexandra, The Honorable Mrs. Collier, names that summon up an Edwardian dinner party—went out sometime around World War I, to be superseded by the Spencer hybrids, bred for large ruffled flowers, and by other strains whose emphasis was on early blooming, dwarfness, or some other quality, not scent. According to the R.H.S. journal, *The Garden* (July 1979), the impression that they steadily lost perfume in the process isn't 'just a prejudice in favor of old-fashioned flowers.' When a modern Spencer cultivar, Leamington, sported back to the grandiflora form a few years ago, the scents could be directly compared. In Leamington, the smell was 'pleasant but weak'; in the sport, 'strong and heady.'

In England efforts have been made to preserve some of the older varieties (Thompson & Morgan carries a selection called Antique Fantasy), even those that antedate the grandifloras: Painted Lady, grown since the eighteenth century, and Original, a cultivated throwback to the red and blue Mediterranean species. In the United States we have to make do with the modern hybrids, and I don't think they pay their way. There are three kinds: the vine types, five to ten feet; an intermediate bush type called, I'm afraid, Knee-Hi; and the eight- to ten-inch varieties that form little mounds. The climbers, of course, need a trellis, and so in my opinion do the intermediate varieties about two-and-a-half-feet tall that are said not to. They sprawl. All three require what is called adequate soil preparation, a tactful way of describing a trench two feet wide and one foot deep filled with 40 percent cow manure, 40 percent loam and 20 percent sand, to a level four inches short of ground level. The seeds should be inoculated with a specially purchased culture of nitrogen-fixing bacteria, then soaked in tepid water before planting, in very early spring. As the seedlings sprout and start to grow, soil is added to the trench at the rate of one-half inch for every two inches of growth. Pinch the seedlings to induce branching, mulch and water regularly.

Those are the directions. Follow them carefully and if you live in the far north you may get flowers for most of the summer. (Night temperatures must fall below 65 degrees, though there are one or two varieties advertised as heat-resistant.) Or you may not. The only times I tried modern sweet peas, they were miserable disasters. I don't feel too badly about this because I can tell from books that they are now classified as temperamental. *Wyman*, for one, remarks that, 'As the varieties introduced became larger, it seemed they became more difficult to grow in the out-door garden.' In other words, they have graduated from the back-yard to the greenhouse in a couple of generations. No wonder I almost never see them any more. The hybridists are to be con-gratulated.

Here again, memory supplies a totally different picture: a few seeds pressed into one's hot little hand, a few bits of string tied to a fence, and *voilà*—a crop of lovely flowers for one's very own. I'm sure I'm not wrong that sweet peas were often given to children to grow, presumably because they were so easy, and that I grew them. I have no recollection of trenches or inoculants, only of lovely colors and a never-to-be-forgotten scent. The colors are still there, but the last time somebody brought me a bunch of florist's sweet peas and I smelled them—what a dusty little madeleine! No power there to summon the memory of things past.

--- ⌒ ---

TOADS

Bufo vulgaris is the rude Latin name bestowed on this little am-phibian, indicating that it has had a poor press for a long time. A 'toad' is 'a person considered as an object of contempt or aversion,' a 'toadeater' an 'obsequious parasite, a sycophant,' a 'toadstool' supposed to be an inedible or dangerous mushroom—though toad-stools and mushrooms are one and the same. I can't think what toads have done to earn such opprobrium. They are wholly bene-ficial presences in the garden and in greenhouses are considered a necessity, so much so that some books advise introducing them if they aren't already there, though how to go about this isn't stated. Small boys used to catch toads, and be warned they would de-velop warts in consequence. I don't see small boys catching toads these days, or small boys with warts, so perhaps there was some-thing to the theory. Alas, I no longer see the toads either in my own garden. A former colony was possibly destroyed by the cat, and I miss them.

Toads feed on slugs, sowbugs and other nuisances and should be encouraged to take up residence. They hunt at night and during the day like warm, dark places. An inverted flower pot with a hole knocked into it to make a door, set in a sheltered place, will attract a toad if it is already in the neighborhood. But toads don't seem to have the communication system that birds do. The birds discovered at once that the cat is no longer with us. The toads continue to absent themselves. Obviously, a creature with such a loathsome reputation wouldn't figure on the endangered list. Too many people would say good riddance. But I wonder about them. *Are* they dying out? I pray not. I want my vulgar little buffoons back.

———— ∾ ————

TOMATO
(*Lycopersicum esculentum*)

————

The decline and fall of the commercial American tomato is a *cause celèbre*, but the tomato isn't the only vegetable to have suffered from modern methods of growing and shipping. Iceberg lettuce; topless carrots and half-spoiled spinach packed in plastic bags; turnips and cucumbers dipped in wax; overgrown string beans—not to speak of melons and stone fruits shipped so unripe they would make effective ammunition in a street fight—all these are evidence that Americans, basking in the belief that they are the best-fed people in the world, will put up with almost anything. How wonderful that we can buy tomatoes and corn on the cob in January! Wonderful indeed, until you taste them. The corn is bad enough. The tomatoes make a more vivid symbol. Green when picked, prematurely ripened with shots of ethylene gas, stored in coolers at 38 degrees before they are put on sale, sometimes also dipped in wax to make them shine, they are the nadir of insulted nature. Yet millions buy and eat them, and I have actually heard people say they prefer them to the drippy home-grown product.

Home-grown tomatoes nevertheless keep their prestige. They

are the most widely raised of all vegetables and so far have been largely immune to the outrages committed on the commercial types. But there are signs that this is changing as corrupted taste goes about the task of corrupting absolutely. High-quality fruits and vegetables in America have traditionally been sold—and eaten—by first-generation immigrants, people who apply old-world standards to produce. With succeeding generations, these standards tend to disintegrate and the inferior becomes the norm. Worse, clever merchandising convinces the ignorant that defects are virtues. I am thinking, for one example, of mozzarella, in Italy a cheese that tears into soft, wet ribbons, in America a dessicated lump. Yet one brand proudly announces itself as 'low in moisture,' another as 'moisture free.'

Now I see the same insidious method being applied to tomatoes in the seed catalogues, where the distinction between fruit raised for the home garden and for the commercial market used to be clear. In some, it still is. Stokes carries the infamous Square Paste, an accurate name for a repulsive product, but does state it to be for bulk harvesting. Another commercial variety called Basket Vee is said to have 'excellent tolerance for cat-facing.' Tolerance for, in seed catalogue jargon, means the opposite: resistance to—and you will read that a tomato has tolerance also for fusarium wilt, which doesn't signify that it takes kindly to the wilt. What cat-facing means I'm not sure—I might be tempted by a tomato with a face like a cat's. In any event Basket Vee isn't for me. It is advised for 'green ship picking,' and I do know what that means.

More disturbing is Stokes's claim that it is better than Red Pak in most areas. Now Stokes doesn't carry Red Pak. Harris, however, does, and commends it highly for home gardens, and given the comparison with Basket Vee, it sounds like a commercial tomato. The description bears this out: 'Almost solid meat . . . can be kept much longer after picking too.' This is getting dangerously close to supermarket standards, and Harris, I'm sorry to say, isn't alone in commending the tomatoes with 'practically solid flesh,' 'solid meat with fewer seed cavities.' (Gurney even offers a 'hollow' tomato, all wall with no flesh or seeds, a prefabricated receptacle for tuna-fish salad.) But the flesh of a good eating tomato *shouldn't be solid*. It should resemble an archipelago broken up with lakes of seed—which are vital to flavor. Peeled and salted and left to stand for a few minutes, such a tomato exudes a good tablespoonful of juice and is slippery as an eel to handle. It is also sublime, but how will future generations, raised on the juiceless, seedless slab, know that?

Just as ominous is the emergence of the home-grown tomato with keeping qualities, the equivalent of the long 'shelf-life' desired by all producers of food in America. Burpee introduced a variety bred especially for storage in 1979. It is called Long-Keeper, and though it 'can't compare with the ripe, juicy Big Boys and Big Girls eaten fresh from the vine,' the claim is that Long-Keeper is superior to store-bought fruit in winter. I don't doubt that—no lower standard of comparison could be found—but in winter I eat tomatoes out of a can or not at all.

Then there is 'acid.' Many of today's tomatoes are touted as being 'low in acid,' or having 'a rich, sub-acid flavor,' an oxymoron. A tomato without acid is practically tasteless, and incidentally poses a threat of botulism when preserved that wasn't present in the older varieties. Presumably the word 'acid' is in itself objectionable, with connotations of the 'stomach acid' that haunts the TV screen. Or does the national sweet tooth actually demand a sugary tomato? Both Burpee and Harris carry a cherry tomato called Sweet 100, and several other varieties are recommended for 'sweetness,' alternatively 'mildness'—in either case sounding more like pipe tobacco than a once robustly acidulous fruit.

For all these reasons, I study catalogues carefully before ordering seed, or (as I now do) buying plants at the garden center. Faced with several dozen varieties and a salesperson hired for the summer, consequently with no more knowledge of plants than of cabinet-making, one needs to know by name what one is looking for, and why. For instance, and in addition to their other qualities, are the plants determinate or indeterminate? The trouble with growing a common vegetable is that one tends to assume there isn't much to be learned about it and doesn't consult books. It never occurred to me to look up tomato culture, and so for years I didn't know there were two kinds of tomato vine. I did notice that some stopped growing and producing rather early in the season while others threatened to climb the walls and fruited until frost; but I put the difference down to chance or having bought a lemon. Not so. Early tomatoes are determinate, meaning that they grow to moderate size, make their crop, and die. They don't take up much room and rarely need staking. Main-crop tomatoes are indeterminate, i.e., will grow until the tops are pinched out to stop them, and require large stakes or wire cages, whichever you prefer by way of support.

They also need pruning—another aspect I failed to investigate and hadn't heard of until someone said casually, 'I see you don't prune your tomatoes.' Ashamed to confess I didn't know what he was talking about, I agreed that pruning wasn't my policy—then hastily tried to remedy my ignorance. I didn't get very far. 'Pinch out all lateral or side shoots as they develop,' said one book. But wouldn't that leave the vine denuded? 'Pinch off all suckers that form between the fruit cluster and the flower cluster higher up, except the one immediately below the fruit cluster,' said another, and I couldn't make head or tail of that, though at least I had learned the purpose of pruning: Unpruned, indeterminate tomatoes sprawl all over the place, an individual plant covering as much as nine square feet, and they can't be staked as I had always tried to do, gathering the whole, unwieldy mass together and lashing it to a giant pole or poles which sooner or later collapsed under their weight.

Pruned tomatoes, which are really a form of espalier, are confined to no more than three fruiting stems and are therefore easily trained to a pole. They produce less fruit than the jungle-like, unpruned vines, and you make up for that by putting in more plants, which can also be planted much closer together—eighteen inches or so—than the ones left to run riot. Thus you arrive at a neat, easily cultivated and managed row of vines instead of a daunting sprawl—not an important consideration if you are growing tomatoes on a farm, but in a small vegetable plot like mine one that makes all the difference.

How to go about this famous pruning? It shames me to admit that it wasn't until the publication of Thalassa Cruso's *Making Vegetables Grow* (1975) that I fully grasped the principle, there set forth in plain English with an accompanying diagram. Twenty-five years is a long time to wait, but for those who are as dim as I am about these things, here it is. 'Main-crop plants grown in a small yard do best if pruned to three stems and tied to a trellis. The pruning consists of allowing the two lowest shoots that appear in the leaf axils to remain and turn into fruiting stems that are also tied in. *The shoots grow in the crotch where a leaf stalk meets the main stem* (my italics). Except for those that are to remain, all the others should be snapped out with a downward motion while they are still small.' (To this, I would add only that the fruiting stems that are allowed to remain also produce shoots or suckers that grow at a 45-degree angle between the leaf stalks and the main stem and that these must also be removed, so that the pruning must in fact go on all summer.)

I read of all sorts of menaces to tomatoes, including the risk that because mosaic virus is present in tobacco, and as I am a heavy smoker, I might transmit the infection through my hands. (Thus far I have seen no signs of having done so.) As to bugs, tomatoes possess a built-in repellent called solanine that protects them from many pests. Not, however, from the hornworm, in appearance the most frightening of creatures, a green-and-black-striped dragon with horns that if it were a foot long would send one screaming for help. At two inches, he is so brilliant an example of camouflage that it is possible to look right at him for many minutes without seeing him, obvious though his presence is from the gnawed leaves and fruits that accompany his progress. Sprays will kill the hornworm. I brace myself and cut him in half with scissors. He is the only enemy I recognize as such, and he doesn't come every year or in any quantity. Of blights I know nothing. We are perhaps a lucky neighborhood: I don't hear of them elsewhere in the village either, and most of us grow tomatoes if little else in the way of vegetables. That fact speaks for itself. At one time, when decent commercial tomatoes were still available, not many people grew them, and I made friends by giving my surplus away. Today, even those who garden reluctantly have been driven to put in a plant or two. To that extent the debasers of this noble fruit are perhaps to be thanked. They may have started a counter-revolution.

TOOLS

Of all implements, those used in gardening have changed the least. The hoe, equipped with a shell, antler, or animal scapula before the development of bronze or wrought iron, is prehistoric. Wooden rakes were known to the earliest Egyptians. Spades, sickles, pruning knives, all are of extremely ancient origin. Down the ages, wherever garden work is illustrated, the tools are instantly recognizable. Farmers and gardeners are notoriously conservative, but this is a simple matter of form following function, and since the functions have changed little, so have the forms—infinite though the variations are from country to country to country, and in Europe, even within a country. According to Anthony Huxley's *Illustrated History of Gardening* (1978), a book no gardener should deny himself, every county in Britain once had its distinctive spade and to a lesser extent still does; while in Belgium twenty-two patterns are currently available. Some nations prefer long handles, others short, etc., but serious structural changes are rare, and significant improvements rarer still—something to keep in mind before plunging into new gadgetry. If anything the trend has been downhill since the end of the nineteenth century, showing a steady decline in ingenuity and specialization.

One of Huxley's illustrations, for example, shows an array of equipment sketched by John Evelyn in 1656, and with the exception of a lawn mower it includes everything the modern gardener could reasonably require, and then some. The pruning shears mounted on a pole and operated with a pull-cord look more efficient than the cumbersome affair that lives in my shed; so does a swan-necked trowel—and here is the two-wheeled cart so many of us prefer to the wheelbarrow, but that wasn't available in this country until the last decade. The double-spouted watering can looks handy too. Elsewhere in the book are sophisticated fruit-pickers for harvesting delicate fruits like pears and grapes, one with little paddles covered with soft leather (early nineteenth century); glass tubes fixed to metal rods, into which a piece of paper with the name of the plant could be inserted and sealed—these from the Pitti Palace in Florence; a beautiful leaf-gathering net from old China, with a drawstring to close it when full (why cannot some present-day genius reproduce that?), a folding ladder mounted on a wheel for easy transport (ditto).

Modern gardening implements are supposed to be improvements on the old in two important ways: the use of stainless steel rather than iron and the addition of power. I can accept stainless steel, and even admit that a stainless steel tool probably *is* better than iron. But they aren't going to separate me from my heavy old iron trowel with an ash handle, or my ancient rakes and spades made of the same materials. Power tools I loathe, and except for power saws for the limbs of large trees, won't admit they do a better job than their predecessors. Electric hedge trimmers and edgers are easily defeated by heavy growth, gnawing rather than cutting the foliage, and if battery-operated, can be counted on to run out of juice long before the project is complete. Those to be hooked up to an outlet aren't practical either unless one is prepared to electrify the garden, which I neither want nor can afford; and the alternative is hundreds of feet of cord to be dragged across flower beds and around shrubs and trees in order to reach the areas most in need of clipping. Of power mowers I speak elsewhere (see LAWNS).

Now and again, centuries of inconvenience do inspire someone to conceive a genuine improvement. That has apparently happened to the long-armed pruner made of heavy wooden sections awkwardly fitted together, with a cord guaranteed to twine itself around the pole as you pull on it to activate the parrot's-beak pruner at the end. The original model seems to have been around since Roman times and I have never looked at mine without wondering why they couldn't design a telescopic aluminum pole with the cord inside. Well, I have had to rewrite this essay to include the information that somebody has. Brookstone's 1980 summer catalogue contains that very thing—brand-new, for it certainly wasn't there last year or I would have ordered it. What is wrong with it, and something is bound to be, remains to be seen. Meanwhile, we continue to be afflicted with watering cans with handles too close to the opening to fit conveniently under a faucet, hoses that develop instant leaks and freeze into coils like a serpent with rigor mortis, toppling 'tomato towers.' The list is endless. Everything made of plastic is of course abominable, but poor design is the real root of one's frustrations. One has only to look at some of the devices on the market to see that they won't work. Others, more irritatingly, betray their flaws only after a little use. Take the sprinkler that sends a fan of water waving over a lawn. The settings are increasingly hard to adjust and after a year or so can't be read because the lettering has worn off. Another, called Water Bird, is a superior article that can be made to water a whole circle or a segment of one. But it takes a good fifteen minutes and the risk of a soaking to get the settings right and the spray is difficult to control. Canvas soakers kink unless set in a straight line, and impede the flow of water. And these are marvels of design compared to sprayers for the home garden, of which the worst is the type that must be pumped to the explosion point before it will release the spray. I believe I have tried them all and I haven't found a single one that didn't have a defect. The one I now use, a plastic container attached to a simple trombone pump (which, however, leaks in some unfixable way) is light and works fairly well. It is also too small and marked for litres, not very helpful to someone like myself who still lives in the dark age of pints, quarts and gallons.

That Americans aren't a race of gardeners is evident enough from the range of tools offered in most stores. But something more is involved. Senseless fiddling with objects of proven worth is characteristic of our society. Plumbers and electricians tell me they have the same problem, and the automobile industry has gone bust on the principle. The voice of experience is never consulted, and the gardener is no more slighted in this respect than the builder, the driver, the housewife. They don't ask *us* because we would either declare ourselves satisfied with what we have, or suggest changes that would be pronounced infeasible. W. H. Auden says somewhere that men should be allowed to invent whatever they like but women be the ones to decide how it is used. Yes indeed, and I would attach a further amendment: Let the engineers design whatever they want to, but make them use it themselves before it is put on the market.

For gardeners, the situation is compounded by our being too few to make an impact. Cooks do better, because so-called gourmet cookery is now an occupation worth catering to. As with automobiles, the pattern was set by large numbers of people buying imported products: ten years ago every sophisticated kitchen tool came from Europe or Asia, and the Cuisinart gained ascendancy at about the same time as the Toyota and the Volkswagen. With the same result: the belated recognition by American manufacturers that consumers (what a word, really) aren't idiots and may actually know what they want and why. And at this point American copies of foreign models began to flood the market. Unfortunately, I don't see the same thing happening to us gardeners. Ours is a dying art, and though we, too, seek foreign-made implements (I think of English copper watering cans; Wilkinson Sword Blade pruners), no American manufacturer is likely to notice and try to satisfy us with homemade equivalents. For one thing, few if any companies can be identified any more with garden tools. Sprayers are made by the manufacturers of pesticides and weed-killers; spreaders (which I don't use and so can't judge) by a division of the chemical company that wants you to use its fertilizer. Plastics manufacturers looking for new markets get into all sorts of areas they don't understand, or care to. Nine-tenths of what they produce is junk and recognized as such by those who buy it because they don't know where to turn for something better.

All my basic gardening tools (trowel, spade, shovel, rakes, claw for cultivating, secateurs, hoe) were bought more than thirty years ago from the kind of store that used to be a sort of hardware heaven. Vast, ill-lighted, manned by laconic staff who wouldn't have dreamed of boasting that they, in fact, could provide just about anything you had in mind—if not on the main floor, somewhere in the cavernous attic, where a friend of mine once ran across an ancient hay wain—this dream-palace stocked hand-cranked ice-cream freezers, pronged ice-shavers, stone crocks, coal scuttles, as well as every imaginable old-fashioned and solidly made garden tool, right up to the black day in the late 1960's when they went out of business and were replaced by a store called Unisex, whose specialty was blue jeans. It was a blow from which a lot of us have never recovered. My tool purchases of any consequence are now few and far between and all confined to firms in Vermont and New Hampshire that are the last bastions of quality. (Brookstone is one; Garden Way Research, the source for two-wheeled carts, the other—see CATALOGUES.) I'm sorry about this élitism, and would be happy to widen the field if that were possible. And anyone wanting to get into the specialized business of manufacturing well-designed garden tools has my cantankerous and opinionated services at his disposal—for nothing.

———— ❧ ————

TREE HOUSES

In my youth, when Kipling's *Jungle Books* were still part of literate Anglo-Saxon children's imaginations, to have access to a tree house was to join the happy tribe of Bandar-log—monkeys who enjoyed a freedom none of the other animals did. Never mind that in hindsight they were, with their gibbering, mischief-making ways, clearly meant to represent the 'natives'—just as Bagheera, the black panther, embodied the ideals of the public-school boys who administered the British Raj. One loved and honored Bagheera, but for oneself the monkeys, swinging from branch to branch and commenting on events below, had the best of it. To climb up, up, among the leaves, beyond the reach of intervention, must be the oldest, most joyous instinct in the world, the next best thing to flying. I can recall few keener pleasures and climbed trees until well past the age when it was decent to do so. (One's own children with their embarrassed wails soon put an end to that sort of thing.)

To find a resting place about half way up, somewhere to stop and dream and read, or perhaps eat lunch, is an enjoyment no child should be denied—and I am tempted to say, no adult either. When I spot a tree house on someone's property, I know civilized people live there, people whose idea of happiness goes beyond the provision of color TV. At the very least, they have made the gift of privacy and independence to a child, and if the child rejects those, he is past saving.

Tree houses acknowledge that we are still apes at heart. That hasn't prevented them from being highly sophisticated structures. The Mogul emperors sat on *chabutra*, 'garden thrones' high in the boughs of their beloved plane trees. The Japanese built 'tree walks' on tall stilts the better to admire the autumn foliage. In Europe, simple seats in trees go back to Roman times, and in the Middle Ages monks and hermits frequently retired to them. And by the sixteenth century the Italians with their genius for pruning had had the most sensational idea of all: By judicious cutting of boughs and interweaving of branches they converted the whole tree into an arboreal room. A famous one was in the *giardino segreto* at Pratolino, where it enchanted Montaigne and other travelers; and another existed, says Georgina Masson, at the nearby Villa Petraia until quite recently. They seem to have been a Tuscan specialty, these green rooms—and perhaps a Piedmontese one as well. I have before me an engraving of a maple actually carved into a three-story pavilion complete with windows and a roof with a finial. It is dated 1841, which means this entrancing art survived for three centuries at least—though I have been unable to discover exactly what were the techniques employed. The training of that maple must have been begun at the end of the eighteenth century. (The tree house at Pratolino was built between 1568 and 1580—and lasted an unknown length of time.) None of these structures was of course designed for children. I don't know when tree houses for adults went out of fashion—and still less why. I myself would rather have an arboreal retreat than a swimming pool any day, but evidently my sentiments aren't widely shared. Tree houses today are exclusively for children, and as often as not constructed by them too, out of old boards or whatever comes to hand.

They needn't be. My son became the proprietor of a one-room tree house in our ash tree when he was about six. It was a simple but handsome building on stilts, with a rope ladder that could be pulled up in emergencies, and it was made for him by his grandfather. I have the impression that he enjoyed it more than any present he received in his childhood. The disadvantage was that it attracted every little ruffian in the neighborhood and eventually, after my son had outgrown it and gone away to school, two of them climbed up to do a little illicit smoking. They succeeded in setting fire to it. In those days we weren't full-time residents and it was reluctantly decided we couldn't take the risk again. The tree house was dismantled. But if anyone under the age of ten were to live here in the future, I would certainly have it rebuilt. A tree house still seems to me a feature that every pleasure garden should have.

TREES

But it wasn't only the exotic trees she liked: the palms of various species, the *Howaenia dulces*, which produced deformed tubers full of a honey-flavored pulp, the American aloe shaped like the candelabra of the *menorah*, which—she told me—flowered only once every twenty or twenty-five years, and then died; the eucalyptus, the *Zelkoviae sinicae*, with their small green trunks flecked with gold (she never told me why, but she felt curiously uneasy about the eucalyptus, as if through the years something not at all pleasant had happened between them and her, something that mustn't be brought up again).

For an enormous plane tree, with a whitish, blotchy trunk thicker than that of almost any other tree in the garden, and, I think, the whole province, her admiration overflowed into reverence. Of course, it wasn't 'grandmother Josette' who had planted it; but Ercole I d'Este himself, or Lucretia Borgia.

'Do you realize? It's nearly five hundred years old!' she murmured, her eyes widening. 'Just imagine all the things it must have seen, since it came into the world!'

And it seemed as if it had eyes like ours, the great ugly beast, that gigantic old plane tree: eyes to see us as well as ears to hear us.

GIORGIO BASSANI
The Garden of the Finzi-Continis

————— ◇ —————

TULIPS

Most people have heard of tulipomania, the craze that struck seventeenth-century Holland and caused men to ruin themselves for a single bulb of Semper Augustus (red-and-white stripes) or Viceroy (white streaked with purple) and other particolored tulips of the type known to the trade as Rembrandts—heaven knows why since Rembrandt was one of the few Dutch painters who *didn't* paint tulips. Nothing quite like it has happened before or since and it would be gratifying if love of flowers had been the cause. In fact it was more nearly the kind of speculative scandal that can strike any commodity market: wheat or hogs. Tulips were first brought to Europe from Turkey by the Austrian ambassador to the court of Suleiman the Magnificent, and like any new and exciting plant fetched high prices among collectors. But the speculators weren't dealing with collectors, or, toward the end, with tulips. At the height of the craze, 1634–37, neither buyer nor seller possessed the bulbs. What was being traded was 'tulip futures'—pieces of paper. Naturally, there was a crash.

There was, however, a botanical phenomenon behind the uproar. Cultivated monochrome tulips, called breeders, have the peculiarity of producing, and no one can predict when it will happen, a brand-new flower marked like a Joseph's coat of many colors. This is known as a break, and broken tulips were those most prized. They were also what turned tulip breeding into a game of chance. Anyone could buy a bulb, plant it, and gamble that he would get a new tulip that might bring him as much as $30,000, or the equivalent in wheat, oxen, a mortgage on a house. We now know that breaking is usually though not invariably caused by a virus disease spread by aphids. Here something of a mystery develops—for me, at least. The original Turkish tulips were apparently monochromes, or so it would appear from the standards set forth by the 'tulip chief' or head gardener of Sultan Ahmed III (1703–30): 'The petals,' he wrote, 'should be stiff and smooth and of one color. . . . The flowers should resemble an almond. The petals should look like a dagger or a needle. If the tulip has not these petal characters it is a cheap flower. The tulip with the needle is the better of the two; if it has both dagger shape and needle point it is priceless.' The sharp-eyed will notice that in addition to being of a single color the tulip described isn't the shape of the ones we are most familiar with, patterned or not. It is the lyre-shaped flower, somewhat akin to the species, which is depicted over and over in Turkish textiles and ceramics—slender, indented, pointed, with at most a thin line down the center of each petal. It isn't a type that breaks.

There is footnote to this. According to *Time-Life*'s *Bulbs*, the early Dutch growers developed tulips with rounded rather than pointed petals, double tulips, and 'the flamboyant multicolored types'—in short, flowers quite unlike the classic Ottoman tulip; and when these new, Europeanized flowers made their way back to Turkey they set off a frenzy like that of tulipomania in Holland a century earlier, inaugurating what is called 'the tulip epoch' in Turkish history: 1718 to 1730. So what price the virus and its effects? The inference has to be that both were unknown in Turkey during the several hundred years that preceded the tulip's discovery by Europeans. And if that is so, it must mean that in the interval between the arrival of tulips in Holland in the late 1500's and the onset of tulipomania sixty years later, two things occurred: The Dutch developed new varieties of garden tulip; and these turned out to be susceptible to a virus not present in Turkish soil. (*Bulbs* also states that Turkish gardeners unaware, like Europeans, that breaks were caused by disease, nevertheless developed a method of spreading it. They ground diseased bulbs to a powder which was then spread on healthy ones. But if I read the text correctly, the technique dates from the eighteenth century and not earlier.) Yet no book I know of puts forth any such thesis.

Wilfred Blunt's *Tulipomania* (1950), a much-quoted source, has nothing to say about the return of Europeanized tulips to Turkey (and mentions the virus only in passing). It does, however, confirm the revival of interest in tulips in the reign of Ahmed III, marked by celebrations dazzling even to Louis XV's ambassador. Lighted with lamps and mirrors, hung with cages of singing birds, the tulip gardens of the seraglio became a fairyland marred only by the booming of cannon and the frantic conduct of the harem women. Half-crazed by their year-long imprisonment, these wretches often fell on the flowers and tore them to pieces. The tulip varieties that so much excited them still seem to me open to question. If they were the Europeanized forms, fringed and streaked like those in Dutch paintings of the same period, one would expect to see some evidence in Turkish art. It isn't there. This is perhaps attributable to the fact that the original, lyre-shaped Turkish tulip had long since been adopted by the reigning Osmanlis as their emblem, just as the fleur-de-lis, which is an iris, had become the symbol of the French royal house, and therefore stylized to the point where it was no longer the portrait of a flower and subject to change in the interests of realism. But there are still the texts that emphatically do not describe the rounded, open, extravagantly patterned forms beloved of Europeans. That of the 'tulip chief' already quoted, written in the eighteenth century, differs not at all from the picture of a large, albeit artificial, tulip that was the object of a celebration at the court of Murad III in the 1500's. As for the 'tulip epoch,' I doubt that it was comparable to tulipomania in Holland—where the principal cause was capitalist speculation in a new product. Nothing of the kind occurred in Turkey. There the rise and fall of a flower's popularity was subject to the whims of sultans, and that alone. Thus, Mohammed IV (1648–87) wasn't interested in tulips. He preferred the ranunculus, and rare specimens were collected for him all over the Levant. In 1700 a visiting French botanist reported that the Turks were neglecting their flower gardens in favor of melons and cucumbers. Ahmed III happened to have a passion for tulips, and given the character of Turkish society, there need be no more to the 'tulip epoch' than that.

Meanwhile there is the virus, bound to be a worry to those of us who prefer the broken tulips to all others. I ask myself why, if monochrome tulips could be counted on to break with such regularity for the seventeenth-century Dutch burghers, they never do for me? What of the presumably infected Rembrandts I grow? Are they a danger to their neighbors? I do wish somebody would clear up this matter of the virus once and for all. Catalogues are naturally of no help. They don't mention the virus for obvious reasons: it is an alarming word to gardeners familiar with botrytis blight and another called 'fire' that afflicts tulips but is apparently something else, and certainly doesn't cause breaking. However, the Department of Agriculture has addressed itself, after a fashion, to the question and this is what it says: 'Many dealers sell Rembrandt or "broken" tulips. These bulbs are infected with a virus disease that gives flowers a "broken" (striped, blotched, or mottled) appearance. Virus from these diseased bulbs will infect healthy tulips and lilies that are planted close to them. Diseased plants get smaller every year, die within 3 to 5 years. If you want to grow healthy tulips, you must keep "broken" tulips away from the healthy ones.'

That is clear enough, except that, as noted, nothing of the sort has happened in my garden in the thirty years or so that I have been growing both kinds of tulips, and in close association with lilies. As for the statement that diseased tulips diminish in size and die within five years, it isn't diagnostic. *All* tulips do that. It is their nature to multiply and divide underground and unless the bulblets are dug up and replanted to grow as new individuals, they become extinct—or rather cease to flower, which comes to the same thing. A way around this is to plant them twice as deeply as the six inches usually called for. I do this and some of mine, including the broken types, have lasted as long as ten years. But it has no connection with the virus problem, since it works with both types.

Given all the confusion, I was gratified to see that Katharine White, who loved the Rembrandts as I do, was equally struck with the peculiar fact that a flower condemned on the one hand as a disease-ridden menace should on the other have been successfully grown for hundreds of years, and by named varieties at that. With a diligence I admire more than I have the energy to emulate, she launched on a correspondence with various authorities here and abroad in an effort to get answers. I paraphrase from her report in *Onward and Upward in the Garden*, the collected edition of her *New Yorker* essays: According to Dr. E. van Slogteren of the

Flower Bulb Research Laboratory at Lisse, Holland, the virus is real enough and can be transmitted, not only by aphids but by using the same pair of scissors on diseased and virus-free flowers. Furthermore, at the time of writing (1961), Dutch bulb growers had for more than a year been required by law to separate plantings of the two by a distance of a hundred feet, and many were phasing out their broken tulips. There may have been second thoughts about that as there seems to be no shortage of Rembrandts on the market today—but how sad, how ironic, that the very tulips that made Holland famous should after three hundred years be under a cloud and in danger of extinction. Another expert, however, was less pessimistic. Mr. Degenaar de Jager, president of a well-known bulb-growing firm, told Mrs. White that 'The danger is within limited scope. If it were not, the whole of our stocks would have been infected and subsequently lost, since we have been growing a collection [of broken tulips] for over forty years among our other tulips, but have never found a spreading of the virus to the other varieties.' (But, one wonders, why then the law? Have other growers been less fortunate?) And now the plot thickens. Mrs. White also learned that not all particolored tulips owe their markings to disease. Some are natural mutations. And how does one tell the difference? Apparently by name alone, though it isn't clear to me where one would obtain a list of virus-free cultivars, and moreover the gentlemen didn't agree on a celebrated tulip called Zomerschoon, in cultivation since 1620. One said it was diseased, the other said it wasn't, and I rather fancy such disagreements might be prolonged indefinitely. So much for consulting the experts.

Let me introduce another mystery, which could be called *The Case of What the Interpreter Said*, and concerns the name 'tulip.' According to the *Oxford English Dictionary*, it derives from 'vulgar Turk. pronounc. of Pers. *dulban*, "turban," which the expanded flower of the tulip was thought to resemble.' A. W. Smith, whose *Gardener's Book of Plant Names* is one of my bibles: 'The Latin version of the Arabic for turban.' *Webster*: 'Turk. *tulbend*, turban, from Per. *dulband*, so called for its likeness to a turban.' Plain enough, except that according to Wilfred Blunt the Turkish and Persian word for tulip is *lalé*, which means I know not what. Blunt has an ingenious explanation for the discrepancy. He thinks that the Austrian ambassador, Ogier Busbecq, who first observed near Adrianople 'an abundance of flowers everywhere—narcissus, hyacinths, and those the Turks called *tulipam*' was misinformed by his interpreter as to the correct name. Probably, says Blunt, the man was only trying to compare the shape of the petals to that of a turban (*dulband*). Based on my own experience with Turkish interpreters, I don't believe a word of it. 'What is the name of that big mountain?' I asked at Bursa. 'We call it big mountain,' was the reply, and I damned him for a fool. But he was right. The mountain's name is Uludağ and it means big mountain. Turks are not overly imaginative, and I have difficulty believing that Busbecq's interpreter was moved to launch on comparisons to turbans if the name had no connection with them; and in any event, Busbecq had ample opportunity in the course of his mission to learn of his error, if it was one. He spent a lot of money on tulips and took them back to Vienna with him. Nor, surely, were subsequent dealers in tulips likely to have consistently used the wrong name for them. Finally, I have another reason for thinking the ambassador got it right the first time. Hungary was occupied by the Turks for nearly two hundred years, and the languages are closely related. And in Hungarian the word for tulip is *tulipan*.

What I guess, and it is only a guess, is that both names were used. A recent report in *The New York Times* says there is a struggle now going on in Turkey between those who would remove foreign words from the language and return to 'pure' Turkish, and those who would retain the innumerable accretions (Persian, Arabic, etc.) of the Ottoman period, which have resulted in the modern idiom called Osmanlica. If that is true it could easily mean that there were all along two words for tulip: one plain Turkish, the other fancy and derived from the Persian. After all, do we not have our common and our Latin names for the same flower?

Or is Blunt just mistaken about *lalé*? I think not, but must admit my confidence in his linguistics is shaken by other passages in his book. He recounts, for instance, how at a flower festival at the Turkish court the Grand Vizier awarded a diploma to the grower of the certain flower, and this diploma was 'drawn up in purest Persian and Arabic.' Now I am no scholar, but I do know that one of these languages is Indo-European and the other Semitic and that in spite of borrowings in both directions, they aren't the same or even related, and I submit that the Grand Vizier couldn't have composed a document in a mélange of the two that could correctly be described as the purest form of either. (Why the Turkish

Grand Vizier wasn't writing in Turkish—which belongs to yet a third family of languages—is a complication that Blunt leaves alone, though one knows more or less why. Persian and Arabic were to the Turks what Latin and Greek were to Europeans in the Middle Ages: more civilized and literary languages than their own. But that would only make it the more probable that the tulip, common in its wild forms to the chillier uplands of Persia and Anatolia alike, had both a Turkish and a Persian name.)

Linguistics and unclassifiable diseases aside, tulips are one of the gardener's joys and I can't imagine anyone with even a patch of ground not growing them. Unlike most northern gardeners, I'm not much moved by the first crocus, poking its brave little head up among the dead leaves; or indeed by any of the other little spring bulbs, which only make me wish I were somewhere else. I plant them of course—one has to have something to look at. But the tulips are what I wait for—the species types with a stripe down their spines that are the earliest arrivals. They are followed by the Darwin hybrids, the Darwins themselves, and—crescendo—my favorites: the modern version of the Ottoman tulip (now called lily-flowered, a misnomer; it doesn't look at all like a lily); the Rembrandts (also known as Bizarres or Bybloemen, sometimes Bijbloemen); and lastly the feathered and extravagant parrots (which really do have the feathery texture and colors of a parrot's plumage—the exception being my favorite 'black' parrot, which has the iridescent ink-purple sheen of a raven's wing and looks absolutely marvelous combined in vases with sprays of lilac).

But I don't choose tulips with any regard for periods of bloom and succession. I look at pictures in catalogues and buy for beauty; and one way or another I get more than six weeks' worth. I don't put them in separate beds either, where to my mind they acquire a regimented, municipal look and are a nuisance. The disadvantage of tulips is that the foliage must ripen—a polite way of saying that it must be left to wither and turn brown in order that the bulbs be nourished for the following year. In a bed with nothing in it but tulips, the drawback is magnified. For whether you dig and store them for replanting in the fall or leave them, you must have an instant supply of annuals to take their places and/or mask their unsightly decline. Whereas in a perennial bed, where mine are planted, clumps of tulips in addition to being the only flower that will make a handsome display between mid-April and the end of May can, with a little juggling, be made practically invisible as they ripen. I plant them among the June and July lilies (so much for the Department of Agriculture's advice), or next to a gypsophila that will soon draw a veil, or close to Oriental poppies whose foliage conceals theirs in no time. And how ravishing they are, especially in the early morning and late afternoons, when their chalices catch and hold the light as if it were wine. And though they are said to be scentless, I find that they have a faint perfume. Not that it matters. The hybridists have been at work on tulips for three hundred years and with the possible exception of the doubles that look like peonies, haven't yet succeeded in debasing their forms or their colors—on the contrary, this is one case where we are heavily in their debt. The modern tulips are exquisite variations on a theme that has kept its authenticity.

TWO GARDENERS

If you were to ask the average American gardener to name the finest twentieth-century garden in England and the one he would most like to see, the chances are he would say Sissinghurst, the joint creation of Victoria Sackville-West and her husband Harold Nicolson — joint because the plantings were hers and the layout his. The reason, of course, is her books, or more accurately the anthologies of the articles she wrote over a period of years for the London *Observer*, and the innumerable photographs that have appeared of the garden itself. Through these we feel we know every corner of it, the one-color 'rooms' in white, purple, or yellow-and-orange, the lime walk, the yew hedges. And we are familiar with her principles such as they were: Don't hang on to a plant that hasn't satisfied you; don't strive for too much tidiness; let the ramblers ramble and the self-sowers sow. Pay attention to scale, both in mass and height. Don't be afraid to experiment.

At the same time we realize that she wasn't a theorist in the tradition of Gertrude Jekyll and William Robinson and for all her knowledge of plants, not a collector or breeder. In short, she was an amateur of a very English kind: imaginative, informed, but eschewing the perils and penalties of professionalism. And indeed she didn't claim to be more. According to her daughter-in-law, her short pieces were written off the top of her head with only brief pauses to check a name or a date in a horticultural dictionary, or a quotation in a Shakespeare concordance. Her style is informal, chatty, direct, and she tried hard not to put down the reader with humbler resources than hers.

All this, together with an historic name, glamorous background, striking person and well-known literary friendships, made her famous. It also tended to inflate the reputation of Sissinghurst and to disguise the fact that for all its great charm it isn't the most remarkable modern garden in England or the most original. That honor belongs to Hidcote Manor in the Cotswolds. It was to Hidcote that Sissinghurst owed the novel conception of many gardens within a garden, and the growing of rare and sophisticated plants in cottage-garden–like casualness and profusion. Hidcote, begun in 1907, is a mine of ideas to this day. There is the extraordinary double line of hornbeams, clipped to look like green boxes standing on stilts; the 'bathing pool' I can't do better than to let Russell Page (in *The Education of a Gardener*, 1962) describe:

At one point we come through a yew arch into a tiny square hedged-in garden filled with so large a circular pool that there is barely room for the narrowest of paths between it and the hedge. This raised pool, perhaps twenty foot across, looks all the larger for being so compressed, and the unusual proportion of the whole breaks down, for a moment, the mechanism of one's habitual criticisms and judgments. One is free to accept this little scene as intensely real; the pool becomes like a sea which reflects the sky and floating leaf . . . time and space change scale.

Without being in the least surreal or deliberately eccentric, Hidcote reveals at every turn one of the most innovative gardening minds the twentieth century has produced and what is much rarer in any age, combines intense originality of design with a deep knowledge of plants. The two have not often gone together. The plantsman and the landscape architect have for the most part lived in different worlds, and the best one can hope for is a collaboration between the two—as, for example, that between Jekyll and Edwin Lutyens (or for that matter V. Sackville-West and Harold Nicolson), while in the remoter past even that was missing. The great garden designers of the seventeenth and eighteenth centuries, who worked with stone, water, native trees and evergreens, had little or no interest in the extraordinary botanicals flooding Europe from every part of the French and British empires—which from Le Nôtre onward they simply ignored.

In the nineteenth century, the opposite occurred. Plants became paramount but no gardening style that could compete in aesthetic importance with those of the flowerless past was devised to cope with them. The so-called gardenesque, described by J. C. Loudon, its chief promoter, as 'a garden for displaying the art of the gardener,' which flourished in the 1830's and 1840's, was a step in the right direction but marred by quaintness—winding paths and rootwork summerhouses—and was essentially middle-class and suburban in tone. The formal carpet-bedding that followed was recognized by gardeners of taste even at the time as an affront and collapsed of its own weight. But the universally acclaimed informal style of planting, characterized by Jekyll's herbaceous borders, Reginald Farrer's rock gardens and the folklorically inspired discovery of the cottage garden, didn't quite balance the equation either. Too much was sacrificed: the pleasures of topiary, the intellectual stimulus and surprise of perspective, the magic of water not handled naturalistically.

It remained for the creator of Hidcote to imagine an entirely new way to bring these disparate and hitherto warring elements into harmony. Hidcote was unique in its day, and in many ways still is, though that fact seems even now to be recognized only by a discriminating few. Not that it lacks publicity. Thousands of gardeners from all over the world visit it year after year, and every gardener who grows lavender knows that the best variety is the deep-purple called Hidcote.

It has been described many times, by V. Sackville-West among others, but to my knowledge no one has written the detailed study it deserves, and only a few conveyed a proper idea of its historical importance. None that I know of has had anything to say about the man who made it beyond stating that he was an American called Lawrence Johnston. Who was he, why did he make a garden in what was then a fairly remote part of England, where did he acquire his fantastic knowledge of plants? These questions appear to have interested nobody sufficiently to try to answer them, and I was prepared to have my own curiosity about him go unsatis-

fied until there appeared in the November 1978 issue of the R.H.S.
journal, *The Garden*, an unfortunately all-too-brief article about
him, from which I now quote freely.

In a way, it only deepens the mystery, for the author (Alvilde
Lees-Milne) admits that little is known about many portions of his
life, and this in spite of his having lived very much among worldly
people. He was a friend of Edith Wharton (Russell Page says he
helped her with the design of her 'blue' garden outside Paris),
and of the gardening Vicomte de Noailles who was Wharton's
neighbor in the south of France. He was apparently intimate with
the blatantly fashionable Lady Colefax. In fact his friends were
legion and adored him—which may mean they conspired to shield
him from the publicity he loathed. Many of the plants he introduced to cultivation bear the name of Hidcote, but only one or
two his own (and since my source doesn't list them, I don't know
what they are). His modesty and shyness were at any rate pro-
verbial, and it does seem that he went out of his way to conceal
or gloze over certain aspects of his career, his military exploits in
particular. In 1900, he joined the Imperial Yeomanry as a trooper
and went off to the Boer War, nobody knows why—or what happened to him in Africa. He didn't retire from the army, and when
the First World War broke out he was commissioned a major and
sent to France. There he was twice wounded and once left for
dead, saved from premature burial only by a friend who recognized him and saw him move. In short, he must have been something of a hero but of all that he seems never to have spoken, and
it can't easily be fitted in with the picture one gets of a small,
gentle man of faultless taste, devoted to gardening.

Johnston was what the English call a Henry James American—
meaning that he was accepted as not your typical transatlantic
boor. He was born in Paris (in 1871) of cosmopolitan parents. His
father was a Baltimorian, his mother was born Gertrude Cleveland
and may have been related to the president of that name. Early
widowed, she married again one Charles Francis Winthrop of a
good New York family, who however also died almost at once.
Mother and son remained in France, where says Mrs. Lees-Milne
with transparent meaning he 'must from an early age have been
accustomed to being surrounded by beauty and culture.' (Elsewhere, she says that he remained at Hidcote during World War II,
where he struggled to keep things going 'and had some Americans
billeted on him.') One takes her point, and it isn't a bad one. From

an early age he was saturated with French civilization—he was educated by a French tutor as well—not subjected to crass American influence. But it is also clear that he was the classic expatriate with all that implies of alienation. He wasn't American, nor yet French. It is unknown when he first went to England, only that he matriculated at Trinity College, Cambridge, in 1898 and was naturalized a British subject two years later. But that didn't make him English either. And there were other and familiar stigmata. At an early age he was converted to Catholicism. (A charming anecdote has him visiting the Vatican gardens and unable to resist picking a piece of water ranunculus. 'Excuse me,' he said to his companion, 'I must go and light a candle.') Finally, it is plain from his obsessive devotion to his mother, described as 'quite a character,' the fact that he never married, and other details, that he was homosexual in inclination if not in practice. In other words, he was and remained an outsider. This would account for the uniqueness of Hidcote, which is much more a French garden than an English one, yet has no counterpart in France either. Johnston's originality was the product of his curious life between worlds, and of divisions within his own character: half stay-at-home aesthete, half adventurer.

There were, for example, his plant-hunting expeditions, both highly romantic. In 1927, he made a four-month trip from Capetown to Victoria Falls, climbing the Drakensburg mountains along the way and accumulating a vast and valuable amount of living material that was sent to the Royal Botanic Garden at Edinburgh —and some later to Menton where he made another garden, his last and the one where he ended his days. Johnston traveled in style. He took along his Italian cook and a chauffeur-valet, though one assumes they didn't accompany him on his second expedition, which was to Yünann with the celebrated George Forrest. The trip killed Forrest and almost killed Johnston, who was taken ill and had to come home before it was over. But from that one, too, he brought back valuable seeds and living specimens, among them two mahonias and *Jasminum polyanthum*, beloved of all gardeners in warm climates. His garden at Menton, called the Serre de la Madone, aside from being a dream of beauty, was also his laboratory for these tender plants, which couldn't live at Hidcote except under glass. After his death many of them were shipped back to the Cambridge Botanic Garden, and Mrs. Lees-Milne says the list is staggering. Unhappily, she also says that few have survived.

(Why?) Johnston died on 27 April 1958 and is buried at Hidcote.
He is still an enigma and likely to remain so.

Very different is my next gardener—the grand, somewhat tragic,
more than a little hateful woman whose garden at Warley Place in
Essex was famous throughout Europe and America between 1890
and 1914. Miss Ellen Willmott (1858–1934) didn't doubt she was
the queen of British horticulture, and so in a way she was. She
stands at any rate as the supreme example of a type not to be
found elsewhere: the English lady gardener—though even then
not many can have had her resources. At Warley Place (once the
property of Evelyn, a fact she made much of), as many as eighty-
five gardeners cared for *one hundred thousand different kinds of
plants*, many of which came from remote parts of the world and
flowered there for the first time in cultivation. Nor was that all.
Like Johnston she had another garden in France (hers was at Aix-
les-Bains and is now a public park), and still another in Italy, at
Ventimiglia. She must at one time or another have grown virtually
every species of flowering plant that can be grown in the temperate zone, but her passion was roses, and in these she outdid even
the Empress Josephine, with whom it is more than probable she
identified herself. She, too, was the *grande dame* interested in botany, with money to burn on the rarest acquisitions, and she, too,
was to commission a work on roses that was no doubt intended to
be the twentieth-century successor to Redoubté and Thory's *Les
Roses*.

Miss Willmott's *The Genus Rosa* (published between 1910 and
1914) was in twenty-five parts and two volumes, with illustrations
especially painted for her by Alfred Parsons from specimens in her
own garden and descriptions mostly by the Kew botanist John Gilbert Baker. According to an article about her in the June 1979
issue of *The Garden*, it isn't a scientific monograph in the modern
sense. Indeed, since no mention of Baker appears on the title page
and the dedication to Queen Alexandra strongly implies she wrote
the whole thing herself, one gets the impression that it was a self-
glorifying monument. She must nevertheless be given credit for
having produced a beautiful work. And for other things: She was a
generous supporter of plant-hunting expeditions, particularly
those of E. H. Wilson. It is true that this paid off. There was no
hanky-panky about *her* services to horticulture not being recognized. Dozens of plants are named for her or for Warley, including
numerous roses, a narcissus, a peony, a potentilla, a phlox, an

epimedium, a lily, a scabiosa, a white lilac, many more. But these trophies were well-deserved. She came honestly by her fame.

It is nevertheless apparent that she was an insufferable woman, unkind to the young wife of E. H. Wilson, stupidly hostile to Reginald Farrer, whose classic *The English Rock-Garden* may have irritated her by its evident superiority to her own magnum opus. She was spiteful, and a terrible, pretentious snob. Her dedication of *The Genus Rosa* is bloodcurdling. It begins: 'Herewith I lay at Your Majesty's feet a Book of Roses, wherein I have striven to set down, with such poor skill and diligence as has been vouchsafed to me, all that I have learned of that most Royal Family of the Kingdom of Flowers . . .' She even compares herself to Sappho: 'And albeit such a task might appear too high for such an one as mine own self, and albeit I might seem unworthily and presumptuously to vie with that Greek poetess of old, of whom it was said "she hath left little, but all Roses"; yet, being mightily encouraged thereto by Your Majesty's gracious countenance . . .' and so on.

Like all gardeners, I have encountered Miss Willmott's name again and again, and my image of her was that of a gentle, learned spinster, rather plain, carrying a silk umbrella. Well, she was a spinster all right, and she may have carried a silk umbrella. But she wasn't gentle, and in her youth she was a beauty. The only man she seems to have cared for didn't care for her, and so she didn't marry, though with her looks and colossal wealth she certainly could have. Her capacity for love must have been transferred to her gardens, and that was her tragedy, because she lost them all. Most of her money had been invested in Germany (it isn't clear why), and the First World War all but wiped her out. The foreign gardens had to go. Warley remained, but as the ghost of its former self. The weeds moved in with the departure of the eighty-five gardeners, the house fell into disrepair, and she was reduced to selling off her possessions—in secret because her pride wouldn't acknowledge her losses.

But even in full retreat, she had to fire her whiff of grapeshot. The loss of her rose garden she blamed not on the war or the consequent loss of help, but on a certain Lady Angela Forbes to whom Warley was let. 'She completely destroyed it and when she was turned out she had made no attempt at cultivation and nettles and thistles had taken the place.' What exactly the wretched Lady Angela could have done otherwise she didn't consider. She even had a bad word for Baker, who had written the technical part of her text in *The Genus Rosa*, and one can guess what a time of it he must have had—the imperious amateur changing her mind every two minutes, the wealth of disorganized thoughts pouring in on him. 'Mr. Baker's work was too diffused,' she wrote, 'and he certainly never had a grasp of the rose situation. M. Crépin wrote me that he was lost in the mass of new material coming in.' Since he was a thorough professional, who had first written on the genus *Rosa* in 1864, the nature of his problems with Miss Willmott can be read between the lines.

All the same, there is something grand and sad about her. On Lawrence Johnston's grave is written, 'Deeply loved by his friends,' and his wonderful garden is more or less intact. No such epitaph was carved for Miss Willmott, and hers has long since gone to ruin. No particular moral is to be drawn. 'To make a great garden, one must have a great idea or a great opportunity,' wrote Sir George Sitwell (*On the Making of Gardens*, 1909, 1951). Lawrence Johnston had the first, Ellen Willmott the second, and both made the most of it. But for a garden to survive, another factor must be present—luck.

VEGETABLES

Never would it occur to a child that sheep, pigs, cows or chickens were good to eat, while, like Milton's *Adam*, he would readily make a meal off fruit, nuts, thyme, mint, peas and broad beans, which penetrate further and stimulate not only the appetite but other vague and deep nostalgias. We are closer to the Vegetable Kingdom than we know; is it not for us alone that mint, thyme, sage, and rosemary exhale 'crush me and eat me!'—for us that opium poppy, coffee-berry, tea-plant and vine perfect themselves? Their aim is to be absorbed by man, although they can achieve it only by attaching themselves to roast mutton.

CYRIL CONNOLLY
The Unquiet Grave

The vegetable patch began like so many others in the village as a victory garden in World War II, and in our innocence of what was needed to feed a small family, let alone an understanding of the ratio between labor and produce, we devoted a quarter of an acre to it. We didn't plant it ourselves. That was done by contract while we were still in the city, and the consequence was an overloading of crops like potatoes, onions and far too many beans that came all at once. By August, there wasn't much left but tomatoes, and meanwhile we had weeded (not in the contract) and picked ourselves to exhaustion with only a heap of not very desirable vegetables to show for it.

This grotesquely sized plot was halved even before the end of the war, but it still left much to be desired and might have gone to grass, as most such gardens did soon after V-J Day. We were summer people in those days; I came only for weekends, and weekends were short—why spend them in manual labor? I can't remember exactly when the tide turned in favor of keeping the vegetable patch. Perhaps there never was any serious thought of abandoning it, because I was, by then, already and incurably a gardener. Lying in my New York bed at night, I would go over every inch of the place in my mind, tearing up some shrubs and planting others, changing the contents of the perennial beds, wondering who I could find to construct bean trellises. And because it is impossible to garden for only three months of the year, the old schedule of opening the house on Memorial Day weekend and closing it right after Labor Day was gradually scrapped. No more teams were hired to come in to plow up the soil and put in potatoes. Once I had mastered the organic method, the soil didn't need to be turned; and I put in peas and lettuces and other spring vegetables myself—arriving earlier and earlier in order to do so, until St. Patrick's Day became the official date for opening the house. Friday nights would find me on hands and knees, aiming a flashlight at vegetable plot and flower beds to see what had come up during the week. The other end of the season prolonged itself in the same way, and it was Thanksgiving before the last rose had been picked, the last Savoy cabbages and Brussels sprouts harvested.

All that has changed. I am a full-time resident now and not as hell-bent as I used to be. I have cut down on many things, but nothing short of total decrepitude could make me decide to give up the vegetables. Ordinary greed comes into it, of course, and the bolstering of insecurities: Scarlett O'Hara grubbing for yams evidently made more of an impression than I realized at the time. But most of all they bewitch me with their textures, infinitely varied forms, even their sounds—the silky rustle of cabbages, the rattle of peas in their pods. Whether in orderly rows in the garden or lying in a heap on the kitchen table, they are almost too beautiful to eat, which at least proves that one isn't just a hog. Given the aesthetic choice, I prefer vegetables and fruits to flowers. I am hardly the first to experience this half-worshipful emotion (think what Chardin could do with a scallion or a plum), but it is undoubtedly sharpened by the premonition that I may be among the last. The seven-year-old son of one of my garden helpers brought this home to me the other day. An intelligent child, he wanted to know what were the pea pods he saw lying on the compost heap. I explained. Still a blank, and it came to me that although he knew perfectly well what peas were, he had supposed they came out of a cardboard box, frozen. And there will soon be many more of him than of me. Already I am something of a freak in the community on account of my vegetables, herbs and fruits. I foresee the day when I graduate from freak to witch.

The patch at half its wartime size isn't very large, perhaps twenty by sixty feet—yet it produces four or five times what it did then, partly because it is at work longer. Many people still talk about getting in their harvest by Labor Day and thereafter expect little but a few lingering tomatoes. Our patch has a good two months to go at that time, and that isn't counting the leeks, carrots (and sometimes parsnips) that will stay in the ground all winter under hay wraps. On Labor Day, the bean trellises (haricot and limas) are producing heavily and will until frost. So will the Swiss chard and late-planted lettuces. The celeriac roots are beginning to swell underground and green rosettes to appear on the stalks of the Brussels sprouts. The Savoy cabbages now look exactly like their imitations in Portuguese pottery; and if I have planted purple cauliflower that year, mauve curds are forming at the base of the huge green leaves. The Belgian endive, on the other hand, won't be ready to pull and store for another six weeks. We haven't come to the end of the French potatoes and the last of them won't be dug until October.

Midsummer would seem to be the high season for the kitchen garden but as a matter of fact the vegetables that like extreme heat are few. Even tomatoes don't set fruit well in excessively hot and humid weather, and they are tropicals. Hot weather hastens the demise of the pea vines, causes lettuces to bolt and green beans to mature too quickly for most of us to keep up with them—whereas midsummer plantings of all these will produce early fall crops that linger much longer. The cabbage family, too, prefers a chill in the air. Cabbage heads crack open in the heat, and broccoli must be timed to head either before or after midsummer or all you will have is bunches of pretty little yellow flowers.

Getting vegetables to grow for six months of the year is largely a matter of planting them in succession. We all know this in theory. Practice is another matter, and books are of little help, at least not to me. An example is *Home Gardening at Its Best,* by Sal Gilbertie. Mr. Gilbertie is a professional market gardener who obviously knows his business and he gives the reader exact information on all standard vegetables, how long they take to mature, when to plant them, etc., plus elaborate diagrams to show how various shapes and sizes of kitchen garden can be managed, suggested groupings of vegetables for all seasons, and much more. Only an idiot could fail to profit from this copious and careful book, yet I find it practically useless—though it is one of the best of its kind. The diagrams refuse to impose themselves on my garden; the vegetables aren't in the right quantities or the choices I would make. And when you come to think of it, how could they be? Only the gardener can know how much of a given vegetable his family can or will eat, and—by trial and error—how many plants it takes to produce that amount. Inevitably he will overdo it. I know perfectly well after all these years that six tomato plants, two each of early, middle and late varieties, is enough for us, yet a seventh almost always creeps in, just in case. The same with Savoy cabbages. A dozen is sufficient: Fourteen will be planted. But it takes no more than a season or two to learn which vegetables will occupy their spaces all season long, and which will be transients to be replaced with something else at midsummer. You also learn *how big things get,* a lesson not found in books. Purple cauliflower plants, for instance, are so enormous you may find the space they need not worth the medium-sized head you eventually harvest; broccoli is smaller and relatively economical because it goes on producing side shoots for a long time after the center is removed. On the other hand, it isn't as good.

Space is altogether such an imperative (second only to considerations of labor and time), that it is too bad so many gardeners persist in raising staples like potatoes, onions and squash. Not only do they take up a huge amount of room, they aren't vegetables whose quality depends on absolute freshness. Gardeners in an earlier day raised them mostly for winter storage—not now a necessity, and in a modern cellar, even a problem. I have come to take quite a different view of the kitchen garden. I don't expect it to supply us with everything. I regard it in the light of a fancy market specializing in more or less exotic produce, such as I would find in a large, cosmopolitan city. This means, first, vegetables that aren't sold in local markets; second, those that are available but generally over-age or of poor quality; and finally, those that shouldn't be picked until—as the old saying goes—the water to cook them is boiling on the stove.

No two households would make the same choices under this system, but for what it is worth, here is my list. In the first category: celeriac, Swiss chard, fennel, Savoy and Chinese cabbage, shallots and Japanese bunching onions, *jaune d'hollande* potatoes, purple cauliflower, miniature white corn (which also qualifies in the third category)—and an occasional flyer like cardoons, cultivated dandelion greens, *flageolets*. In the second group are: carrots (unacceptable in plastic bags and without their feathery tops), cucumbers (now that shippers have thought of coating them with wax), leeks (seemingly no less than two years old and filthy dirty), Brussels sprouts, broccoli and early green cabbage, Bibb and other loose-leaf lettuces (not bad at the market, better at home), Belgian endive (O.K. from the market and a lot less trouble but horrendous in price). Lastly: all the bean family, corn, peas. I'm not sure where to list tomatoes because the market carries fine, locally grown ones in season and I don't know that mine are appreciably better. The point is that I would be humiliated to be seen buying them.

Some omissions may need a word of explanation. Much as I love the fresh-picked and detest the bagged stuff, spinach isn't a crop for a small garden. A whole row of it stuffed into a pot will reduce itself to barely enough for a small dinner party. Then I am invariably asked why I don't grow snow peas. The answer is we don't care for them much and especially not in competition with Harris's forty-year-old Lincoln variety of green pea that matures at the same time. The new so-called Sugar Snaps were tried and found to combine the worst of both worlds—the peas themselves second-rate and the pods tough and inedible. I grow no celery either, though I would very much like to lay hands on a white European variety and try my luck. In general, though, celery is strictly for professionals, requiring a lot of care, watering and protection from disease. I have also given up eggplant and peppers, which don't do well for me unless I raise them from seed myself, a chore I am now reluctant to undertake. I would blame my failure on the weather, or the stock I have bought, or any handy culprit if it weren't that several neighbors whose gardening skills I frankly consider inferior to my own didn't produce splendid specimens from plants bought at the same sources. Beets aren't on the list either, and only partly because the ones at the store are just as good. I'm sorry to say I like canned beets better than fresh ones (and am only moderately fond of beet greens). I used to think this a secret vice until the fussiest gastronome I ever knew, who kept a legendary table, tersely told me that of course canned beets were better. Everyone knew *that*.

The absence of squashes in any and all forms explains itself, given the criteria. I defy anyone to tell the difference between a store-bought squash and a home-grown one. The possible exception is zucchini, and that is a matter of size alone. In Italy (or France, where it is a *courgette*), this vegetable is eaten when it is the size of a small pickle, and not a centimeter more. It is then sautéed in butter or stuffed whole, a tricky job requiring a special tool. Under no circumstances is zucchini made into bread or relish or some other dreadful concoction. In America, we let them balloon to colossal size, publish cookbooks for the desperate, and doorstep them like unwanted kittens, hoping somebody will give them shelter. Not me. I just might grow zucchini if I had room for it but I doubt it. To me it is one of a number of marginal vegetables that I quite like if they are well cooked, yet now reject when the day of judgment arrives with the filling of the seed orders. Parsnips and salsify are others, also kohlrabi—a detestable vegetable in most hands, though my Hungarian cook could do wonders with it. I can't.

I have made such a point of space that the knowledgeable may wonder why I don't make use of the method called French-intensive, though it is as much Chinese as it is French and wasn't originally designed to save space. The purpose of French-intensive gardening is to increase yields and improve their quality without farm machinery or a large investment, but in practice it can quadruple the production of a pocket-sized kitchen garden. Those who remember France before the war, when Paris was surrounded by market gardens, will know what such a system of cultivation

looks like—and how beautiful it is with its rectangular beds full of
closely planted vegetables, usually one of a kind to a plot, and so
neatly cared for they seemed to have been stitched together with
needle and thread. The whole thing is a vision of horticultural
order. This vision has never appealed to Americans whose use of
garden space is as wasteful as every other aspect of our society
and therefore it is rarely to be seen here except on the West Coast,
where Orientals practice a form of intensive vegetable gardening.

The key is the raised beds, separated by paths—therefore not
walked on or compacted, quickly warmed and drained, and the
sole recipients of water, fertilizer and the gardener's labor, all of
which are to some extent wasted in the conventional layout where
every row of vegetables is, in effect, bordered by a path on either
side. Moreover, the plants can and should be very closely spaced,
their leaves when mature barely touching each other, which con-
serves water and almost eliminates weeding.

So demonstrably superior is this system that it would seem no
vegetable gardener in his senses would practice any other. And
indeed no year goes by that I don't seriously think of it. The hitch
occurs when I reread the directions for making a raised bed. Let me
quote from the *Encyclopedia of Organic Gardening:*

The primary method of preparing a raised bed is a technique known
as double digging. Dig a trench (12 inches wide and 12 inches deep)
the width of the bed. Set the soil aside, outside the bed. Use a spade
or pitchfork to break up the soil in the trench until it is loose and
crumbly to a depth of 12 inches. Move the top layer of soil (12 inches
wide and 12 inches deep) from the next trench into the first trench
and spade the lower level of the second trench to a depth of 12 inches.
Repeat this process until the entire bed is dug to a total depth of
24 inches. [Thus far, by the way, the process is the same as that for
preparing an English herbaceous border.]
Let the bed rest for a few days. . . . This time, again remove the top
layer of soil and loosen the bottom layer. As the topsoil is returned
to each trench, nutrients are added at different levels . . . bone meal
first (four pounds per 50 square feet), a little topsoil, a 4-inch layer
of compost, some more topsoil, about 2 inches of rotted manure, some
more topsoil, and a small amount of wood ashes (three pounds per
50 square feet). Cover with soil and rake the surface well. Soil
conditioners are added to the upper layers of the bed only, as is done
in nature. By working manure and compost into the topsoil layers
you protect these layers from nutrient leaching, drying and other ills

they are exposed to at the surface. The top of the bed should be raised some 4 to 8 inches above ground level when everything has been added.

Well, there it is. If you are up to it, or have a strong arm to help you, no better or more aesthetically satisfying way of growing vegetables can be found. Add a few trellises for the climbers and you have my dream of a kitchen garden. Dream it remains. All I aspire to is the grouping of the long-term vegetables in a vague sort of way into blocks, as if they were in raised beds, with fewer lines of demarcation than the usual way of planting them in rows; and even that breaks down in practice. What happens in the end is the profligate piling of the whole space with compost, salt hay, seaweed—and I am grateful when I can find someone willing to do *that*. A notable fertility I think I can say I have achieved. The ingredients I use are, after all, the same as those called for in the recipe for the raised beds, though one could quibble with details. The cow manure I manage to find in off-years isn't well rotted, and is therefore composted, but it comes to the same thing. Seaweed isn't mentioned but would probably be incorporated in a coastal area, certainly not frowned upon. And so on. The method is essentially organic and would never work with artificial fertilizer—one reason why this noble and ancient form of cultivation, which produced the finest vegetables in the world in its day, is on its way out even in the countries whose pride it once was.

Those kitchen gardens supplying the Ile de France were to me at one time a symbol of western civilization, as they have been to others. When I made the long voyage from east to west via the Orient Express, from Hungary to France before the war, a passage from a certain unremembered novel used to ring in my ears:

At daybreak on the morning of her arrival, as she passed Château-Thierry, she pressed her forehead to the windowpane, which had been growing brighter since the train had crossed the French border. Its blanket of frost had melted away. The melon frames, the lettuce frames, the hotbeds for growing violets all reflected the 'fair but cloudy' sky of the Paris Basin. The trees spurted up, like geysers covered with bark, or like barometers showing the atmospheric pressure of the Ile de France. Little walls formed espaliers, where the best peaches and pears in all the world are ripened. France is a modulated country; after a Poland without modulations, it seemed a symphony . . .

Substitute Hungary for Poland and that is what I felt about a landscape now crisscrossed by superhighways and *peripheriques*, where the fields are the right size to be plowed by tractors.

Kitchen gardens are burgeoning I'm glad to say—they are the only kind of garden that is. But the trend isn't likely to last unless the legions of new gardeners take more trouble than we did during the war—another boom period—to master the techniques of raising good vegetables. Home-grown produce isn't ipso facto better than what you find at a good market, and can be worse. If you count on chemicals to do the job for you, don't attend to the health of the soil, don't pick the vegetables when they are young (and with most of them that means when they are about half the size of the store-bought), make dull choices, you will end up finding the whole business a bore, just as so many victory gardeners did. Fifty pounds of potatoes, a few lettuces and a lot of overgrown green beans aren't worth a summer of hoeing and weeding—though of course if you garden organically you can avoid those chores. But not all chores. Mulches don't solve every problem, and a good deal of effort goes into making, finding and spreading them. You have to have a real passion for vegetables, and to be a good cook, which is to say one with a dedicated interest in what you and your family consume, not for health's sake—I take that for granted, and a lot of so-called health food is grim stuff—but in behalf of excellence. If you don't terribly care what you eat, or enjoy preparing it—forget about making a kitchen garden. Once you start thinking of it as work, or a duty, it's all over.

VINES

I wish the growing and training of vines were given more attention than it is in books, for it is really a separate branch of horticulture, an advanced exercise in the *Gradus ad Parnassum* of the gardening arts if not actually right up there with topiary and espaliering. Seldom is it treated as such. (The exceptions are grape and wisteria, whose training is usually described in some detail.) Ordinarily we are informed that there are three types of vine: those that climb by twining, those that send out tendrils, and those that cling to surfaces with discs or holdfasts, and that about completes our education. As to pruning and training, encyclopedias either fall silent or put the information in a form quite useless to the average gardener.

Take clematis: According to *Hortus III*, there are three groups: the Florida, blooming on old wood in summer; the Patens, flowering on old wood in spring; and the Jackmanii, flowering on new wood in summer and autumn. The first two are lightly pruned—it doesn't say when—the last cut to the ground during the dormant period. But to which type does my *C. montana* belong? No word on that. Many cultivars are also mentioned by name, but it so happens that my 'Will Godwin' isn't among them. What do I do with him? (And while I am at it, I would like to inquire what Mrs. George Jackman is doing in the Patens group? Shouldn't she be with the Jackmaniis?) In any event, no catalogue follows these classifications. In the Wayside catalogue, the large-flowered clematis are simply described as 'European treasures' and are listed apart from the species types—which is correct since they are hybrids but doesn't help with the pruning problem. Nor does the description 'old wood'—which is intelligible when it applies to a trunk or branches thick enough to be called 'wood' but not to the tangle of wiry stems that constitutes my large-flowering clematises. Study them as I will, I can't determine whether the flowers are blooming on 'wood' that is old or new; and as a result I don't dare put the secateurs to any of them, scraggy though they are.

I could go on. How and when do you prune a trumpet vine—always provided we mean the same thing by this term? The trumpet vine I knew as a child was a bignonia, and it rampaged all over our back fence in Washington. Only after a series of ridiculous mix-ups did I discover that it isn't hardy in the North and that what I wanted wasn't *Bignonia* or any of its bewildering Latin aliases but one or another species of *Campsis*, which are 'members of the Bignonia family.' To my untutored eye, they look as nearly alike as makes no matter, but let that go. I am still in the dark as to how to manage the vine I have at last obtained. All this family are rampant growers and capable of burying a small building in a few years, and I will have to take action sooner or later. I am still searching for precise instructions.

Then there is ivy. Surely everybody knows how to prune ivy. Or do they? I'm not at all sure I do. The ivies I have—and God knows

what they all are, since I didn't plant any of them—vary considerably in size and growth rate and clearly can't be treated alike.
Some have to be pruned because they threaten the neighborhood;
others move so slowly they never have to be pruned at all—unless
of course pruning would hasten their growth. Would it? And
when, if ever, should it be done? No one can tell me.

Roses are another puzzle. One says 'climbing roses,' but of
course they aren't vines. They have no inbred instinct to mount, no
twining tendencies and no tentacles to hold them upright. They
are just roses with tremendously long canes that man long ago
decided to prop up in various ways. That is far from the end of it.
Tough old roses can be more or less left to their fate, tied to their
supports and in spring pruned back to undamaged wood. That, at
least, is what I do, and in fact it isn't right. You are supposed, with
ramblers, to distinguish between the current season's flower-
bearing canes and the new growth. The canes that have borne flowers are then removed in late summer, and the new canes (which
will bear next year) raised up and secured in their places. All I can
say is, try it—and hope to escape without a mortal wound. You
may then move on to the large-flowered climbers, either the once-
or the everblooming; and if you can decipher the directions you
deserve to succeed.

Hardly ever can I get a vine of any kind to do what I want it
to—if a so-called climbing rose to clamber, if an ivy to cling to the
surface I have in mind, if a clematis to gather itself on a trellis and
toss its mantle in all directions. I use an infinity of equipment:
nails, wires, staples, not to mention ladders, secateurs and ham-
mers as indirect accessories. Vast quantities of material are carried
off to the dump. Yet summer's end always finds me with an overgrown wisteria headed in the wrong direction; the clematis called
Traveler's Joy condemned by the telephone company because it is
weighing down (and looking absolutely beautiful—a waterfall of
fragrant white blossom) the cable that leads into the house instead of following the route I have indicated for it. A neighbor has
actually cut down his *Hydrangea petiolaris*, that glorious climber
with its flattened inflorescences like so many lacy pincushions, because the tentacles were reaching into the clapboards of his
garage. Now it happens that I am willing to pay the price and am
trying to persuade mine to do that very thing—mount the side of
the house. It will not. It has decided instead to compete with the
hemlock hedge: its growth is lateral and contrary to all rules,

headed toward the dark interior of the hedge instead of upward toward the light and those vulnerable clapboards.

Still, I rather like wrestling with vines. Of all plants they are the most vigorously, visibly alive, uncannily so. A silver-lace vine that has foamed twenty feet over a trellis in the space of a summer is little short of astounding. Look, it seems to say, only look at me— and indeed one does look, with something of the awe one feels at an acrobatic feat. But when it has risen as high as the roof-tree— don't ask me what you do with it then.

———————— ❧ ————————

WEEDS

While I was at Coudray I fell asleep in the deep grass and slept there for some time. As I roused myself and lay half awake, with eyes smarting from the sun's heat and with vision clouded by the hot vapor which the hay exhales at noontime, I found myself possessed by an amusing illusion. Lying close to the ground as I was, the high grass overtopped my face and limited my view to a narrow bit of space where grass and field flowers were silhouetted against the transparent blue of the air.

For the moment I lost all sense of dimension, and those tenuous weeds took on enormous proportions. Their slight bodies seemed to me transformed into various trees which the grasses resemble in minia- ture. One was the tall, slender palm, another the weeping willow. A blade of ripe oats above my head seemed ready to crush me by letting fall its gigantic fruit, and in the distance—of a few feet—I caught the vision of other superb trees. Serried rows of purple sumac and of spiny aloes, cactus, cedars of Lebanon, banana trees with their volup- tuous, outspread leaves, orange trees in flower, luxuriant catalpa, robust oaks and pale olive trees took the place of tiny field flowers, fine aigrettes and delicate filaments, silky tufts and dangling seed pods in which the meadows abound. The space between their stems was filled with short grass like a thick undergrowth. As I looked at those weeds, which a hot breeze stirred feebly, they seemed to me an immeasurable forest which bent beneath the force of a powerful storm. Its heavy branches were shattered by the tempest, and the lofty tree-tops crashed with a terrifying noise. In the midst of this tumult a dull roaring came to my ears. Gripped by terror at the approach of a lion, I leaped to my feet—and it was well that I did, for a big hornet was buzzing under my nose. But alas, the virgin forest and the mighty exotic trees had disappeared. I found myself surrounded by nothing more intimidating than clover, alfalfa, grass and other kinds of fodder.

So that was the end of my solitary journey into the wilds of the New World.

GEORGE SAND
Intimate Journal.
Translated by M. J. Howe

If we could bring ourselves to see weeds like this, we might be in less of a rush to get rid of them; and organic theory does in fact hold that they constitute a mini-ecology that should be respected. They put nutrients into the soil as well as taking them out, preserve tilth, and some are useful in insect control. The green lacewing, for example, whose larvae devour many pests, itself feeds on the nectar of nettles, lamb's-quarters and dandelions—all of which happen to make delicious soups and salads as well. The distinction between weeds and wildings is therefore far from clear, and in some countries is scarcely made.

Italians are by our standards wonderfully indifferent to weeds. Once in Amalfi I lived by a garden that descended in innumerable terraces to the sea, each planted with lemon, orange or olive trees and under them artichokes and asparagus, lettuces, every sort of vegetable growing in a blooming tangle of plants classifiable as weeds because they were obstructing the vegetables. I climbed those terraces every day and every day my hand went irresistibly to root up a wild pea, a clover, a valerian. Once I weeded a whole bed of lettuces, and left my little bundle on a wall as a hint to the gardener to mend his ways. He didn't of course, being content to hoe the rows at long intervals, and to smile tolerantly when he saw me at work. It wasn't my garden after all, and moreover he was right. They can raise three crops a year in that fertile volcanic soil and turning under the weeds enriches it further. No doubt the gardens of Armida weren't weeded either.

I think of that Amalfi garden and others like it when I read the lists of 'weeds' in American encyclopedias. They include black-eyed Susan, buttercups, white clover, crane's-bill geranium, nettles, mallow, St.-John's-wort, celandine, *Veronica officinalis*, tansy, yarrow, sorrel and many other wild flowers and potherbs; and an appalling assortment of weedkillers is needed to eliminate them—

none of which I would touch, not since my one and only betrayal of organic principles. That year's help was flatly opposed to weeding the lawn by hand and I myself recovering from an operation. I accordingly applied the type of herbicide that is combined with fertilizer, and was properly punished. Mild though the application was, owing to my qualms, it finished the weeds all right, and grass too; but the worst was yet to come. The following year the weeds returned in redoubled numbers and the grass was in such a terrible state that compost had to be applied like compresses on a wound.

I recognize of course that some weeds have got to go, those in the lawn especially, though I wouldn't count buttercups, clover or oxeye daisies among them; and my worst lawn enemy doesn't appear on weed lists. Star-of-Bethlehem (*Ornithogalum umbellatum*) is a pretty little item in bulb catalogues, who sometimes offer it as a bonus on a large order. Don't touch it. It will invade every part of the garden, choking out everything in its path, and like many undesirables is cunningly constructed to thwart easy extraction—the slippery foliage when tugged instantly separates from the bulblets, leaving them snugly far below ground. I have a theory that every garden harbors its own particular weeds, and usually this is owing to somebody's stupidity. The Star-of-Bethlehem must have been planted by some misguided soul, and so must the semi-wild campanula known as creeping bluebell, which my wild-flower books say is a garden escapee. Like all campanulas, it is very pretty but don't be charmed by that, or it will creep into every clump of perennials, turn up in every unoccupied corner and drive you crazy. Pulling up does no good here either, nor does digging with a trowel unless you persevere and locate the turnip-like taproot, sometimes six inches down, that is the source of endless smaller dependencies—which will in the course of time produce taproots of their own. Nobody, on the other hand, can have planted the deadly nightshade imbedded in the stone wall behind the vegetable garden, which by now has reached the stage where only a blast of dynamite could dislodge it. Rock salt and boiling water it loves, and cutting down only stimulates it to greater efforts. To that one I bow in defeat.

These are the worst kinds of weeds in that they can't be killed simply by burying them under a heavy mulch. The majority, however, can. I use salt hay, seaweed, compost and buckwheat hulls (see MULCHES), but any substance applied to a depth of four to five inches will, by depriving the plant of light and air, kill it off. Or if not, those that can battle their way through can usually be lifted rather than hauled out. In general I wish we could restrain our hysteria about weeds, and when serious weeding *is* necessary, be cautious about attacking George Sand's miniature universe. I have discovered tiny hollies, asparagus fern, the offspring of my silk tree, even a Norfolk Island pine while weeding, these seeded by the birds. Other plants self-sow in the area immediately around them, and if these come from hybrids, they aren't worth saving. In most cases they will revert to inferior ancestral types. In others, you may be doing yourself and everybody else a favor if you save them. There is a disturbing rumor to the effect that when a tree is about to die it showers seedlings around it—disturbing, that is, to atheists because, like the statistic that more boy babies are born during wars, it implies that somebody up there is watching, and trying to compensate for impending loss. The fact remains that our doomed elms in their penultimate days did produce an unusual number of seedlings. A lot of them came up under my hemlock hedge and I have been careful to see that they aren't weeded out. One has fought its way through four or five feet of impenetrable hemlock growth and reached the light. My hope is that by the time it is ready to call itself a tree, a cure for Dutch elm disease will have been found, and in that case I will have a vigorous specimen on hand. Too assiduous weeding would have eliminated it.

--- ❧ ---

WILD FLOWERS

Study a book on wild flowers (I can commend *Wildflowers of Eastern America* by Klimas and Cunningham) or for that matter walk out into the woods and fields, and you wonder why you go to the trouble of sowing seed, ordering plants, when the countryside is alive with flowers that are identical with or sometimes superior to their domesticated cousins. Wild bluebells (*Mertensia virginica*), bee balm (*Monarda*), the common bleeding heart, Jacob's-ladder, false indigo, passion-flower and lots of others differ in no important respect from cultivated varieties. Still others are uniquely themselves and therefore unobtainable except in the wild, among them our native orchids: the exquisite pink lady's-slipper that really looks more like a little satchel to carry satin dancing shoes than the shoes themselves; the white fringed orchis (*Habenaria blephariglottis*), hooded plumes collected on a spike; the rosebud orchid, poised like a hummingbird on its stalk; the three-bird orchis. Cattleyas grown under glass are coarse by comparison. The golden *Iris Pseudacorus*, wild blue flag, *Iris prismatica* and the crested dwarf iris make all but certain Japanese and Siberian varieties look vulgar. Wild flowers are never vulgar. One and all they have an elegance and restraint to their design that ought to give the hybridists pause as they go about their work: Fabergé would have been proud to produce the nodding bells of *Clematis viorna*, purple enameled on green gold; Grinling Gibbons pleased to have carved the wild-ginger flower, a three-cornered brown box whose petals open to reveal the surprise at the bottom—pistils incised like a cameo. Wood lilies are so refined in their beauty that if Jan de Graaff, for one, hadn't been born, I would say that they too couldn't be improved upon.

There was a time when one could have looted all this natural beauty without compunction. It had, in fact, to be done, or we would have had no flowers to grow in our gardens, since all are descended from some wild variety that caught somebody's eye. But—it can't be too often emphasized—that time has gone. No longer is it permissible to venture forth with a trowel and a view to improving a naturalistic patch in one's own garden. Remoteness of the site is no justification, rather the opposite. To remove a plant from a spot where 'no one will notice' is a greater risk than to dig up something by the roadside. The chances are excellent that the hidden specimen is the rare one, perhaps the only example to have survived for miles around, while the one by the roadside is nothing more than an escapee from a lost farm. Even then, one should proceed with caution. I can remember, and it isn't longer than twenty years ago, when Turk's-cap lilies abounded in this part of New England. Now they are gone, raped, many of them, by passing motorists who treated them as cut flowers and didn't even plant the bulbs when they got home. They are of course on the endangered species list—as are all the orchids I mention. But those who go out to bag wild flowers are hardly ever the same people who know or care about endangered species.

A middle ground exists between the extremes of letting all wild flowers strictly alone and robbing them indiscriminately, and I tread it uneasily. What if you happen to know that a certain area is threatened with 'development' and the wild flowers in it are sure to be destroyed? I am thinking of a miniature swamp close by one of our back roads where each June a lake of *Iris prismatica* comes into bloom, and every time I pass it I whisper to myself, why not? The tide of tacky little houses has all but reached this point and if not this year, then next or the year after, the iris will be gone. Why not, in the meantime, dig up a few and preserve them, as it were, in my garden? The problem is exactly analagous to that of what to do with wild animals. If man is going to destroy their habitats, making survival impossible, is it or isn't it a good idea to preserve and try to breed a few specimens in zoos? Any answer you can think of is repulsive. Extinction is almost too awful to contemplate, but are a few survivors preserved in memoriam any better? I don't know. So far, I have left the *Iris prismatica* to its fate.

The decision, I have to confess, isn't exclusively on moral grounds. Like wild animals, wild plants often sicken and die in captivity. Nobody understands exactly what combinations of soil and soil bacteria, of moisture, light, heat or cold are responsible for their success in a given place; whereas with domesticated plants all these factors are to some extent predictable in their effect. Those wild flowers that grow from bulbs or tubers are the least risky to tamper with. Usually they can be transplanted with fair hopes that they will accommodate themselves to a new environment. The commoner ferns are equally adaptable. With others, the issue is in doubt. Wild flowers seem tough a priori to the ignorant: If they weren't, they wouldn't have managed so well without the helping hand of man. So goes the reasoning and it is false. Wild flowers do best when they are allowed to make their own choices about where and how they will grow, and the best that man can do is try to emulate those conditions. As often as not, he fails, and the lover of wild flowers would do better to join a conservationist society than to try to start his own sanctuary for endangered species.

Some nurserymen offer wild flowers by mail. (See CATALOGUES.) To be consistent, I suppose one should inquire into precisely how the plants were obtained, and if it were admitted that those on the endangered list were collected in the wild, refuse to order them.

I've not gone to that length, and have done fairly well with the few I have ordered. Trilliums seem to transplant easily, as do Virginia bluebells, wild columbines and Jack-in-the-pulpit. But with me it has been precisely the threatened orchids that fare badly—likewise the fringed and closed gentians and trout lilies (also called dogtooth violet, *Erythronium americanum*), all on the list. None of these can I claim to have 'saved,' and so probably shouldn't have sent for them in the first place. As I say, I don't know the answer to this dilemma.

WOMAN'S PLACE

There are the husband's apple and pear trees, twined by the wife's clematis; his cabbage beds fringed with her pinks and pansies; the tool-house wreathed with roses; his rougher labor adorned by her gayer fancy, all speaking loudly of their hearts and tastes . . . We trust the cottager's wife will love and care for the flowers and we are sure if she does that her husband's love and esteem for her will be heightened and strengthened.

From an English gardening magazine, 1848

A charming sentiment on the face of it, but what about that veiled threat at the end? Why should the cottager's love and esteem for his wife be contingent on her care for the flowers? And if he neglected the apple and pear trees—would she then be entitled to think less of *him*? It may come as a surprise that sexism should play any part in horticulture but the more you read of gardening history the more convincing the case for it becomes, and the less you are ready to see the cottager as a chivalrous male doing the hard work while indulging his wife in her 'gayer fancy.' Divisions of labor there have been, but not nearly as simple as that, while the whole business of women's supposed devotion to flowers may need another look.

At Woburn Abbey in the seventeenth century there was a famously lifelike statue of a woman weeding, and records of English estates show that from a very early period this chore was almost exclusively performed by females. It is, says my source (who is, naturally, a man), 'a task at which they have always been pre-eminent,' and this is an assessment with which male gardeners have long agreed. La Quintinie, who was in charge of Louis XIV's *potagers* and otherwise an adorable person, recommended the hiring of married men rather than bachelors (as was the usual custom), on the ground that wives would be available for weeding, as well as cleaning and scraping out pots. In the Orient, women weed the rice paddies in water up to their knees. In general, it is to be observed that men plow while women sow; prune fruit and nut trees but leave the harvest to women; and most men like working with vegetables (all, that is, but the weeding). Other crops appear to be largely in the hands of women. In that part of Turkey where tobacco is grown, I saw them patting together the raised beds, setting out seedlings, and of course weeding, while the male population sat under pergolas playing tric-trac. But why pick on Turks? In other parts of the world women are thought to be pre-eminent at hauling brushwood on their backs. Russian grannies sweep leaves in parks and streets.

Altogether, it is pretty obvious that relative physical strength isn't the determining factor in most cases of divided labor but rather which tasks men prefer to do and which they have decided to leave to women. The man in charge of our Hungarian vineyard was the envy of the neighborhood on account of his ten terrific daughters, who could and did get through twice the work of any male, and he didn't hesitate to lay it on them. In peasant societies nobody worries very much about overtaxing women's strength. I doubt if they do in any society. What men fear is competition and losing the services of women as drudges. Thus, La Quintinie must have known that women could be trained as well as men to perform a hundred more exacting and interesting horticultural tasks than scraping out pots.

This is all the more striking when you consider that it was women who invented horticulture in the first place, women who ventured into field and forest in search of wild plants, and women who domesticated them while men were still out chasing wild beasts. Women were the first gardeners; but when men retired from the hunting field and decided in favor of agriculture instead, women steadily lost control. No longer were they the ones to decide what was planted, how, or where; and accordingly the space allotted to them diminished too, until flowers and herbs were the only plants left under their direct management, while their former power passed into myth. The inventor of agriculture became the goddess of agriculture, her daughter the bringer of spring, when plants come to life; and each of these had a flower or flowers assigned to her—almost certainly by men and as a form of propitiation. For make no mistake: Men were always half in a terror of women's complicity with nature, and the power it had given them. The other face of the goddess belongs to the witch brewing her spells from plants, able to cure and also curse with her knowledge of their properties. In some societies this fear of women amounted to panic. It was believed that their mere presence could blight vegetation. Democritus wrote that a menstruating woman could kill young produce 'merely by looking at it.' On the one hand, the benign giver of life and fertility; on the other, the baneful caster of withering spells—it's a tall order and no wonder that men were inclined to confine such a dangerously two-faced influence to a safe place.

For that is how I have come to interpret the two-thousand-odd years of women's incarceration in the flower garden. The superstitious fear that women were in league with nature in some way that men were not was thus simultaneously catered to and kept in check. Flowers are of all plants the least menacing and the most useless. Their sole purpose is to be beautiful and to give pleasure —which is what one half of man wants from woman (the other, it is needless to say, asks for qualities more practical and down-to-earth)—and as such they are the perfect combination of tribute and demand. A gift of flowers to a woman implies that she is as deliciously desirable as the blossoms themselves; but there may be another and hidden message, contained in old-fashioned phrases like 'shy as a violet,' 'clinging vine,' not originally conceived as pejoratives, that tells more of the truth—which is that flowers are also emblems of feminine submission. In the western world, this is rarely explicit. In the Orient, where fewer bones are made about the position of women, two examples may be cited. The art of Japanese flower arrangement, *ikebanu*, whose masters are male, was originally imparted to women as a means of silent communication with stern samurai husbands to whom words, and especially plaintive words, would have been an intolerable presumption; whereas an iris and a pussy willow and perhaps a convolvulus, arranged in the right order, conveyed a world of meaning. In China, we find another example, one that borders on the atrocious: the bound foot, to be encountered as late as the 1920's. My Chinese amah's feet were bound, and filled me with fascinated horror. What unspeakable distortion lay inside that delicate little slipper that caused her to sway (seductively to men, that was the point) as she walked? She would never show me but I have seen photographs since, and learned that the hideously crushed mass of flesh and bone was compared by Chinese poets to a lotus bud.

With this in mind, one may feel that those paintings of Chinese gardens in which exquisitely clad ladies float about tending to potted peonies depict scenes less idyllic than they appear. What we are seeing is a sort of floral cage—one that in the Hindu and Moslem world was an actual prison. Purdah and the harem were mitigated for their captives by the presence of many beautiful flowers. The illiterate women in the Ottoman seraglio even devised a 'language of flowers' (described with some scorn by Lady Mary Wortley Montagu in her letters from Turkey and later all the rage among European females with nothing better to do) to take the place of the written language forbidden them. But there was no escape from the famous tulip gardens of the seraglio (see TULIPS for the way their confinement affected these wretches). Call them what you will—and as everybody knows the word 'paradise' derives from the Persian word for garden, an idea later expanded in Moslem usage to mean a heaven where male wants were attended to by ravishing and submissive houris—one of the principal functions of the Oriental garden from Turkey to China was the incarceration of women.

To equate European gardens with any such purpose might seem to carry feminist interpretation too far, and obviously the differences are great. Garden plans nevertheless suggest a similar if less drastic impulse on the part of men. The Roman atrium was a flower-filled enclosure chiefly for women's use, and it is in marked contrast to the pleasure grounds laid out by a rich Roman gentleman and intellectual like Pliny, who makes it perfectly clear that his were entirely for male diversion. Those pavilions for reading and sunbathing, dining with friends, those philosopher's walks, were for himself and his male companions. Possibly there was somewhere an inner courtyard where the women of the household could spend their leisure time, and more than likely it was filled with flowers, if only those that would be picked for the house; but except for his violet beds, he doesn't speak of flowers—or of women.

Medieval gardens repeat the pattern of the *hortus conclusus*, with the difference that they are more elaborate and better adapted to feminine comfort. Trellised walks, turf seats, tiny flower beds, all mark a female presence that is borne out in the illuminations and tapestries where we almost invariably see a lady stooping to pluck a strawberry, a rose, or at her ease with embroidery and lute. So plainly were they designed for women that they even convey an illusion of female supremacy at last—and it wasn't entirely an illusion. The mass folly of the Crusades occupied European men for the better part of two hundred years, and with her lord away at the wars the chatelaine did often manage his estate at home, and not badly either. She lived behind fortified walls nevertheless, and it isn't hard to conjecture that her garden was in the nature of a chastity belt, locking her in until the return of her lord and master. 'A garden inclosed is my sister, my spouse; a spring shut up, a fountain sealed,' says the Song of Solomon—to all of course but him. That feminine purity is only to be preserved within four walls is another ancient idea, and in the late Middle Ages it found indirect expression in those curious paintings of so-called Mary gardens, which show the Virgin seated in a castellated enclosure surrounded by richly symbolic fruits, vines and flowers. But the fortified walls came down with the return of something like peace and leisure, and the Renaissance garden with its magical perspectives, its cascades and fountains, was another story altogether—a celebration of humanism—except that in Italy at least it always had an odd little appendix attached, as it were, to the grand design: the *giardino segreto*.

Garden histories don't try to account for the *giardini segreti* except to note that flowers, largely absent in the rest of the garden, grew in them. To me it is at least plausible that these fossilized remnants of the medieval garden were for women, intended to be so, and that in fact they kept alive the tradition of the flower-filled feminine ghetto.

'Know that it doesn't displease but rather pleases me that you should have roses to grow and violets to care for,' wrote a fifteenth-century French merchant to his wife, sounding the note to be heard again and again for the next three hundred years. From 1500 to 1800 was the great age of garden design: visions of what a garden should be shifted like scenery upon a stage, theories multiplied and books on the subject poured from the presses. But in England only two were in all that time specifically directed to women, and both assume her province to be flowers and herbs. Lawson's *Coun-*

trie Housewife (1618) gives her a list of sixteen flowers for nose-
gays, five kinds of bulbs including 'Tulippos,' and twenty-six
herbs. Charles Evelyn's *Lady's Recreation* (1707) discusses most
of the same flowers while permitting a fountain and 'an excellent
contriv'd statue.' He also allows her a wilderness where 'being no
longer pleas'd with a solitary Amusement you come out into a
large Road, where you have the Diversion of seeing Travellers
pass by, to compleat your Variety.' Why she should be solitary and
driven to watch travelers in the road he doesn't say. His whole
tone, however, is one of a patronage that is echoed elsewhere. Sir
William Temple (*Garden of Epicurus*, 1685): 'I will not enter
upon any account of flowers, having only pleased myself with seeing or smelling them, and not troubled myself with the care, which
is more the ladies' part than the men's . . .' John Lawrence (*New
System . . . a Complete Body of Husbandry and Gardening*, 1726)
adds to patronage something like a scolding: 'I flatter myself the
Ladies would soon think that their vacant Hours in the Culture of
the *Flower-Garden* would be more innocently spent and with
greater Satisfaction than the common Talk over a Tea-Table
where Envy and Detraction so commonly preside. Whereas when
Opportunity and Weather invite them amongst their Flowers,
there they may dress, and admire and cultivate Beauties like
themselves without *envying* or *being envied*.' Here the argument
for keeping women shut up with flowers is almost entirely trivi-
alized. The Virgin's bower is now a school for decorum.

What amazes me is the way female scholars have failed to notice the implications of statements like these. Eleanor Sinclair
Rohde (*The Story of the Garden*, 1932), to whom I am indebted
for many of my quotations, gives no hint that she catches their
drift. She takes no umbrage at her adored Parkinson (or perhaps
doesn't choose to understand him) when she quotes a passage like
this from the *Paradisus*: 'Gentlewomen, these pleasures are the
delights of leisure [*sic*], which hath bred your love and liking to
them, and although you are not herein predominant, yet cannot
they be barred from your beloved, who I doubt not, will share
with you in the delight as much as is fit.' Not the cleanest prose in
the world, and Mrs. Rohde construes it as a tribute to the central
place of women in seventeenth-century gardening. I read it as the
opposite: a warning to wives with ideas about garden layout to
leave that area to their husbands, who know best but will, if not
aggravated, allow a share in the result.

Whichever of us is right, history is on my side. Not until the twentieth century did any woman play a recognizable part in garden design. We know why, of course. The great gardens of the world have been reflections of men's intellectual and spiritual experience: visions of Arcadia, hymns to rationalism or the divine right of kings, Zen parables—and the well-known reasons for our failure to compose symphonies, paint masterpieces, conceive the Einstein theory, apply equally to our failure to produce a feminine incarnation of, say, Le Nôtre. One or two great gardens *were* made for women, who were queens or the equivalent; but as they were always in the prevailing fashion it isn't possible to tell to what extent they conformed to the client's particular wishes. In one case we know they didn't. Marie de Medici's ideas for the Luxembourg were resolutely opposed by her designer, the incomparable Boyceau, and he had his way (much to posterity's gain, it should be said). We know, too, that Marie Antoinette's *hameau*, arranged in what she imagined to be the English style, was done in a taste all her own, but that sad spot, so out of place at Versailles, doesn't say much in favor of feminine theories about design.

Malmaison might be a happier example. It, too, was laid out for a woman, and given the Empress Josephine's character, one can be sure she got what she wanted. Malmaison, however, isn't outstanding for its design but for the millions of roses that grew there, probably the greatest collection the world has ever seen; and this was generally true of all gardens made by or for women of which we have any record. Flowers were, and until the twentieth century remained, the theme. In the eighteenth, the Duchess of Beaufort grew exotics, as did Mme. de Pompadour in all the many ravishing gardens given her by Louis XV—she adored the white, highly scented tropicals, gardenias and jasmine especially, brought to her from all parts of the French empire. Lady Broughton specialized in alpines, and was one of the first to grow them outdoors in a rock garden; Lady Holland introduced dahlias to England and grew them in her greenhouses.

Here, a new note was introduced, for it was at about this time that women were allowed to embark on the study of botany—not too seriously and rather late in the day; and it is notable that various writers should have seen their studies in much the same light as pottering in the flower garden itself. J. C. Loudon, for one, recommended botany as 'a charming and instructive female exercise,' or a grade or two above the netting of purses, and in the hands of the upper-class young ladies who went in for it, that was about what these studies amounted to. In fact, they mostly consisted in the coloring of flower engravings, and counting stamens according to the newly introduced Linnaean system of classification, which made everything wonderfully simple. Honorable exceptions there were, mostly royal. The dowager Princess of Wales founded the great botanic garden at Kew in 1761; and Queen Charlotte was accounted a passionate student, though how she found time for her researches in the course of bearing her sixteen children is a wonder. The *Strelitzia* or bird-of-paradise flower, however, is named for her (she was born Mecklenberg-Strelitz), as were four varieties of apple—hence, it is said, Apple Charlotte, the dessert.

Women in humbler positions, who might have contributed rather more to the science, did not fare so well. One of them was Jane Colden, the daughter of a lieutenant-governor of New York, who lived near Newburgh-on-Hudson and who ventured into the wilderness at a time when that was neither easy nor safe. By 1758 she had compiled a manuscript describing four hundred local plants and their uses, illustrated by herself. It was never published. During the Revolution it fell into the hands of a Hessian officer who was interested in botany. He took it back to Germany where it was preserved at the University of Göttingen. Evidently it was important enough to have been purchased at a later date by Sir Joseph Banks, the most influential botanist of his time; but he didn't try to have it published and it reposes in the British Museum to this day. Nor is any flower called *Coldenia*, the accolade regularly bestowed by botanists on those of their tribe who have made important contributions to science. (That those standards have been less than strict is, however, obvious even where men's names are concerned: The *Montanoa*, a species of shrub, appears to have been named for a Mexican bandit-politician. As applied to women, names seem chiefly to have been bows to rank: *Victoria amazonica*, that water-lily whose pad is the size of a dinner table, was of course named for the dear queen; while the *Cinchona*, from whose bark quinine is derived, was called after the Condesa de Cinchon, Vicerene of Peru, who in 1638 was cured of malaria by a decoction of what had previously been called Peruvian bark.)

Given the circumstances—circumscribed travel, the reluctance to admit that female minds could cope seriously with science—it isn't surprising that no woman made a name for herself in botany.

That her accomplishments in the breeding and cultivating of plants should also be a well-kept secret is another matter. 'In March and in April from morning till night/In sowing and seeding good housewives delight,' sang Thomas Tusser (1524–80) in his rhyming calendar for gardeners. Even in Tudor times England was famous for the beauty of its flowers, especially doubled varieties— columbines, primroses, violets, marigolds and campanulas—but also striped and unusual colors, which included sports such as a reddish lily-of-the-valley. Foreigners attributed these variations to the damp English climate which allowed for year-around planting, but also noted that the selection and cultivation were done by housewives rather than professionals—at that period well behind their French and Dutch colleagues. In the seventeenth century, the great age of English plantsmanship, when collectors like the Tradescants began to range the world, these accomplishments receded into the background—where they remained for another two hundred years. What the Victorians called 'old-fashioned' flowers were really housewives' flowers, grown continuously and in defiance or ignorance of fashion—including the landscape movement that destroyed so many of England's finest and most characteristic gardens and prohibited so much as a cowslip from showing its pretty head above ground. In the feminine domain called the cottage garden, which a modern state might designate as a preserve with plants whose removal would be punishable by law, grew such otherwise lost rarities as blue primroses, Parkinson's 'stately Crown Imperial,' and the fairy rose (not to be confused with the modern polyantha of that name), many violas and pinks long since vanished from cultivation in the gardens of the rich and those desiring to be *à la page*.

The cottage garden was rediscovered toward the end of the nineteenth century—mostly by women like Mrs. Juliana Horatia Ewing, who founded a Parkinson Society 'to search out and cultivate old flowers which have become scarce,' and of course Gertrude Jekyll, who reintroduced the fairy rose. But although these gardens clearly pointed to the role of women as important conservators as well as breeders and cultivators of plant species, no one pursued the obvious conclusion that what had happened in the nineteenth century might also be presumed to have occurred in others as well. No writer I know of has, for example, enlarged the thesis that in the Dark Ages it was monks in monasteries who preserved such species as survived in those parts of Europe not fortunate enough to be conquered by the garden-loving Arabs (Spain, Sicily, etc.). Why not also nuns in nunneries? It is known that they grew flowers in profusion for the adornment of churches and herbs for simples, just as the monks did. Indeed it was one of their functions to school ladies in the uses of cooking and medicinal herbs (which then included flowers like marigolds, poppies, even roses and honeysuckle), especially the latter because it was the lady of the manor who compounded and administered medicines, though she wasn't of course honored with the title of physician, and the few venturesome women who did try to set themselves up as doctors were promptly squelched.

With all the vast amount of writing about gardens that has appeared in the last hundred years, much of it by women, you might expect somebody to have devoted a book to women's place in gardening history. If anyone has, I haven't heard of it, and it must be admitted that the difficulties of research would be formidable. Where would the documentation come from? In England, the earliest herbal published by a woman was Elizabeth Blackwell's in 1737. The earliest essay on gardening itself is probably Lady Charlotte Murray's *British Garden* (1799); in America, Mrs. Martha Logan's *Gardener's Kalender* (known only through republication in a magazine around 1798). What the library stacks of other countries would yield I can't say; the pickings would presumably be even slimmer. Private correspondence would be a richer source, if one knew where to look. (There are, for instance, tantalizing hints in Mme. de Sévigné's letters that in the age dominated by Le Nôtre's geometry she had ideas about *la nature* that anticipated Rousseau's—as when she told her daughter that she had spent the morning on her country estate 'in the dew up to my knees laying lines; I am making winding *allées* all around my park . . .') Novels by women could also be studied in this light. Jane Austen has a great deal about the theory and practice of gardening, especially in *Mansfield Park*, where a part of the plot hinges on Mr. Rushworth's determination to have Mr. Repton remodel his grounds, though in fact every novel has its gardens and each is made to say something about the character and social situation of the owner. (Elizabeth Bennet isn't entirely joking when she says she must date her falling in love with Mr. Darcy to her visit to his 'beautiful grounds at Pemberley.')

Diaries and notebooks would be another source, not forgetting *The Pillow Book of Sei Shōnagon*. In the remoter past, the body of feminine knowledge was locked away under the anonymous heading of old wives' tales, a phrase I have always found offensive. Assume that 'old' doesn't mean the woman gardener was a crone but refers to 'old times.' The expression still implies a combination of ignorance and superstition peculiarly female—and never mind that a thirteenth-century church father like the Abbott of Beauvais testified that a decoction of heliotrope could produce invisibility or that St. Gregory the Great believed the devil hid in lettuce heads. Women will have shed their superstitions at about the same time men did, and what many an old wives' tale really refers to is orally transmitted information, as often as not the result of illiteracy, not inborn backwardness. Women weren't stupider than men; they lacked the means of expressing themselves, and instead of writing herbals or treatises on what is called (note this) husbandry, they told one another what experience had taught them about plants, medicines and many other things. This is also called folk wisdom, and it can be as discriminatory as the rest of human history: How many people know, for instance, that the subtly constructed tents of the Plains Indians were designed and set up entirely by women?

To remedy these deficiencies wouldn't be easy, but I wish somebody would try. The story could end well, too—up to a point. In the spring of 1980 a symposium was held at Dumbarton Oaks whose subject was 'Beatrix Jones Farrand (1872–1959) and fifty Years of American Landscape Architecture.' The setting was appropriate: Mrs. Farrand designed the beautiful garden at Dumbarton Oaks and many other famous ones as well. She was the only woman among the eleven original members of the American Society of Landscape Architects, founded in 1899, and the first to demonstrate that women could design gardens as well as plant flowers. (Jekyll, remember, worked in collaboration with the architect Edwin Lutyens.) She was a thorough professional and inaugurated a period of great brilliance for women as landscape architects. Ellen Biddle Shipman, another of them, told a reporter in 1938 that 'until women took up landscaping, gardening in this country was at its lowest ebb. The renaissance was due largely to the fact that women, instead of working over their boards, used plants as if they were painting pictures and as an artist would. Today women are at the top of the profession.'

That, alas, is no longer true. Not only are the gardens designed by those women for the most part in a sad state of neglect, the profession itself leaves something to be desired. It has, so it seems, gone back to the drawing boards. Many universities now separate courses in design and horticulture into different academic departments. We are where we were in earlier centuries when the designer and the plantsman lived in different worlds—an extraordinary step backward. Does it also represent a resurgence of male chauvinism, a return of the old idea that flowers and plants are a province less worthy than that of stone and water? Not overtly so perhaps. But the lack of interest in horticulture shown by liberated women, including liberated women architects, suggests that they recognize, however subconsciously, the link between flowering plants and old-style femininity as opposed to feminism, and if forced to choose between the two courses, as I gather the students more or less must, would opt for the 'higher' (i.e., male-dominated) one of landscaping. If so, though we have come a long way from the statue of the female weeder and the cottager's wife, it isn't far enough.

Catalogues

Blackthorne Gardens
48 Quincy Street
Holbrook, Massachusetts 02343

Although I hate this catalogue, which costs $2.00 and is crowded, confusing and just about everything a catalogue ought not to be, it is worth struggling through for its offerings of wild American lilies and their so-called Cape Cod lilies, which are exceedingly tough (and exceedingly expensive). Anyone living in the icier regions of the country would do well to look into these. Blackthorne also carries an unusually large and varied selection of Hosta lilies (*Funkia*), those wonderfully resilient and disease-free plants, and is to be complimented for having straightened out the appalling mess of their botanical nomenclature, which other catalogues have yet to do.

Brookstone Company
127 Vose Farm Road
Peterborough, New Hampshire 13458

Hard-to-find tools are the specialty of this house, and that means everything from clock-oilers to logger's hooks. I stick to the garden and greenhouse section for top-notch pruning saws, English dibbles, weeders and the like. Just about everything I have ordered from them has been excellent, and the service is so fast it takes your breath away in these days of botched mailings and delayed deliveries.

Burpee Seed Co.
Warminster, Pennsylvania 18991

One of the oldest and once the best all-around seed houses in the country, Burpee in recent years has been trying to be all things to all gardeners and now carries plants ranging from roses to shade trees. You could order a complete garden from their catalogue. The point is, would you want to? Their prices are consistently higher than those of their competitors: the quality isn't. Examples: The new Sugar Snap pea introduced in 1979 was $4.25 a pound at Burpee; $3.75 at Park; $3.19 at Gurney; $2.50 at Harris. (Smaller packets run 5 to 30 cents higher for all vegetables and most flower seed than they do elsewhere, and the 'handling charge' is stiffer too.) The prices of shrubs, fruit trees, berries, etc., also compare unfavorably with those of firms specializing in these things and offering more sophisticated choices. A rhododendron from Burpee will cost about the same as one from Wayside, though smaller in size and of a commonplace variety. Stark Bros. will sell you 10 Heritage raspberries for $10.90; Burpee charges $14.95—and Stark is a specialist in small fruits. I hate to knock Burpee. They were part of my gardening education. But the overpricing and the fact that their seed is no better than anyone else's have turned me away from this respected old firm. On the other hand, February wouldn't be February if their catalogue didn't arrive on schedule.

J. A. Demonchaux Co.
827 North Kansas
Topeka, Kansas 66608

In spite of my strictures on hygroponically grown endive (which see under ENDIVE) for which this firm supplies seed and directions, they are a source to know about for authentic French vegetable seed: real *haricots vert*, sorrel, Charentais melons, etc., and they send a good planting guide with their orders.

Far North Gardens
15621 Auburndale Avenue
Livonia, Michigan 48154

For primrose fanciers, I am told this is it, and I am sure they know all about it. But Far North Gardens also deals in other kinds of rare flower seed. Their collector's list runs into the hundreds and makes me long for a greenhouse. Unfortunately, they don't ship many plants but those they do include such wonders as the gold-laced polyanthus and the double bloodroot (*Sanguinaria canadensis flore pleno*). Probably a house for professionals rather than the everyday gardener, but a fascinating catalogue.

Garden Way Research
Dept A 335
Charlotte, Vermont 05445

Other firms sell the big, two-wheeled carts that should supplant the wheelbarrow for all gardeners. Wheelbarrows, unless you are a builder who needs a container for bricks, etc., that must be guided over a narrow plank, or have a need for the little plastic 'ball-barrow' that has a pneumatic ball for a wheel, and leaves no mark on soggy springtime lawns, really are rendered obsolete by these capacious wagons that don't require human arms to maintain their equilibrium and can be pushed and hauled in all directions with a minimum of effort. They are, of course, about as new as the Roman Empire but their manufacture in twentieth-century America is of fairly recent date. Garden Way Research is my source—not often, since the carts last for years—and also publishes paperbacks such as *Secrets of Companion Planting* (1975) which I find fascinating.

Gurney Seed and Nursery Co.
Yankton, South Dakota 57079

Gurney's huge, full-color catalogue printed on inelegant paper transports one at once to a Middle Western farm kitchen of fifty years ago. Everything is crammed together—apples, potatoes, bush beans, flowers, trees, vines, house plants, in a glorious hodgepodge. Plants are, of course, not properly identified but called by their common, even local names: velvet cloak for the smoke tree, beauty bush for kolkwitzia; lilacs are lilacs, 'grandmother's favorite.' Yet there are some goodies not easily found in other catalogues: My *jaune d'hollande* potatoes, smuggled from France, proved to be available here, where they are called 'lady finger' potatoes—and they carry also the rare Blue Victor potato. Here too are Swedish brown beans, beloved of Scandinavians, and dewberries. I have a wonderful time with this catalogue but don't often order from it. What I have sent for has been good.

Joseph Harris Co., Inc.
Moreton Farm
3670 Buffalo Road
Rochester, New York 14624

Only flower and vegetable seed here but those of the finest quality and very reasonably priced—few exotics or surprises. My choice for vegetable seed, if only because they don't run after novelties at the expense of the tried and true, like Lincoln peas, which some of us think can't be bettered and are now hard to find. Harris also fills orders promptly and correctly, a rarity today. If wild flowers interest you, they have them—though I quarrel with their definitions. Since when are dame's rocket, coreopsis, monarda, classified as wild? Never mind. This is a first-class house.

Le Jardin du Gourmet
West Danville, Vermont 05873

An unpretentious list in spite of the name, includes herbs (and herb plants), Egyptian onions, shallots, etc. For me, the chief virtue is that they carry a number of seeds from Vilmorin, the great French seed house—and unless you send for the Vilmorin catalogue direct (a tiresome and expensive business) there is no other way I know of to obtain the seed for French gherkins (*cornichons*), *mâche*, salad dandelions, *flageolets*, and among the flowers the incomparable French forget-me-nots (I don't know why these are better—they just are).

Johnny's Selected Seeds
Organic Seed and Crop Research
Albion, Maine 14910

An extremely interesting small catalogue that seems to be aimed at the sophisticated organic homesteader. Many foreign seeds: Oriental greens, beans and melon; Dutch and Danish cabbages and cucumbers —and American varieties they call 'heirloom' that have been lost or aren't carried by commercial houses. E.g., Jacob's Cattle shell beans, Champagne pole beans, Mandan dry corn, Black salsify, Inverno leeks. They also specialize in vegetables suitable to the far north, and carry grains and herbs. I am eager to give this house, which is new to me, a try, for they sound like innovative and deserving amateurs (in the best sense of that word).

Kitazawa Seed Co.
356 W. Taylor Street
San Jose, California 94110

The excellence of Japanese vegetables is now so well established that many American seed houses have incorporated them into their stock. Here, however, is indubitably the real thing and many items that won't be found except at an exclusively Oriental house—such as the edible-leaved chrysanthemum.

Henry Leuthardt Nurseries Inc.
Montauk Highway
East Moriches, New York 11940

As far as I know, this is the only nursery in the East to sell full-grown classically trained espaliers, chiefly apples and pears. They always have been surprisingly reasonable in price, and today are extraordinary. In the 1979 catalogue, a six-armed Palmette Verrier, that is, a candelabrum 65 inches wide and 5 to 6 feet tall, an ornament to any wall, was $60—and that, believe me, is quite a bargain. These beauties arrive lashed to a framework, and all you have to do is untie and plant them against a wall or wire frame. Leuthardt also carries a fine choice of wine and table grapes, berries and dwarf and semi-dwarf trees that aren't espaliered, including some almost lost varieties like the Atlantic Queen Pear. The hitch is that you must order the espaliers long in advance as they are quickly sold out.

Makielski Berry Farm
7130 Platt Road
Ypsilanti, Michigan 48197

This little company has a list, not a catalogue, and wouldn't be worth mentioning except that they carry the only decent gooseberry I have been able to discover in America. The name is Poorman, and while not comparable to the English fruit, it is far better than the dreary and ubiquitous Pixwell.

New England Rootstock Association
Christian Hill
Great Barrington, Massachusetts 01230

A modest selection of wild flowers and ferns, rootstock only, native to New England but presumably growable elsewhere. I have had splendid results from their trilliums, trout lilies and wild iris. A charming little catalogue, and fair prices.

North American Fruit Explorers
c/o Robert Kurle
10 S. 55 Madison St.
Hinsdale, Illinois 60521

A regional association, whose members grow fruit as a hobby and don't supply the public commercially. Membership lets you get in touch with people who may be willing to sell you rare varieties they are working with—'old' apples, etc. Still another way to locate unusual fruit stock is to write the Information Office, Agricultural Service, U.S.D.A., Washington, D.C. 20250 for a copy of *Fruit and Tree Nut Germ Plasm Resource Inventory*, which off-putting name signifies nothing worse than a listing of all fruit and nut varieties now being grown on government research stations. Serious growers can get in touch with the nearest such station and obtain scionwood of varieties that interest them.

Geo. W. Park Seed Co., Inc.
Greenwood, South Carolina 29647

Park's catalogue is fascinating, offering both seed and plants and specializing in miniature vegetables, out-of-the way annuals and perennials, unusual house plants, southern vegetables like cowpeas and peanuts (yes, peanuts are a vegetable). I spend much time studying their Japanese chrysanthemums, Madagascar palms and green amaryllis, but must report disappointments at the lower level: packets mislabeled (laced pinks at 10 cents a seed that turned out to be common Cheddar); low viability in the seed; poorly rooted cuttings. An uneven performance. Many of their plants have also turned out well for me. Good wild-flower mixtures here.

David Reath
Vulcan, Michigan 49892

Peonies only, and as stated in my article on peonies I have my doubts about these peony specialists. I find Reath's catalogue confusingly written—it is by no means always clear which peonies are the tree type and which herbaceous, and prices are high. All illustrations, however, are in full color and though it takes a while to figure it all out (prices, for example, are listed separately from pictures and descriptions), I think it's worth a look, and perhaps an order.

Rex Bulb Farms
P.O. Box 774
Port Townsend, Washington 98368

My one and only for lilies, which is all they sell. The catalogue requires hours of study, being divided into many categories and offering an array of choices so large as to bewilder the greedy—who will want them all. A wide range of prices too, depending on bulb size and rarity: A Harlequin hybrid will go for $1.25, while the precious species lily *L. occidentale* costs $11.00. But whatever they cost, Rex lilies can't be bettered.

Roses of Yesterday and Today
802 Brown's Valley Road
Watsonville, California 95076

The successor to Will Tillotson's old firm, this is the only source I know to offer such a comprehensive selection of antique roses, and the prices are amazingly low. The catalogue, too, is beautiful, a joy to browse through even if you aren't ordering that year—and as old roses last practically forever, you may well not be.

Stark Bros.
Louisiana, Missouri 63353

Not a glamorous house but their fruit trees, berries and nut trees seem to be sturdy and reliable. Many of their peaches are exclusively their own, and they have greengages, the Japanese Shiro plum, and the exquisite Reine Claude—all these, alas, ruled out for me because they carry only standard size trees in this category, no dwarfs. Their dwarf trees are considerably less interesting but anyone with space for large fruit trees will find good choices here.

Stokes Seeds, Inc.
737 Main Street, Box 548
Buffalo, New York 14240

A dense and not alluringly presented catalogue slanted toward the commercial rather than the home gardener. Stokes's offers a staggering variety of vegetable seed (fewer flowers) and a lot of information—not all of it pleasant reading. Here you will find the decline and fall of the American tomato documented in phrases like 'our best basket tomato for green-pick shipping,' and learn how many sprays are used on commercially grown cauliflower. Still, every detail on fruit size, height of plant, number of seeds to the packet, etc., is meticulously given and the language is no-nonsense. I haven't tried the seed but others commend it.

Thompson & Morgan, Inc.
P.O. Box 100
Farmingdale, New Jersey 07727

This English firm's American catalogue is a prettied-up, much truncated version of the copious and sober original—a reflection, I'm afraid, of the relative gardening skills of our two countries. The snappier American edition isn't better than its American counterparts and I have experienced long delays in seed deliveries. Altogether, I would rather order direct from England but suppose this can no longer be done.

Tsang and Ma International
1556 Laurel Street
San Carlos, California 94070

A source for Chinese vegetables like gai lon, a broccoli, dozens of Chinese greens, and cee gwa, the Oriental okra that becomes a luffa sponge when dried. Not being a particular fan of Chinese food, I haven't ordered from here, but those who have tell me the seed is fine. They also caution that you had better know exactly what the names mean or you may end up with several packets of the same vegetable.

Van Bourgondian Bros.
P.O. Box A
245 Farmingdale Road, Rt. 109
Babylon, Long Island, New York 11702

Dutch bulbs and a few other plants, mostly wild flowers and ferns. Nothing special but everything good and very cheap. Their $2.50 specials of mixed bulbs, and lilies at less than $2.00 apiece (not all are this low) are a boon to anyone looking for a quick effect at low cost.

Wayside Gardens
Hodges, South Carolina 29695

Wayside prints the handsomest catalogue in the country, in full color on glossy stock, and offers de luxe plants—no seed—to gardeners in search of out-of-the-ordinary shrubs, trees, perennials, etc. I always want practically everything they have, and I wish I didn't have to report serious problems with wrongly labeled plants, late deliveries and the sudden announcement, six months after a plant has been ordered, that it is sold out. Refunds are prompt, but that doesn't help the gardener who has lost a season of bloom. It is very much to be hoped that the situation is temporary and Wayside gets its act together. Otherwise, I won't know where to turn for such things as *Anemone vitifolia*, *Althea zebrina*, standard lilacs, many more. Which of course only makes the fouled-up delivery system the more exasperating.

Weston Nurseries Inc.
East Main Street, Route 135
Hopkinton, Massachusetts 01748

In southern New England, we rate Weston pretty well tops for ever-greens, trees, and flowering shrubs—though they also carry roses, perennial and rock garden plants and fruit trees. The catalogue is a model of businesslike concision and clarity, and alas, unless you know exactly what you are looking for, something of a bore. There are no illustrations, not even a line-drawing—nothing to lure you into a purchase. Yankee-style, they tell you what they have, and if you aren't interested, they couldn't care less. First-class stock, reasonable prices, and everything is hardy unless they tell you otherwise.

White Flower Farm
Litchfield, Connecticut 16759

Wayside's nearest rival, though the catalogue isn't a patch on Wayside's and the selection much narrower. However, it makes good reading. As to the actual plants—I haven't ordered any for years. They never did well for me, and I found the tone of the establishment decidedly arrogant. Friends tell me that it is best to go directly to the farm, which is all right if you happen to be within easy driving distance. I am not. I also have good reports of the bulb collections they offer at reasonable prices. But as I am never in need of that many bulbs I haven't tried them myself. This is a firm that I feel very much overrates itself via the catalogue and the ads it runs in *The New Yorker*. But their continued success shows that many people disagree.

Index

acanthus, 142
Acosta, José de, *Natural and Moral History of the Indies*, 48
Adams, A. W., *The French Garden, 1500–1800*, 183
Addison, Joseph, 181, 185; *The Spectator*, 183
Adonis gardens, 202–3
agapanthus (lily-of-the-Nile), 38; *A. orientalis*, 38
ageratum, 4, 6
Ahmed III, Sultan, 230
Aix-les-Bains, Willmott's garden, 240
Albertus Magnus, 112, 121
Alcott, Bronson, 44
aldicarb (Temix), 167
aldrin, 168
Alexandra, Queen, 240, 241
almond, flowering, 210
alpine plants, 190
alstroemeria (Peruvian lily), 63–4
Amalfi, garden, 254
amaranth, 45
American Peony Society, 158
American Rose Society, 194
American Society of Landscape Architects, 269
Ames, Oakes (quoted in Edgar Anderson, *Plants, Man and Life*), 146–7
Anderson, Edgar, *Plants, Man and Life*, 146–7
andromeda, 59
Andropogon (firm), 113
Anne, Queen, 183
Anthemis tinctoria, 84
apples, 15
apricots, 68, 69
arborvitae, 63; American, 60
armadillo, 114
Arnold Arboretum, 123
artemisia, 13, 162; *see also* tarragon
artichokes (*Cynara scalymus*), 8–9; Jerusalem (*Italianthus tuberosus*), 8, 10
ashes, 9–10
asparagus, 10–12

asters (*Aster, Callistephus chinensis*), 7, 12–14, 211; *A. amellus*, 13; *A. novae-angliae* (Michaelmas daisies), 13, 164; *A. novi-belgii*, 13; Stokes, 36
astilbe, 85, 165
Attar of rose, 198
Aucuba japonica, 96
Auden, W. H., 108, 224
Augustus, Emperor, 10
Austen, Jane, 19–20, 33, 268
autumn, 14–17
azaleas, 18–21, 59, 61, 212; *A. arborescens*, 19; *A. calendulacea*, 18; *A. indica*, 19; *A. schlippenbach*, 20; *A. viscosum*, 19; Exbury, 18; Gibraltar, 20; Japanese, 20–1, 61; Knapp Hill, 18; Stowhead, 19; Villa Lante, 19
Aztecs, 50

bachelor's buttons, 4
Bacon, Francis, 113
Bagatelle (Comte d'Artois), 122
Baker, John Gilbert (in Ellen Willmot, *The Genus Rosa*), 240, 242
Banks, Sir Joseph, 266
Banvel, 168
Baptisia australis (false indigo), 31, 256
barberry (*Berberis*), 63; *B. gilgiana*, 77; *B. thunbergii*, 77; *B. verruculosa*, 77; *B. vulgaris*, 77; hedges, 63, 75, 77
barley, 47
basil (*Ocimum*), 85, 98–100; *O. basilicum*, 99; *O. minimum*, 99; purple, 99–100
Bassani, Giorgio, *The Garden of the Finzi-Continis*, 227–8
bay (*Laurus nobilis*), 87, 96, 210
bay laurel (*Umbellaria californica*), 87, 96
beans, 21–4, 171, 243–6; fave, 21; flageolets, 21; French horticultural, 22; lima, 21–4; pinto, 21; snap, 22–4, 171; soybeans, 21, 166, 206

Beaufort, Duchess of, 265
Beauvais, Abbot of, 269
Beckford, William, 122
bedstraw, 84
bee balm (*Monarda*), 256
beeches (*Fagus*): copper, 63, 76; in hedges, 76
beets, 26, 247
begonias, 31; wax, 4, 6
Belgian fence, 24–5
Benson, E. F., *Mapp and Lucia*, 107–8
Beston, Henry, 94; *Herbs and the Earth*, 85
biennials, 25–8; perennials distinguished from, 27; transplanting, 16; vegetables, 26
bignonia, 251
biological control, 174
bird-of-paradise flower (*Strelitzia*), 266
birds, 23, 28–30; feeding, 29–30
black-eyed Susan (*Rudbeckia hirta*), 254
Blackthorne Gardens, 273
Blaikie, Thomas, 122
bleeding heart (*Dicentra spectabilis*), 164, 256
blessed thistle (*Cnicus benedictus*), 126
bluebells: creeping, 255; Virginia (*Mertensia virginica*), 36, 256, 259
bluebirds, 28, 29
blues (blue flowers), 31–8
Blunt, Wilfred, *Tulipomania*, 230, 232–4
Boccaccio, Giovanni, 112
Boland, Brigid, *Gardener's Magic and Other Old Wives' Tales*, 85
Bomarzo (monster garden), 189
bone meal, 134
borage, 34
Boucher, François, 106
boxwood (*Buxus*), 62–3, 183
Boyceau, Jacques, 265
bricks: for paths, 155; for perennial borders, 164
Bridgeman, Charles, 182
broccoli, 245, 246
Brooklyn Botanic Garden, 192
Brookstone Company, 223, 225, 273
Broughton, Lady, 265
Brown, Lancelot (Capability), 182
Brussels sprouts, 243, 244, 246
buckthorn (*Rhamnus frangula*), 76–7
buckwheat hulls, 132
Budding, Edwin, 110
bugloss, Italian (anchusa), 165
Burlington, Richard Boyle, earl of, 181
burnet, 113
Burpee Seed Co., 27, 33, 204, 206, 207, 219, 273–4
Busbecq, Ogier, 232–3
buttercups, 175, 254, 255
butterflies, 13

cabbage, 171, 211, 243, 244, 245; Chinese, 246; early green, 246; Savoy, 244, 245, 246
cactus gardens, 138

California: climate, 149; landscape gardening, 61, 138; Spanish horticulture, 51
Cambridge Botanic Garden, 239
camellia, 138
camomile (*Anthema nobilis*), 112
Campanula, *C. carpatica*, 35; *C. glomerata*, 35; *C. medium* (Canterbury bells), 25, 26, 204; *C. persicifolia*, 35
camphor balsam, 85
Campsis, 251
cannas, 162
cardoons, 246
carnations, *see* dianthus
carpet-bedding, 5–6, 162, 237
Carroll, Lewis, *Alice's Adventures in Wonderland*, 209
carrots, 17, 26, 244, 246
Carson, Rachel, *Silent Spring*, 47
caryopteris, 39; *C.x clandonensis*, 39
Castor, Antonius, 121
castor bean, 176
Caswell-Massey, apothecaries, 99
Cather, Willa, *Death Comes for the Archbishop*, 138
Catherine of Aragon, Queen, 50
Cato the Censor, 10, 121, 127
cauliflower, purple, 244, 245, 246
Cavanilles, Abbé, 49
cedar, red (*Juniperus virginiana*), 60
celandine, 254
Celanese, 206
celeriac, 204, 244, 246
celery, 246–7
centaureas, 165; *C. moschata* (sweet sultan), 4; *C. montana*, 34
cerinthe, 85
Cervantes, Vincente, 49
chalk garden, 36
Chambers, Sir William, 191
Chamonix, Mer de Glace, 189
Chanel, Coco, 196
Chao Ch'ang, 104
chapparal, 138
Chardin, Jean Baptiste Siméon, 244
Charles II, King, 183
Charlotte, Queen, 266
chemicals, *see* fertilizers; pesticides
chervil, 94–5
chicory (*Cichorium*), 57; *C. endivia*, 57; *C. intybus*, 57
Child, Julia, *Mastering the Art of French Cooking*, Vol. I, 87, 180
China: bound feet in, 261–2; gardens, 262; rock gardens, 190–2
chinch bugs, 173
chives, 94
chlordane, 168
Christie, Ella, 191
chrysanthemums, 13, 64, 164
Churchill, Winston, 123
Ciba-Geigy, 206
Cinchona, 266
clary, 91
clematis, 251, 252; *viorna*, 257
cleome, 7

clethra, 141
clover, white (*Trifolium repens*), 115, 254, 255
cocoa hulls, 132
codling moth, 173, 174
Colden, Jane, 266
Colette, 160
coleus, 4
Colfax, Lady, 238
colors of flowers, favorite, 31
color vision, 141–42
columbine (*aquilegia*), 165; wild, 259
Columbus, Christopher, 50
Columella, 211
comfrey, 85
Common Catalogue in Common Market countries, 104
companion planting (interplanting), 170–2
compost, 15–17, 39–46, 249; ashes, 9–10; in asparagus beds, 12; for disease control, 169; Indore system, 43; mulch and, 130, 132, 133
Compton Wynyates, topiary garden, 74
conifers, *see* evergreens
Connolly, Cyril, 124, 242
coral bells (*heuchara*), 165
coriander, 84
corn (maize), 47, 71, 207, 217, 246; miniature white, 246; planting time, 152
Cortes, Hernando, 47
cosmos, 49
costmary, 85
cotoneaster, 210, 212
cottage gardens, 259, 267–8
Cowell, F. R., *The Garden as a Fine Art*, 50
crab grass, 108, 135, 136
Crescenzi, Pietro de', 112
Crockett, James, 11, 12, 27
Cruso, Thalassa, *Making Vegetables Grow*, 31, 56, 95, 220
cryptomeria, 61
cucumbers, 171, 246; hygroponically grown, 58
Cuisinart, 224
cumin, 84
Cupid's dart (*Catananche caerulea*), 37
currants (*Ribes*), 72–3
cynidin, 33–4

daffodils, naturalized, 137
Dahl, Anders, 49
dahlias, 31, 46–54
daisy, oxeye, 255
dame's rocket (*Hesperis matronalis*), 26
dandelion greens, 246
Daphne mezereum, 176
Daphnis, Nassos, 158
Davis, Adele, 46
daylilies (*Hemerocallis*), 54–5; escaped from cultivation, 136; *H. flava*, 54; *H. fulva*, 54, 55, 136
DDT, 168

deadly nightshade (*solanum dulcamara*), 176, 177, 255
defoliants in Vietnam, 41, 168; Agent Orange (2, 4, 5-T), 167–8
de Graaf, Jan, 117, 257
delphiniums, 36–7, 165; Blackmore & Langdon hybrids, 37; Connecticut Yankee, 36; giants, 36–7; Pacific hybrids, 26, 37
Democritus, 261
Demonchaux, J. A., Co., 58, 274
Department of Agriculture, U.S., 167, 205, 231, 235
Désert de Retz, 189
Deutzia gracilis, 212
dianthus, 27; carnations, 141; laced pinks, 204; paisley pinks, 204; sweet William (*Dianthus barbatus*), 25, 26, 164, 204
dichondra, 109
Dieffenbachia seguine, 176
dieldrin, 168
dill, 92–3; in trap-cropping, 172
disease-resistant plants, 170
diseases, *see* pests and diseases
dittany (*Origanum dictamnus*), 93, 94
dogtooth violet (trout lily) (*Erythronium*), 259
dogwood (*Cornus*), 152; Chinese (*Cornus kousa chinensis*), 62, 116
Domoto, Toichi, 158
dormant oil spray, 175
Douglas, David, 116
Douglas fir, 116, 138
dove tree (Davidia), 116
Downing, Andrew Jackson, 60, 62, 185
Drake, Sir Francis, 48, 50
Dumbarton Oaks, 269

earthworms, 40, 55–7
Edinburgh, Royal Botanic Garden, 239
eelgrass, 131
eggplant, 169, 172, 204, 247
electric power, 149–50
electric tools, 223
electroculture, 45
Eliot, Jared, 16
elms (*Ulmus*), 152; seedlings, 256; Siberian (*Ulmus pumila*), 76
Encyclopedia of Organic Gardening (Rodale), 44, 45, 132, 171, 175, 248–9
endive, 57–8, 244, 246; *see also* chicory
endrin, 168
Environmental Protection Agency, 167, 168
Erythronium americanum, *see* trout lily
espaliers, 186–7; Belgian fence, 24–5
eucalyptus, 138
euonymus, 210; E. fortunei, 75; *E. vegetus*, 75; sarcoxie, 75
Evelyn, Charles, *Lady's Recreation*, 264
Evelyn, John, 74, 122, 222, 240
evergreens, 59–63; American, as exotics in Europe, 137–8; in hedges, 74–9; Japanese technique with, 60–2;

evergreens (*continued*)
planting, space in, 59–60; pruning,
61; in winter, 60–1
Ewing, Juliana Horatia, 267

Fabergé, 257
failures, 63–6
fall (autumn), 14–17
false cypress (*Chamaecyparis*), 61, 63,
212; Hinoki (*C. obtusa*), 61, 62;
Sawara (*C. pisifera*), 61
Far North Gardens, 274
Farrand, Beatrix Jones, 269
Farrer, Reginald, 116, 237, 241; *The
English Rock-Garden*, 190
Faustinius's villa, 189
fennel, 66–7, 172, 246
fenugreek, 84
ferns, 258
Ferry-Morse, 206
fertilizers: chemical, 131, 133–4, 167,
206; figures showing content, 134
field salad, 176
figs (*Ficus*), 47, 51, 212
flax (linum perenne), 35; tumbleweeds
in seed of, 136
fleur-de-lis, 230
Folie de Saint James, 189
Forbes, Lady Angela, 241
Ford, Ford Madox, 71
forget-me-nots (*Myosotis*): alpine
(*M. alpestris*), 26; woodland (*M.
sylvatica*), 26
Forrest, George, 116, 239
forsythia, 77, 152, 186
Foxfire Books, 128
foxgloves (digitalis), 26, 31, 136, 176,
177
Fragonard, Jean Honoré, 106
fraises des bois, see strawberries
French-intensive gardening, 247–9
Freud, Sigmund, 43–4
Friar Park, 189
Frost, Robert, 185
frost, 67–8
fruits, 68–70; borers, 69; dwarf trees,
standards, 210; grafting trees, 211;
planting trees, 152
fuchsias, 48, 212
fungicides, 167, 206
Funk Seeds International, 206

Garden, The (R.H.S. journal), 215, 238,
240
gardenesque style, 237
gardenia, 31
Garden Way Research, 225, 274–5
genetics and hybridization, 102
gentians (*Gentiana*), 38; closed (*G.
andrewsii*), 259; *G. crinita*
(fringed), 38, 259; *G. septemfidae*,
38
geraniums, 4, 171; crane's-bill geranium,
254; standards, 210, 212; white, 172
germ plasm, 102
Gibbon, Edward, 189

Gibbons, Grinling, 257
Gide, André, 101, 103, 104
Gilbertie, Sal, *Home Gardening at Its
Best*, 245
ginkgo, 138
gladiolas, 31, 32
Glasscock, Lyman, 158
globe thistle (*Echinops*), 34
golden-rain tree (*Koelreuteria paniculata*), 138
goldenrod (*Solidago*) in English gardens, 138
golf greens, 109
gooseberries (*Ribes*), 72–3
grafting: compatibility, 211; standards,
209–12
grapes, 47, 51
grasses: bent, 109; bluegrass, 113; fescue, 113; lawn, 113; meadow, 113;
paths, 155–6; perennial rye grass, 113
Gratwick, William, 158
Gregory I, St., Pope, 269
grottoes, 189
ground covers, 111–12
Guillot, J. B., 201
Gurney Seed and Nursery Co., 275
gypsophila, 13

Hadrian's villa, 189
Hampton Court, 183
Handel, George Frederick, 137
harems, 230, 262
Harris, Joseph, Co., Inc., 4, 23, 27, 218,
219, 246, 275
Haughton, Claire S., *Green Immigrants*,
49, 136
Hawkins, Sir John, 50
hawthorn (*Crataegus*), 170, 211; *C.
crusgalli*, 78; *C. laevigata* (*oxycantha*), 78
Hazan, Marcella, *The Classic Italian
Cookbook*, 8, 87, 97
hedgerows, 77–8, 137
hedges, 62, 63, 74–79
Hemerocallis, see daylilies
hemlock (*Tsuga*), 62, 74
heptachlor, 168
herbaceous borders, English, 5–6, 116,
161–2, 237
herbicides, 126, 167–8; broad-leaved, 115
herbs, 83–101
Hidcote, 76, 236–9
Holland, Lady, 47, 265
holly (*Ilex*), 58; English, 75; hedges,
74–5, 76; *I. crenata* (Japanese), 61,
75; *I. opaca*, 75; *I. pedunculosa*, 75;
standards, 210, 212
hollyhocks (*Althaea rosea*), 26–7
honesty (*Lunaria biennis*), 26
honeysuckle, 268
Hoole House, 189
hornbeam, 76
horseradish, 171, 175
hortus inclusus (*giardino segreto*), 262–3
Hortus III, 97, 98, 100, 251

Howard, Sir Albert, 45; *An Agricultural Testament*, 42–3
hurricanes, 150, 151
Huxley, Anthony, *Illustrated History of Gardening*, 186, 222
hybrids, 33, 101–4; lilies, *see* lilies; seeds, 103–4, 204–5
hydrangeas, 64, 78; *H. petiolaris*, 252; standard, 210
hygroponic plant growing, 58
hyssop, 84, 85

impatiens, 31
Impressionists, 142
India, farming in, 42–3
indigo, 36
interplanting, 170–2
iris, 112, 164; crested dwarf, 257; *I. prismatica*, 257, 258; *I. pseudacorus*, 257; naturalized, 137; wild blue flag, 257
ITT, 206
ivy (*Hedera helix*), 105–6, 176, 177, 251–2; trees, grafting, 212

jack-in-the-pulpit, 259
Jackson & Perkins, 196
Jacob's-ladder, 256
Jager, Degenaar de, 232
James, Henry, 107–8
Japanese flower arrangement, 261
Japanese gardening: evergreens, 60–2; rock gardens, 190–2; tree walks, 226
Jardin des Plantes, Paris, 122
Jardin du Gourmet, Le, 276
Jasminum polyanthum, 239
Jefferson, Thomas, 123
Jeffrey, John, 116
Jekyll, Gertrude, 5–6, 12–13, 19, 122, 162, 163, 235, 236, 237, 267, 269
Jerusalem cherry (*Solanum pseudocapsicum*), 176
jimsonweed (*Datura stramonium*), 176
Johnny's Selected Seeds, 276
Johnston, Lawrence, 237–40, 242
Josephine, Empress, 47, 240, 265
junipers (*Juniperus*): *J. pfitzeri*, 59, 61; *J. virginiana*, 60
Jussieu, Bernard de, 122

Kawabata, *The Snow Country*, 61
Kensington Palace, 183
Kent, William, 182
Kerria japonica, 212
Kew Gardens, 191, 266
Keystone Seed Company, 206
Kipling, Rudyard, *Jungle Books*, 225–6
Kitazawa Seed Co., 276
Klimas, John E. and James A. Cunningham, *Wildflowers of Eastern America*, 256
kohlrabi, 247
Kublai Khan, 137

laburnum, 175–6, 177.
lacewing, 173, 254

ladybug, 173
lady's-slipper, pink, 257
Lamb House, 108
landscape gardening, 181–7, 267; in California, 61, 138; women in, 269–70
language of flowers, 261, 262
lantana, 176, 212
La Quintinie, Jean Baptiste de, 122, 260
larkspurs, 4, 175; garland, 36
laurel, 75; mountain (*Kalmia latifolia*), 59, 96
Laurus canariensis, 96
lavender (*Lavandula*), 85, 96–8, 162; Hidcote, 237; *L. angustifolia*, 97, 98; *L. dentata*, 98; *L. officinalis*, 97; *L. spica*, 97, 98; *L. stoechas*, 98; *L. vera*, 97, 98; *L. viris*, 84
Law, Donald, *The Concise Herbal Encyclopedia*, 85–6
lawn mowers, 110–11
lawns, 108–15
Lawrence, John, *New System . . .*, 264
Lawson, *Countrie Housewife*, 263–4
leeks, 17, 45–6, 204, 244, 246
Lees-Milne, Alvide, 238, 239
lemons, 51
Le Nôtre, André, 121, 162, 268
lettuce, 47, 144, 243, 244; loose-leaf, 246
Leuthardt, Henry, Nurseries, Inc., 24, 25, 186–7, 276–7
lighting in gardens, 142
Ligorio, Pirro, 121
lilacs (*Philadelphus*), 21, 160; Chinese, 78; grafting, 211; pruning, 17; standard, 187, 210, 212; in weather forecasting, 152
lilies (*Lilium*), 116–20
lily-of-the-valley, 112
lindane, 168
Lindsay, Norah, 162
Lloyd, Christopher, 120
Loden, Harold, 103
Logan, Martha, *Gardener's Kalender*, 268
Lombardy poplars, 170
Longleat, 76
Longwood Gardens, 186
Lorrain, Claude, 59, 182
Loudon, J. C., 153, 237, 265
Louisiana Seed Company, 206
Louis XIV, 260
lovage, 85, 90
love-in-a-mist, 4
lupin, 165
Lutyens, Sir Edwin, 236, 269
Luxembourg Gardens, 265

magic, 123–6, 261
magnolia, 186; grafting, 211
Mahonia, 239; *M. acquifolium*, Oregon grape holly, 75–6
Makielski Berry Farm, 277
mallow (*Malva*), 254
Malmaison, 265
mandrake, 85

manure: in compost, 40–1; in mulch, 131, 132, 134
maples, red, 63
Marie Antoinette, Queen, 265
Marie de' Médicis, Queen, 265
marigolds, 4, 6, 7, 206, 268; history of, 47, 48; in pest control, 171; white, 33
marijuana (hemp, *Cannabis sativa*), 7, 171
marjoram (*Origanum*): *O. majorana* (*Majorana hortensis*), 93, 94; *O. maru*, 85, 87; pot (*O. onites*), 93, 94; winter (*O. heracleoticum*), 93
martins, purple, 29
Marvell, Andrew, 183–4
Mary gardens, 263
Masson, Georgina, *Italian Gardens*, 127, 189, 226
Maugham, Syrie, 31
Mayas, 40
mazes, 130
meadows, 113–14
Medici, Lorenzo de, 183
Meilland, Francis, 194
Mellon estate, Virginia, 186
melons, 169, 211
Mentone, Johnston's garden, 239
Merrill, James, *Nights and Days*, 187–8
Mexico: Aztec gardens, 51; Spanish gardens, 51
millet, 136
Milton, John, 184
mint (*Mentha*), 100–1, 171; water, 113
mistletoe, 176
Mitford, Nancy, *The Pursuit of Love*, 32
mitsuba, 84
Mohammed IV, Sultan, 230
Mollet, Claude, 121
Monardes, Nicholas, 47, 48
Monet, Claude, 12–13
monkshood (*Aconitum*), 36, 177
Monsanto, 206
Montagu, Lady Mary Wortley, 262
Montaigne, Michael Eyquem de, 226
Montanoa, 266
Morris, William, 5
Mount Vernon, Va., 186
mozzarella cheese, 218
mulches, 16–17, 130–5; weeds killed by, 255–6
mulleins (*Verbascum*), 26
Murad III, Sultan, 230
Murray, Lady Charlotte, *British Garden*, 268
mushrooms, 176–7
music, plants responding to, 123–4

nasturtiums, 6, 47, 48, 171
National Academy of Sciences, 103
natural gardening, 138–40
naturalizing, 135–40
nettles, 176, 254
New England Rootstock Association, 277

Nichols, Beverley, *Garden Open Tomorrow*, 63–4, 66
Nicolson, Harold, 235, 236
nicotiana, 7, 31, 141
Nikko fir, 61
Noailles, Vicomte de, 238
North American Fruit Explorers, 277
Northrup-King, 206
Northwest Ornamental Horticultural Society, 139

oaks, pin, 76
okra, 169
oleander, 176
olives, 47
Olmsted, Frederick Law, 123, 185
onions (*Allium*), 26, 47, 143–6, 171, 243, 245; garlic (*Allium sativum*), 70–1, in pest control, 171, 174, 175; Japanese bunching, 246; scallions, 144–5; seedlings, 143; seeds, 143; sets, 143, 144; shallots, 143–4, 246
oranges, 47, 51
orchids, wild, 257, 259; lady's-slipper, 257; rosebud, 257
orchis, 257
oregano (*Origanum*), 87, 93–4
Oregon grape holly (*Mahonia acquifolium*), 75–6
organic gardening, theory of, 39–46; mulch in, 131–5; pest and disease control, 169–75; Rodale's work, 41–6
Organic Gardening (magazine), 41, 43, 44, 103, 113, 114, 115, 125, 132
Organic Gardening and Farming Research Center, 45
Origanum, see marjoram; oregano
origins of plants, 146–7
Oudry, Jean Baptiste, 106

Page, Russell, 76, 153, 154, 155, 162, 238; *The Education of a Gardener*, 19, 236
pak choi, 84
Palissy, Bernard, *The Delectable Garden*, 122
Parc Monceau, 122
Park, George W., Seed Co., Inc., 20, 22, 27, 278
Parkinson, John, *Paradisi in Sole, Paradisus Terrestris*, 264, 267
Parrish, Anne, 108
parsley, 26, 94, 95
parsnips, 17, 187–8, 244, 247
Parsons, Alfred, 240
passion-flower, 256
paths, 153–6
peaches, 47, 50, 68, 69, 211
pears, 47, 68, 69; grafting, 211
peas, 144, 243, 244, 246; Lincoln, 246; snow, 246; Sugar Snap, 205, 246
peat moss, 131, 132
pennyroyal, 100, 155
peonies (*Paeonia*), 156–61; wire hoops for, 165

peppers, 169, 247; hot, 175
Perelman, S. J., 43
perennials, 161–6; biennials distinguished from, 27; blue, 34–8; dividing, 16, 35, 164–5; in fall, 15–16
Pernet-Duchet, Joseph, 195
Perry, Frances, *Flowers of the World*, 49
pesticides, 126, 166–75; conglomerates interested in, 206; organic gardening substitutes for, 169–75
pests and diseases, 166–174; *see also* fruit borers, 69; fusarium wilt, 218; tobacco mosaic virus, 221; tomato hornworm, 65, 172, 173, 221; tulip breaking virus disease, 228–32; wheat rust, 77
Petrarch, 121, 127, 128
petunias, 4, 6, 31, 171, 206
Pfizer, 206
pH, 134
phenology, 151–2
philodendron, 176
phlox, 31, 101–2, 165; *P. divaricata*, 36
pincushion flower (*Scabiosa caucasica*), 4
pineapples, 47
pines: Monterey, 116; Mugo, 61; Taniyosho, 62; weeping white, 62
Pizarro, Francisco, 51
plantain, 135–6
Plant Variety Protection Act, 205
platycodon, 35
Pliny the Younger, 10, 121, 142, 154, 176, 188, 262
Plumier, Charles, 48
plums, *see Prunus*
poinsettia (*Euphorbia pulpulcherrima*), 176
poison ivy, 176
poisonous plants, 175–7
pomegranates, 51
Pompadour, Mme. de, 265
Pope, Alexander, 181, 182, 184
poppies, 177–8, 268; Himalayan (*Meconopsis betonicifolia*), 26, 37–8; Iceland, 26, 178; opium, 7; Oriental (*Papaver orientale*), 164, 178; Shirley, 178, 204
possums, 114
potatoes, 243, 245; aldicarb as pesticide, 167; history, 47, 48; interaction with other plants, 171; *jaune d'hollande* (German fingerlings), 179–81, 244, 246; poison in, 176; trap-cropping, 172
potpourri, 198
Poussin, Nicolas, 182
prairies, 113, 114; tumbleweeds on, 136–7
Pratolino, *giardino segreto*, 226
praying mantis, 172–3, 174
Prevention (magazine), 44
primroses (primulas), 112, 137; evening (*Oenothera*), 26; *Primula bilekii*, 190
Prinsepia sinensis, 76

privet (*Ligustrum*), 78–9, 211; *L. ovalifolium*, 135; *L. vulgare*, 135
Proust, Marcel, 78
pruning, 181–7; city trees, 186; equipment, 222, 223; evergreens, 61; in fall, 16–17; roses, 16–17; tomatoes, 220–1; topiary, 182, 186, 188–9; tree as green room, 226
Prunus; cherries, 50, 68, 69; weeping, standard, 212; plums, 50, 211; *Prunus laurocerasus*, 96; *Prunus lusitanica*, 96; quinces, 68–9
Purex, 206
Pyle, Robert, 194
pyracantha, 186, 187
pyrethrum, 175

quassia, 175

raccoons, 114, 141
ragweed, 114
rain, forecasting, 148, 151
ranunculus, 230
Reath, David, 158, 278
Réunion (Ile de Bourbon), 199
Rex Bulb Farms, 117, 278
rhododendrons, 18–20, 59, 61
rhubarb, 176
right- and left-handedness in plants, 124, 125
Riotte, Louise, *Companion Planting*, 171, 172
Robert, Hubert, 106, 189
Robinson, William, 5, 122, 190, 235
rock gardens, 188–92
Rodale, Jerome Irving, 41–6; *see also Encyclopedia of Organic Gardening; Organic Gardening*
Rodale, Robert, 46
Rohde, Eleanor Sinclair, *The Story of the Garden*, 264
Roman gardens, 262; rock gardens, 188–9
root rots, 169
Rosa, Salvator, 59
rosemary, 91, 171, 210
roses, 102, 162, 193–202, 268
rotenone, 175
Rousseau, Jean Jacques, 106, 183, 268
Royal Horticultural Society, *Dictionary of Gardening*, (R.H.S.), 18, 26, 27, 47, 73, 87, 97, 98, 211
royal poinciana, 138
rue, 84, 85
Ruskin, John, 5
Russell, George, 122
Russian olive (*Elaeagnus*), 76
Ryan, Clarence, 125
Ryōanji temple, Kyoto, 192

Sackville-West, V., 162, 235–7
sage (*Salvia officionalis*), 91–2; pineapple, 91
St. Martin's Day, 151

salpiglossis, 6
salsify, 247
salt hay as mulch, 130, 132–4
salvia, 91; red, 4, 6, 31
Sand, George, 253–4, 256
Sandoz, Inc., 206
Sargent, Charles S., 123
Sauer, Leslie, 113
Saunders, Professor, 158
Saunders, Silvia, 158
Savannah, Ga., Trustees' Garden, 51
Sayes Court, 75
scallions, 144–5
schizanthus, 6
scything, 110, 112–14
seaweed: in fertilizer, 40; as mulch, 130, 133, 134
seeds, 202–7; hybrid, 103–4, 204–5; ordering, 103; patenting, 205–6; seed companies owned by conglomerates, 205–6
seed tapes, 207
Sei Shōnagon, *The Pillow Book of Sei Shōnagon*, 208, 268
senecio, 162
sequoia (*Wellingtonia*), 138
Serres, Olivier de, *Le Théâtre de l'Agriculture*, 122
Sévigné, Mme. de, 268
Shipman, Ellen Biddle, 269
silver-lace vine (*Polygonum Aubertii*), 253
Sirén, Osvald, *Gardens of China*, 153, 191
Sissinghurst, 162, 236
Sitwell, Sir George, *On the Making of Gardens*, 242
Slogteren, E. van, 231–2
Smith, A. W., *Gardener's Book of Plant Names*, 232
snapdragons, 6, 164
snow, 60–1; forecasting, 148–51, 153
soil: analysis ,134; fertilizer ingredients and, 134
sorrel (*Rumex cutatus*), 90–1, 254
southernwood, 85
Spain: dahlias imported from, 47, 49; plants from New World imported to, 47–8
Spanish America, plants discovered and introduced in, 47–8, 50–1
Spathoglottis ixiodes, 190
spiderwort (*Tradescantia virginiana*), 35
spinach, 246
sprayers, 223–5
spraying, 173–5; fruit trees, 69
spruce: Norway, 60; Sitka, 138
Spry, Constance, *Garden Notebook*, 118
squashes, 171, 245, 247
squirrels, 114
staking: dahlias, 53; perennials, 165
standards, 209–12; grafting, 209–12; lilacs, 187, 210, 212; roses, 187, 202, 209–10, 212

Stark Bros., 279
Star-of-Bethlehem (*Ornithogalum umbellatum*), 255
Steichen, Edward, 36
Stein, Gertrude, 213
Stewart Seeds, 206
Stobhill Castle, 76
stocks, Brompton, 26
Stokes Seeds, Inc., 218, 279
Stout, Ruth, 123, 132
straw as mulch, 132
strawberries, 213–14
summer savory, 171
Sun Belt, 149, 185
sunflowers, 211
Sutton Courtenay, 162
swan river daisy, 7
sweet peas (*Lathyrus odoratus*), 4, 31, 214–15
sweet William, 25, 26, 164, 204
Swiss chard, 26, 244, 246
sycamore, 76

Tale of Genji, The, 61
talking to plants, 123–5
tamarisk, 138
tanbark for paths, 154
tansy, 171, 254
tarragon (*Artemisia*), 89–90, 94
Temix (aldicarb), 167
Temple, Sir William, *Garden of Epicurus*, 264
tennis courts, 109
Theophrastus, 121
thistles, Canada, 114
Thomas, Eric, and John White, *Hedgerow*, 137
Thompson & Morgan, Inc., 37, 215, 279
Thoreau, Henry David, 184, 185
thyme (*Thymus*), 85, 87–8; shepherd's, 155; wild, 113
Tillotson, Will, *Roses of Yesterday and Today*, 197
Time-Life Encyclopedia of Gardening, 24, 26, 27, 33, 61, 94, 98, 100, 109, 115, 187, 211, 212, 229
toads, 216–17
tobacco, 47, 261
Toklas, Alice B., 213
tomatoes, 47, 100, 204, 211, 217–21, 243–6; hygroponically grown, 58; interaction with other plants, 171–2; pest and disease control, 169, 172, 221
tools, 221–5
topiary, 182, 188–9
Tradescantia virginiana, see spiderwort
Tradescants, John I and John II, 267
trap-cropping, 172
tree houses, 225–7
trees, 227–8
trilliums, 259
Trollope, Anthony, 51
Trollope, Frances, 185
trout lily (dogtooth violet, *Erythronium americanum*), 259

truffles, 176
trumpet vine, 251
Tsang and Ma International, 280
tuberose, 31
tulipomania, 228–9
tulips, 31, 228–35
tumbleweeds, 136–7
Tusser, Thomas, 267

Union Carbide, 206
Upjohn, 206

valerian, 85
Van Bourgondian Bros., 280
Varro, Marcus Terentius, 121
vegetables, 242–50; biennial, 26; companion planting (interplanting), 170–2; disease and pest control, 169–75; in fall, 17; interaction between plants, 171–2; modern shipping methods, 217; in New World, 47; rotation of crops, 169; seaweed as mulch, 133
Ventimiglia, Willmott's garden, 240
Vergil, 127, 199
veronica, 35; *V. officinalis*, 254
Versailles, 122, 265
vervain, 85
Viburnum plicatum mariesii, 62
Victoria amazonica, 266
Villa d'Este, 121
Villa Lante, 19
Villa Petraia, 226
Vilmorin, seed firm, 145
vines, 250–3

wallflowers (*Cheiranthus*), 25, 204; English (*C. cheiri*), 26; Siberian (*C. allioni*), 26, 204
Walpole, Horace, 122, 181
Warley Place, 240, 241
Washington, George, 123
watering, 130; equipment for, 223; lawns, 109–10
Watteau, Jean Antoine, 106
Wayside Gardens, 13, 38, 63, 158, 187, 196, 212, 251, 280
weather forecasting, 148–53
weeds, 253–6; American, in English flower gardens, 138; in autumn, 16; in meadows, 113, 114; naturalized or imported, 135–7; in perennials, 165; in ruins of bombed cities, 137
weigela, 21
Wellingtonia (sequoia), 138
Weston Nurseries, Inc., 77, 280–1

Wexler, Arthur, *The Architecture of Japan*, 192
Wharton, Edith, 31, 238
wheat, 47, 166, 207
Whisler, Mrs. Dorothy, 33–4
White, Katharine S., *Onward and Upward in the Garden*, 196, 231–2
White Flower Farm, 213, 281
white flowers, 31
"white man's foot," 136
Whole Earth Catalog, The, 128
wild flowers, 256–9; in meadows, 112, 113
wild ginger, 257
William III, King, 183
Willmott, Ellen, 240–2; *The Genus Rosa*, 240–2
Wilson, H. and Leonie Bell, *The Fragrant Year*, 118, 160, 198, 200
Wilson, E. H., 116, 119, 240, 241
Wise, Henry, 122
wisteria, 176, 177, 210
woad, 84
Woburn Abbey, 259
women: as botanists, 265–6; gardens as prisons for, 262–4; gardens made for, 265; as landscape architects, 269–70; magic and witchcraft of, 261; as plant breeders and cultivators, 267–8; work in gardens, 259–60
wood chips: as mulch, 130, 131–2; for paths, 154
Wordsworth, Dorothy, 126
wormwood (*artemisia*), 85, 171, 175
woundwort, 85
Wright, Richardson, *Practical Book of Outdoor Flowers*, 18–19
Wyman, Donald, *Wyman's Gardening Encyclopedia*, 18, 26, 33, 38, 39, 72, 75, 100, 186

yarrow, 254
yews (*Taxus*), 59; hedges, 74; standards, 210; *T. baccata* (Irish or English), 60, 74, 176, 177; *T. cuspidata* (Japanese), 61, 74; *T. cuspidata densa*, 74; *T. x media*, 74
Youssoupoff, Prince, 201
Yüan Yeh, 154, 155
yuccas, 162

Zen, sand gardens, 192
Zinn, Gottfried, 48–9
zinnias, 4, 6, 7, 31, 206; history, 48–9; in trap-cropping, 172
zucchini (*courgettes*), 247

About the Author

ELEANOR PERÉNYI was born in Washington, D.C., the daughter of an American naval officer and the novelist Grace Zaring Stone (Ethel Vance). She grew up in Europe, China, the West Indies and various parts of the United States, according to where her father was stationed. At nineteen she married the late Baron Zsigmond Perényi and lived on his estate in Hungary for several years, a life which she described in *More Was Lost*, published in 1946. For many years she worked on various magazines in New York City; her last job was as managing editor of *Mademoiselle*. She has written articles for *The Atlantic Monthly*, *Esquire*, *Harper's*, *Vogue*, and *Harper's Bazaar* as well as book reviews for *The New York Times* and the *Washington Post*. Her most recent book was *Liszt: The Artist as Romantic Hero*, which was nominated for a National Book Award. She lives in Stonington, Connecticut where the garden described in this book takes up most of her time not spent writing. She has one son, Peter, who is in the U.S. Foreign Service.